The
Economic Gang

One Man's Battle with
Japan, Inc.

T. H. Wang

FIRELIGHT
PUBLISHING

Firelight Publishing, Inc.
226 Division St., SW
Sublimity, Oregon 97385-9637
http://www.firelightpublishing.com

This publication is designed to provide adequate and authoritative information in regard to the subject matter covered. None of the material provided here is intended to serve as the basis for any financial decision, nor does any of the information contained within constitute advice to buy or sell any security.

The material presented in this book is accurate to the best of the author's knowledge. Although the information, data, and dialogues contained in this book are from sources believed to be reliable, the publisher assumes no responsibility for errors, inaccuracies, omissions, or inconsistencies. Any opinions or views expressed herein are not necessarily the views of the publisher.

Printed in the United States of America

Edited by Mark Anderson
Cover design by Richard Ferguson
Interior layout by Firelight Editing & Design

Publisher's Cataloguing-in-Publication Data

Wang, Tseng Hsiang
    The economic gang : one man's battle with
japan, inc. / by T.H. Wang;
edited by Mark Anderson. - - 1st ed.
        383 p. cm.
        Includes index.
        ISBN: 0-9707206-3-7
        LCCN: 2002104439

    1. Economics–Japan. 2. Politics and Business–Japan. 3. Japan–
Economic Policy. 4. Biography. 5. Finance–Investments.
I. Title.
HC462.95.W35 2002   332.6

3 4 5 6 7 8 9 0 1 2

Table of Contents

Acknowledgments

*The publisher would like to thank the following
for their various contributions to this book: Mia Mohr, Karla
Davenport, Bob Smith, Richard Ferguson, Carol Drost, Robert
Wang, Phil Midland, B.K. Ho, and Dennis Wang.*

Foreword

Fortune is a strange thing.

A year ago, when this project was first taking shape, I often wondered, "Why me?" Perhaps that's not the thing to ask when Fortune smiles on you. Or frowns for that matter. It just happens and sometimes there is little we can do other than hang on for the ride. In any event, I have considered myself extremely fortunate to be associated with this project. When I was first approached to do this book, I have to admit that I was terribly daunted in several respects. I am not an expert in Japanese society, there were names and events I'd never heard of and took some time to sort out, and the events in this book dealt with millions and millions of dollars, sums that I—or most people—can only imagine.

But there was one thing that I was certain of, and that is I knew a great story when I saw it. International business, wealthy financiers, extremely powerful people—this had all that and more, and yet, at its heart, this was a very human story: a story of perseverance, hard work, and dogged determination; a story of success and of pain.

In reading his story, I also came to share a certain affinity with Mr. Wang in that, like him, I believe in Fortune, that there is a guiding principle to our lives that we can't always fathom. His life has taken him down some unusual paths; certainly, I did not anticipate having a project of this magnitude drop out of the sky on me. He believes in justice and fair play, an innate sense of right and wrong and of how the world *ought* to be—if only it could be wrestled into place.

These are certainly traits that I aspire to and that I'd like to think we share in common.

I have met Mr. Wang and have also come to know him both in conversations and through his and his sons' writings. I believe him to be a man of his word. He is intelligent, obviously of high moral fiber, and possesses a bulldog's determination. He has a high sense of justice and integrity and lofty aspirations.

Seeing the problems of Japan's financial sector that stem from its society, he has worked for the last two decades to address these problems when it would have been easy for him simply to walk away; to take his wealth and go elsewhere where he would be appreciated. And yet for someone of Mr. Wang's integrity, that was not the easy thing to do because he saw an injustice and he became determined to fix it. I can honestly say that the country of Japan must mean a great deal to him in order for him to put so much of his time, energy, and hard-earned money into helping Japan and her people.

Japan is at a crossroads. It is not in the U.S. news as it was in the 1980s, when the fear here in the U.S.—which sometimes bordered on racism—was that the Japanese were going to take over. It seemed everyday you heard how Japan was buying up U.S. companies and soil, like diners snatching up lobster puffs at an all-you-can-eat café. But since the early 1990s, Japan has somehow slipped into the background.

This is unfortunate because Japan most definitely should be in the spotlight. If Enron, a single company, can cause such havoc in U.S. markets and pension funds, imagine what would happen if the world's second largest *economy* were to suddenly plummet.

This book is based on facts personally experienced by Mr. Wang in the course of his many years of investments in Japanese securities. He made his fortune through good luck, astute business judgment and skill, and, above all, hard work. He considered Japan to be his second homeland and he wrote this book as one of his contributions to a land where he had so many fond memories. It is his sincere wish that this book helps to expose Japan's problems to the world, that it will open eyes, and, hopefully, help to bring about some changes—perhaps even the badly needed reforms to Japan's financial and political system.

Japan is facing the worst financial crisis after World War II. It has bad debts in excess of $770 billion; its national debt, by way of issued bonds, is no less than $5.1 trillion. And though its government is espousing reform, very little real action is taking place. Meanwhile, Japan slips further into debt with no signs of recovery, which is only likely to result in forcing the rest of the world to clean up Japan's mess.

As you'll see from reading this book, many of these debts were caused by unsecured loans made to businesses, corporations, and institutions as a result of the incestuous relationship between politicians, government officials, and the financial sector. Sometimes, these loans were based on fictitious collateral. Together, the Ministry of Finance, the banking sector, and the securities companies were able to freely exploit the system.

President George W. Bush met with two former Japanese prime ministers at the White House and implored them to resolve Japan's bad debt issue as soon as possible. On April 2, 2002, the ministries of finance and chairmen of central banks from other G7 countries also pressed this same issue at their meeting held in Washington. They were unanimous in their view that the sooner Japan rid itself of deflation, the better it would be for all concerned.

Unfortunately, this is easier said than done. For many years, the making of laws in Japan was, and continues to be, unique. Contrary to our concept of the separation of powers among the various branches of government, all legislation in the Japanese Diet—the equivalent of Congress—was subject to the approval of the Liberal Democratic Party ("LDP"), which is the biggest political party in the Diet. Mr. Wang would be the first to say—and I would agree with him—that such a system gave rise to abuse and conflicts of interest. This system has to be changed if Japan is to stand a better chance of creating real and meaningful reforms. (The judicial system, which is described in this book in some detail, is certainly an eye opener in itself.)

What may be even more shocking to the average reader is the way that political parties in Japan have relied heavily on businesses and corporations for their political campaigns and elections. This goes far beyond mere "donations" by corporations as we have here in the States. The associations between business and politicians have been so scandalous they led to the arrest of former Prime Minister Kakuei Tanaka and Shin Kanamaru, a prominent member of the LDP; the resignation of former Prime Minister Yasuhiro Nakasone as a member of the LDP; and the stepping down of Prime Minister Nobolu Takashita. More recently, Yutaka Inoue, the Upper House president, had to resign both as president and as a member of the Diet on account of the scandal involving his secretary in obtaining ¥63 million from a construction company. In this same scandal, former LDP Secretary Koich Kato also had to resign as a member of the Diet.

These types of scandals have been going on for some time and there are no real signs of improvement.

An example of this lack of improvement is one of the companies dealt with in the contents of this book. Saibo Co., Ltd., had substantial latent assets; it was debt free, owning about ¥7.6 billion in securities and valuable real property. Because of this potential, Mr. Wang and his friends acquired about three percent of its shares. Unfortunately, as you will see, this investment led to numerous problems that involved self-dealing in its own shares and several other nefarious activities.

Interestingly, for nineteen years, Saibo's textile department had been running at a total net loss of ¥7 billion, which was eleven times that of its capital (of ¥600 million). Additionally, in its official securities report; Saibo was listed as investing in a Taiwanese company. However, upon investigation by Mr. Wang, the Taiwanese company was actually invested in by Saibo's president, under his own name and not under Saibo's name.

This discrepancy in the securities report went uncorrected for nine years. Saibo's auditor surely should have caught this. In light of this, it seems that there are certainly many questions that Saibo and its auditor need to answer in relation to this investment. Saibo's auditor must have approved, condoned, or at least acquiesced in the clandestine arrangements between Saibo and this Taiwanese company. Or, if the auditor claims not to be involved, they were at least grossly negligent in the performance of their duty as auditor. Currently, Mr. Wang is considering taking action against Saibo's auditor for this and other dubious accounting methods.

The action that Mr. Wang intends to take against Saibo's auditor is important in light of the recent Enron incident in U.S. and their auditor, Arthur Andersen. It's an exact parallel to the Saibo situation and there are many such situations in Japan involving many banks and corporations. In fact, as you read this book you may come to believe, as I do, that Enron simply took lessons from the Japanese who have been doing these types of activities for years.

Serious scandals have also surrounded ten out of the top thirteen Japanese banks and some of these scandals involved direct violations of banking laws. One outcome was that Daiwa Bank was evicted from American soil. Further, the share prices of these banks took a big plunge, causing astronomical losses to Japanese and American investors alike. It is plain that not only Japanese investors needed protection; American investors also fell victim to these wrong doings.

It is because of such things that Japan's credit rating has been reduced twice in recent months, in November 2001 and again in February 2002. The world's second-largest economy now has the same credit rating as Cyprus.

Mr. Wang is not alone in his opinions of the Japanese financial sector. In fact, his opinions on the misconduct regarding his investments in Japanese securities are fully supported by some of the best legal minds in the U.S. and Japan. The following have assisted him in his fight against the Japanese system:

Howell E. Jackson, Esq., Professor of Law, Harvard University

Howard V. Perlmutter, Esq., Professor, Wharton School of Business, University of Pennsylvania

Steve H. Hanke, Professor, Johns Hopkins University

Mark A. Sargent, Esq., Professor of Law, University of Maryland

William L. Reynolds, Esq., Professor of Law, University of Maryland

Kazuo Yamauchi, Professor, Gakushuin University

Masafumy Kaneko, Assistant Professor, Dokkyo University

Katsuro Kanzaki, Professor, Kobe University

Tatsuo Kamimura, Professor, Faculty of Law, Waseda University

Atsuo Mihara, Economic Analyst

Additionally, here in the U.S., his son Robert has spent time and effort to bring the Japanese problem to the attention of Congress, testifying on two different occasions and preparing several White Papers to brief the representatives. Members of U.S. government that have responded favorably to the white papers and supported Mr. Wang's crusade include:

Mr. James A. Baker, III, the former Secretary of State and Secretary of the Treasury

Senator Tom Daschle

Senator Christopher S. Bond

Senator Robert G. Torricelli (also a former U.S. Representative)

Representative Richard A. Gephardt

Representative Robert T. Matsui

Representative Duncan Hunter

Mr. Douglas H. Bosco, a former U.S. Representative

Despite this impressive list, the problems continue in Japan. More action is needed.

If there is one thing I have learned in working on this book, it is that change comes hard in Japan. It is often a long, drawn-out fight because the true power remains in the hands of a few and often they have no motive to change because they have set up the system to benefit themselves. But change *is* possible. It's just that sometimes, like the ships of Commodore Perry in Tokyo Bay, it takes drastic measures and outside pressure to force Japan to change its ways.

It is with this in mind that Mr. Wang and Firelight Publishing present this book to the world in hopes that through exposure and outside pressure, Japan will take a hard look at itself and bring about the necessary changes—for its own sake and that of the rest of the world.

Mr. Wang once said that the purpose of this book would have been well served and his contribution to his second homeland would have been achieved if only one more voice from the readers is raised for change and reform of the Japanese system.

Who knows, perhaps Fortune has put this book in your hands so that you might raise your voice too, and make a real difference. It's hard to say. But what is certain is that a voice never raised is one that always goes unheard.

— Mark Anderson
May 2002

The

Economic Gang

Chapter One

The Essence of Betrayal

I have been wronged.

There's no easier way to put it. I have been wronged. Unfortunately, this mistreatment was not at the hands of thieves or career criminals. Instead, this mistreatment has come from individuals, corporations, the courts, and even the government; a system-wide abuse that has assaulted my friends, myself, and so many others—victimizing thousands of people.

Unexpected twists and turns lie in wait for us. Unfortunate accidents, unforeseen events—these are all part of human life here on this Earth. But how do you cope when you learn that the unexpected twist was a deliberate trap? A betrayal of trust, a miscarriage of justice, a trap that was set by the powers-that-be. Do you put up a fight or do you just give in?

What you are about to read is a true story, a recounting of the bitter experiences and lessons I have personally had through my investment activities in Japan over the past thirty years, although to the Western mindset some of it may seem unbelievable at times. This is because my experiences go far beyond the simple process of investing in a company in hopes of turning a profit. This book is a documentary to bring attention to the cozy and dirty relationships among the Japanese major corporations, bureaucrats, major securities firms, and high court justices; it is about the Japanese stock market that is infested with illegal price manipulation activities and a financial system that is a slave to those lurking in the shadows.

I have recently turned seventy-five. My five sons and three daughters are all adults and are living in the United States and Hong Kong. As for myself, I have virtually retired from business, spending half of each year in Hong Kong, and the other half in the United States and Europe. It would be fair to say that my final years are tolerably happy ones.

However, there is only one thing left for me to do. I am devoting myself to the betterment of Japan, the country of my youth. This is because there has not been one iota of realistic improvement in Japan's unfair economic and social system in the last thirty or even sixty years. Instead, it is still dominated by insiders and the average person is left on the outside to struggle along as best they can.

For more than twenty years I have been trying to arouse public opinion about Japanese society, which is so riddled with abuses. I have published several books in Japan to try to wake the Japanese up to the problems within their system. In 1981, I published *Kabushiki Gaisha Nippon tono Taiketsu* (*Confronting Japan, Inc.*), and from 1997 onward I published four more books: *Akugou* (*Evil Deeds*), *Kinyu, Shoken Houkai no Zenya* (*The Eve of the Financial and Securities Collapse*) *Otonashi-sugiru Nihonjin* (*The Quiet Japanese*), and, in April 2001, *Kenryoku no Giseisha* (*Victim of the Establishment*) . It would be fair to say that I have spent nearly all of the latter part of my life exclusively in these pursuits. I don't have much time left.

Lately, I have been thinking a great deal about life and death. I have come to think of the life that we human beings are granted in this world as a journey through time on Earth. What is the purpose of our birth into the world? What are we supposed accomplish? First of all, the very origin of our lives is an event that is filled with mystery and wonder. One sperm out of hundreds of millions combines with an egg at a certain instant and we are born as a consequence. I believe that this is not so much a matter of coincidence, but of necessity. A cosmic providence has chosen us to exist. The fact that our lives here on this world have been conferred upon us means that each of us has been assigned a role that we are duty-bound to perform.

If we take the average male life expectancy to be seventy-eight years, that means there are still a few years left to me. In the short time that remains, I have to put the finishing touches on my life. Together with my Japanese friends, I would like to devote the rest of my days to doing all that I can for Japan. This is why I would like the people of America simply to hear what I have to say.

The exclusiveness and unfairness of Japan's financial circles, particularly the stock market, are things that they would like to keep hidden. "Dirty linen" such as the lavishing of benefits upon professional corporate extortion artists by Nomura Securities came as no surprise to those familiar with the world of Japanese securities. Such occurrences are, unfortunately, everyday fare that make the Enron scandal seem almost tame in comparison. Certainly, what happened with Enron would not seem out of place in Japanese circles. While the Japanese government and the securities houses intone the mantra of "liberalization and internationalization" whenever they open their mouths, the hard fact of the matter is that severe discrimination and collusion are still rampant at a time when Japan is supposed to be a full-fledged member of the international financial community.

The Japanese government is now saying that the economic situation is showing some signs of recovery from the latest recession and that the reconstruction of the Japanese economy is proceeding smoothly. However, no truly sound economic reconstruction can be expected unless the evils that are the sources of the disease ravaging Japan's society are stamped out. Any doctor knows that to treat cancer, the cancer must be removed rather than ignored. Yet the Japanese government pretends it is not there.

In Japan, there is the old maxim that "You can't fight city hall." It means that it is best and wisest to do what the authorities tell you. This precept suggests how powerful the establishment in Japan really is, and that it has predominated for a very long time. Consequently, the Japanese people do not fight against the establishment and most Japanese feel it is unthinkable to challenge those in authority. This is truly different from Western society that thrives on and even insists on the responsibility of those in power to those who put them there. Having lived in Japan for a number of years, and having had a great many dealings with Japanese people, I am well versed in the Japanese mindset. The Japanese people are often as meek as sheep and will do whatever their superiors tell them to do and as such do not stand up for what they might believe in or what they know to be right.

Such a sheepish attitude has allowed the Japanese authorities to grow presumptuous because they believe that those "beneath them" will not stand up to them. If the commoners do stand up to them, the authorities know they can be quickly beaten back down.

This ugly but pervasive attitude also exists in the corporate world, where authorities, corporations, banks, and others band together in a diabolical form of collusion, protecting one another and protecting their power base. Such collusion can happen at any time, without warning, simply because one or more of these entities chooses to do so. If you try to go against the system or are no longer welcome, they will not hesitate to try to destroy you. As a result, laws designed to protect investors can mean very little in real-life application.

The idea of such heavy-handed, blatant collusion between the various financial and governmental entities may come as a bit of a surprise to the average U.S. reader, due in part to the fact that Japan tries to portray itself as an open market, just like its Western counterparts. As a result, most Americans no doubt believe that Japan is an economy similar to that of the U.S., with capitalistic principals driving the economy and stock market. The truth is far from it.

Here in America, we sometimes take our rights for granted. The very idea that the U.S. Congress, the Securities and Exchange Commission, the FBI, and major corporations could all band together to attack an investor who was simply trying to earn a return on his investment seems completely unreal—like something out of movie or a novel. In reality, of course, that would be unheard of. And if it did happen, Americans would quickly band together and demand justice for the individual, and the media would not let the story rest until those responsible were punished. Yet these very things happened to my friends and me.

Unfortunately, the problems Japan is experiencing and the problems with its financial system are not only problems for the Japanese people. They are international problems. The financial problems that the Japanese are experiencing will certainly have ramifications for the United States as well as the rest of the world. Japan has the world's second-largest economy and you can bet that if it collapses, the "Japanese problem" will very quickly become an American problem. The collapse of Enron—which was just a single company—has left millions of Americans with their pensions in doubt, but the collapse of the Japanese system would have much greater implications for the rest of the world. Something must be done to fix the Japanese problem and it must be done quickly.

What may also surprise you about my experiences is that I am not an average investor. After a life of hard work and astute entrepreneurship, I have made my fortune. I have done a great deal of business in Hong Kong and am part of what is considered to be a very influential investing group. The securities houses in Japan freely welcomed my investments and they treated me with warmth and open arms—no doubt due in part to the large commissions they earned from my transactions. In the ten-year period leading up to the start of my trouble with the system, I had traded 226 million shares with a value of roughly $600 million (¥75.125 billion), and paid $4 million in commissions to six Japanese securities firms with a presence in Hong Kong at the time. All this took place some thirty-five years ago, and those were extremely large amounts of money, especially back then.

Needless to say, the Japanese securities houses treated me as one of their best clients. The top executives of the brokerages would personally fly to visit me in Hong Kong where I lived at the time, bringing me expensive gifts in appreciation of my business.

I was not only a big investor for the Japanese securities companies, but I also helped them in their business. If they needed to meet an important Hong Kong businessman, I would set up the meeting for them; if they hoped to meet new clients, then I would introduce them to other well-to-do investors. Their company's portfolio grew and expanded because of my efforts on their behalf.

I'm not saying any of this to impress you. I say it because if the powers-that-be can take away my rights as an investor and treat me—a wealthy investor—the way that they did, then just imagine the abuse that they are capable of. Imagine for a moment the power they hold over average investors and citizens—combined with the inability of the Japanese to stand up for themselves—and you can begin to imagine the plight of the Japanese people and why I am trying to stand up for them.

Most strikingly, unlike the U.S., the Japanese system does not have a powerful SEC to oversee the fair and proper trading of stocks. In my mind, this is horrifying and frightening, because it exposes investors to abuse by those in power. In Japan, the safeguards that protect U.S. investment do not exist, at least not in practical application. It is a system that is ripe for manipulation.

When I first began investing in Japanese companies, I believed that the companies and individuals I worked with had my best interest at heart. When some of my investor friends and I received a tip from one of the securities companies about a good, established company with a large amount of latent assets but a seriously undervalued stock price, naturally, we jumped at the chance to take advantage of it.

But what had looked so promising turned out to be a trap, one that would send me on a long and sometimes lonely path that in turn exposed me to the very worst of what human beings are capable of doing to each other.

I was betrayed by those I had come to trust. I was lied to and lied about. I was attacked in the media—viciously accused of crimes I did not commit. I was called names, and my reputation and honor were attacked. Even my life was threatened. When I appealed for help from the government that was supposed to protect me, it was denied. Those who were in positions of authority who had the opportunity and ability to help me instead deliberately chose not to. When things eventually came to court, trusted business associates betrayed me or committed perjury to protect themselves.

As painful as this first experience with the system was, I felt I could put it behind me. But as it turned out, I was betrayed and lied to two more times.

It has been more than thirty years of frustration, lies, betrayal, and attacks. They have all been very black experiences that no decent person would wish on another. Not including appeals, I have lodged nearly two-dozen lawsuits in Japan's courts against such unfair conduct by those in power in an effort to correct Japan's corporate culture and to clear away the unwarranted slander and defamation against me. It has been a long, grueling, and expensive fight. Perhaps some might consider it even a foolish fight. After all, you can't fight city hall.

But I steadfastly refuse to believe that the country of Japan I had come to know and love in my youth is incapable of changing, because I believe in the integrity of the Japanese people, and I know that they can make the necessary changes if only they will steel themselves to do so.

It is my sincere hope that this book will help bring attention to these problems and also serve as a reference tool to foreign investors who are thinking of investing in Japanese stocks. I also hope that this book will serve to bring some external pressure to Japan and that it will serve for Japan's national interest in the long run. I believe it is absolutely necessary and critical to fight city hall, especially when individuals are ruthlessly attacked, because that is what happened to me.

I can only hope it stops before it's too late.

Chapter Two

Background

I was born on March 25, 1926, in the city of Sum Gup, Taipei Prefect, on the island of Taiwan. I was the second son of fourteen children. Members of my family were landlords who owned extensive tracts of land; my father himself owned a coal mine and worked near the town of Lung Tum, which was several miles away. So even though my family was large, we were quite well off.

In 1936, when I was ten, my father took me to Lung Tum for school where I stayed until I completed my elementary education in 1938 at Lung Tum School. After that, my father tried to enroll me into a good school. There were two prestigious schools that my father knew of; one was a technical school for coal mining and the other was a famous high school in Taipei, and he applied to both of them for me. But at that time, Taiwan was a Japanese colony so Japanese students had priority in school admissions. As a result, I wasn't admitted to either school. So I went back to Sum Gup, my hometown, to continue my junior high school education and at the end of each year, I applied to the same schools, but each time I was rejected.

I completed my junior high school education in 1940 at the age of fourteen. That was when my mother tried to enroll me into the local high school, but I failed to show up on the day of the admissions test because I thought the test was supposed to take place the following day. My mother was furious with me but there was nothing she could do. Looking back, it was fortunate for me to have missed the admissions test because I was a good student and would have passed the test easily. Had I done so, I might have become a clerk and been one to this day.

Because I'd missed the test, my parents planned to send me to Shanghai over in China—where my uncle was the mayor—to continue my education. But the Japanese colonial authorities in Taiwan refused to let me leave for China because by this time in 1940, Japan was at war with China.

My parents then decided to send me to Tokyo, where my father had a friend. I left for Tokyo in 1941 and through this family friend I was set up in a modest apartment and enrolled in a Tokyo business trading school.

But before the end of 1941, Japan was at war with the United States. I decided to leave school because my friends, who were employees at a transportation company, offered me a job as a bill collector. I worked with that company for about eighteen months, until about mid-1943 when I became aware that my friends were pilfering company money and I decided to leave. By now, I was seventeen.

I went to Kobe with the money I'd saved from my job, knowing that the city was a major port for Taiwanese imports and also because many Taiwanese merchants, my fellow countrymen, were living there. Also, with the war and all, there were a lot of business opportunities in Kobe. I settled into an inexpensive boarding house there and began looking for work.

After some careful study of the situation, I soon became a food broker in Kobe. I would buy food products from importers and then resell them to factory workers and office employees. It was a profitable business and they were always glad to see me arrive at their workplaces. In this way, I also began to make some contacts with the white-collar workers that would later prove to be valuable.

As 1944 grew near, the food situation in Japan grew extremely bad and it was sometimes difficult even for me, a broker, to obtain food to sell—and I was dealing directly with the importers. I took stock of what was happening and I felt I could either continue to struggle or try to do something to improve the situation.

Fresh fish was one of the most profitable items I sold, so I decided to take a huge risk and—with funds borrowed from my father— buy a fishing vessel of my own to import fish into Kobe. Stepping into any new venture is always risky, but this was in the middle of the war so it would be doubly risky. There were probably some people who thought I was crazy, especially since I was only seventeen. All it would take would be one torpedo and my entire investment could end up at the bottom of the sea—to say nothing of my life and those of my crewmen.

I went down to the docks and started to look around. I managed to find a vessel of about forty tons that I purchased from a Korean fisherman and we worked out an agreement that he and his crew would stay on and work for me. Before I could set sail, however, I needed to obtain a license from the Japanese authorities in order to sell fish as an importer in Kobe. Obtaining a license wasn't easy, even though this was in the middle of the war and one might think that they would expedite the process but that was not the case. Fortunately, some of my food customers introduced me to a famous retired Japanese baseball player, Mr. Nidekawa, who later became the head umpire in the Japanese baseball league after the war. Mr. Nidekawa in turn introduced me to a high-ranking Japanese naval officer in Kobe who facilitated the application process for my import license.

Between 1944 and early 1945, I made three trips to Korea on my ship to buy fish. I would set sail from Shimonoseki, which is in Southwest Japan, and head nearly due west toward the port of Pusan in Korea by way of Tsushima. Tsushima is an island that lies in the Korean Straits and is nearly halfway between Japan and Korea. During the Russo-Japanese War in the early 1900s, the Japanese had defeated Russia off this island in an epic sea battle by hiding their ships near this island and then ambushing the Russian battleships.

Sailing under the cover of night was dangerous because Allied submarines could appear out of nowhere, so I had to sail during the day. But even during the day, these were terribly perilous sea journeys because Allied combat airplanes and submarines would attack any ships that originated from Japan. In order to avoid such attacks, we would set sail from Shimonoseki and head for the island of Tsushima, the eastern shore of which was only several hours away. This was the most dangerous part of the journey and those hours seemed to last forever. If we could make it to Tsushima, then we would be relatively safe—or at least as safe as one could be on the open sea in the middle of a world war. Once we reached Tsushima, we would stay overnight and then set out for Korea early the following morning, heading for Pusan, which was the nearest port on the Korean peninsula. It was still very dangerous to be out on the open sea where we might be mistaken for a munitions ship, but having "originated" from Tsushima, we felt a little safer. Once there, we refueled and replenished our supplies before sailing to fishing towns to the north to buy fish.

After we bought the fish, we would sail back to Pusan, and then head back in the same manner to Tsushima and on to Shimonoseki. You cannot believe what a great relief it was to finally come into port, especially since we were arriving on a boat that was riding heavy with food for hungry people.

Because of the extremely dangerous and risky work, I made a large sum of money with the fish that I managed to import into Kobe during this period. People were desperate for food so I felt especially good being able to provide such a basic necessity to the civilian population. It was also a heady feeling. I was young and it was daring work that was highly rewarding.

On one occasion, though, while I was walking around Pusan, a naval officer, who was walking at the head of ten or so subordinates, suddenly saluted me. I wondered who he was and then realized that he was a friend of mine from back home in Taiwan. He'd been a student at Chuo University in Japan, and was now a cadet officer in the Japanese Navy. I invited him over to my hotel in Pusan and we talked all through the night until he had to go back to his ship.

The next day, his ship was attacked and sunk in the open sea off Sai Shu Island, which lay to the south of Korea—only a few hours after I'd seen him.

Things like this make me believe from the bottom of my heart that the destiny of human beings is something we can't fathom. If our positions had been reversed, my boat might well have been the one destroyed.

Around May 1945, I sent the vessel to Korea to buy fish, but this time, instead of going along, I entrusted the money to the captain and instructed him to buy the fish. The vessel never returned. Since the war was ending, I guessed the captain and his crew had remained in Korea along with my ship and money for the fish. There was also the grim possibility that they could have been killed, but I had no way of finding out. In any event, I never heard from them again.

In addition to importing fresh fish into Kobe during the war, I had also started to import and sell other goods from Taiwan such as dried bananas, powdered bananas, and sugared water. At that time, food controls were being imposed in Japan and 100% pure sugar was a controlled substance. However, importing products that were sweet, but not 100% sugar, was allowed. So I imported a sugar syrup that was made with 90% sugar, which did not violate the controls.

This sugared syrup sold like hotcakes in Japan, where there was not only a general food shortage but a real shortage of sweets. Before I knew it, I was clearing around ¥100,000 per trip. This was an incredible fortune at a time when white-collar workers were earning an average salary of ¥100 per month. Through hard and very dangerous work, my business prospered nicely and over the last year or so of the war I succeeded in amassing a small fortune.

When the war finally ended, I called my two brothers over from Taiwan and put one of them through medical school and the other through high school. My brother who went to medical school now owns several hospitals in Japan and employs several hundred nurses. My other brother later went on to study architecture in the U.S. and is now a U.S. citizen. He currently owns and runs an upscale motel business.

As for myself, I decided to stay in Japan and, with the money I'd made, I started a finance business. I knew that now that the war was over, people would settle back into a normal lifestyle, but I also knew that companies would need help with financing and with their day-to-day operations. I bought accounts receivables from established Japanese companies at a discount and then later collected the face value from the original purchaser when they became due. This benefited the issuing company by giving them immediate sources of cash instead of having to wait sixty days or more for the accounts receivable. This again led to some valuable contacts. In fact, one such company that I financed, Tsugami Seisaku Sho, was a large machine manufacturer whose director, Mr. Nobusuke Kishi, later became the prime minister of Japan.

In addition to the finance company, I also started another import business. By 1949, foreigners in Japan were allowed to set up import stores to supply expatriates that were living in Japan with products from their own countries. Since I, too, was a foreigner living in Japan, I obtained a license to start an import store and called it "Lucky Store." I imported mostly food products and textiles, most of which I actually ended up selling to Japanese consumers since they were not able to purchase imported goods very easily.

After nearly fifteen years of living in Japan, I moved to Hong Kong in 1955. I had previously visited the city when I bought merchandise for my Lucky Store and I felt relaxed in Hong Kong. Life in Japan was getting too hectic and I was even suffering from insomnia to the point that the doctor prescribed nightly injections in order to induce sleep. Also, Hong Kong was very business friendly: it had a low tax rate, no tax on foreign income, no tax on capital gains, and no tax on stock dividends.

In Hong Kong, I started a property development business. I guessed—correctly as it turned out—that Hong Kong would develop as a free port and a tourist area. One of my first ventures was in 1956, when I started construction on what would be a first-class hotel on Hing Fat Street, Causeway Bay, to be named the Victoria Park Hotel. However, the project had reached the piling stage when I came to the determination that the location would probably not be as convenient for tourists to Hong Kong as I initially thought since the international airport was then in Kai Tak. Because of this, I changed the project to a residential apartment building. This became Victoria Court, the very first multistory residential building in that part of the Causeway Bay and North Point area, and it is still standing tall and proud even by today's standards.

I then launched into property development around Kai Tak Airport on a large scale. At the time, the area was still very much virgin territory for substantial development or investment, so it was a bit of a risk. I bought the land at auction from the government and erected two blocks of industrial buildings, putting up the Kai Tak Industrial Building Phase One and Kai Tak Industrial Building Phase Two. I also built the Kai Sun Building, which was the first residential building in San Po Kong. There were other projects as well, including various apartment buildings, a school, office buildings, and residential housing. The company I operated, Kai Tak Property, eventually grew into a publicly listed company.

After awhile, I decided to sell my property business and start up an investment company. I had become intrigued with the whole idea of investing when my property investment company went public with its initial stock offering. It was a fascinating process.

I didn't have anyone to teach me how to invest. It was all a self-taught process and the early going was a trial-and-error period, but I applied the same sense of study and hard work into investing that I had applied to all of my business up until then.

One area in particular that I always looked for when I examined a company for possible investing was the company's latent assets. Perhaps this was due to my own land development background or because of my family's history as landowners, but I knew that if the company had a lot of land—perhaps that it wasn't using at all or wasn't using to its best potential—then there was a good deal of profit to be made from that alone.

What I eventually came to develop were five guiding principles for successful investing. First, the market value should be four to five times the reporting value. Second, the business absolutely must have growth potential. Third, the company's products must be competitive with other companies in their field. Fourth, the company should have a low level of debt. And, fifth, always, always review the security reports on the company.

As I became more involved in investing, I thought I should start investing in companies in Japan. In this way, I would be able to share my good fortune with the Japan of my youth. After all, Japan was where I first started to amass my fortune, so I felt it would be good to invest some of my money back into a country that I had great fondness for. Besides, I still had many friends who lived there, as well as family members.

So around 1967, I began to look for Japanese companies to invest in. This was also around the time that Japan started to liberalize investment opportunities for foreigners, whereas up until then it had been a fairly closed market.

I began to make large purchases of Japanese companies' shares. My first investments were in Pioneer Electronic, Tokyo Denki Kagaku (TDK), and Alps Denki. I made some good profits with those companies and then sold my shares. After those, I invested in a number of other Japanese stocks including Isuzu, Nippon Yusen, Fuji Electric, Nippon Steel, Japan Line, Kao Soap, Ajinomoto, Meiji Milk, Snow Brand Milk, Konishiroku, Fujitsu, Fuji Photo Film, Takeda Pharmacy, Japan Cold Storage, Sumitomo Mining, NKK, Mitsubishi Metal, and Fuji Heavy Industries.

Part of my learning process for investing involved learning about the rather unique Japanese investment system. Japan, especially in the late 1960s and 1970s, was not like many other nations when it came to investment. In addition to being largely closed to foreign investment, there were other unique intricacies that I came to learn about.

One peculiarity that I quickly discovered had to do with the securities houses and the vast influence they hold over the financial markets. At the time, there were four major securities companies in Japan, known as the "Big Four." These companies were Nomura, Daiwa, Nikko, and Yamaichi. In addition to the Big Four, there were also four other, smaller companies, but because a substantial portion of Japanese corporations were traded through and by the Big Four, they controlled much of the stocks and had huge influence and sway over the market. As you will see, it is very much an understatement for me to say that the Big Four had influence and sway over the markets because there is so much that happens behind the scenes due to the interconnectedness of the Japanese financial system. In any event, each of these four major securities companies also had many affiliates (also securities companies) throughout Japan and had branches overseas in Hong Kong.

It was these securities companies that recommended concentrated investments—in other words, buying in volume. This is because, for a securities house, the amount of effort involved in dealing in quantities of thousand-share lots with small investors and acting as an intermediary for investors with million-share lots is exactly the same. Obviously, if it takes the same amount of effort, then the securities firms would naturally want to emphasize the million-share investors over the thousand-share investors.

It goes without saying that I was given the royal treatment. Whenever any representative of any of the securities houses came to Hong Kong, they always made a point to visit me personally. I received numerous gifts from them in gratitude for my business. It was a good business relationship for both sides. They helped me with my investments and I helped them with their business as well. For example, when Daiwa's managing director came to Hong Kong, he specifically came to visit me and asked me to introduce him to some valuable contacts, one of which was the Consulate General of the Republic of Nauru. I later discovered through a newspaper article that as a result of this meeting, Daiwa Securities took over the management of a ¥10 billion account for the Republic of Nauru.

I also introduced him to three major businessmen in Hong Kong. One was Mr. Li Ka-shing, the president of the Cheung Kong Group, a multinational conglomerate. (Incidentally, Mr. Li Ka-shing has recently aroused comment by making a profit of around ¥1.5 trillion by selling shares in the British telecommunications company Orange that were held by a subsidiary under his umbrella.) Over the years, Mr. Li has also donated huge sums of money to both Hong Kong and China, which included building a university at his birthplace. The second was Mr. Cheng Yu-tung, president of the New World Development Company Group, with a number of major property companies in Hong Kong that owned the Grand Hyatt Hotel, the New World Hotel, and many other hotels in Hong Kong and China. Like Mr. Li, Mr. Cheng has also donated huge sums of money to both Hong Kong and China, including a high school at his birthplace. This high school is as large as a university. And finally, there was Mr. Henry Y. T. Fok, a major shareholder in Macau Casinos, who had large-scale investments in China. Mr. Fok was considered to be one of the earlier land developers in Hong Kong and has also donated large sums of money to Hong Kong and China, including various sports programs for the people of Hong Kong.

These were three extremely busy and self-made businessmen. I sweated blood to adjust their schedules and somehow managed to obtain appointments with them at one-hour intervals. As a result, Daiwa Securities succeeded in opening their accounts and was able to do a great deal of business.

In addition to my own investing, I persuaded some of my Hong Kong friends and associates to begin investing in Japanese companies. Together, we were some of the wealthiest investors in Hong Kong and we presented a strong investing group. My friends, some of whom rank among the wealthiest men in the world, are all chairmen of well-known, publicly listed companies in Hong Kong.

Even though Japan was beginning to open its markets to foreigners during the late 1960s, we were not allowed to buy on margin. In other words, we had to pay for everything in cash. So we focused on picking up stocks with relatively low share prices that either had large latent assets—including land—or those that were showing improving results.

Because we would buy large blocks of these types of shares, the natural consequence of our investing was that company was bound to take a turn for the better. The share price would pick up accordingly and we would reap a profit. Not only was this beneficial to us, but it also benefited the company itself and other Japanese investors who had invested in the same company as we had.

Besides having to buy our stocks in cash, there were other restrictions on foreign investment in Japan as well. At this time, foreigners were limited to the percentage amount of a single company that they could own. When I started investing in the late 1960s, foreigners were limited to no more than 25% of a Japanese company. This meant that, unlike U.S. companies, foreigners could never buy out Japanese companies. This aspect didn't bother me too much since neither my friends nor I were interested in buying out a company and then having to run it. We simply wanted to find good investments for our hard-earned money that would give us a good return.

What was highly unfair, however, was that when we found a good company that was doing well and our investment was paying handsomely, we were unable to purchase more of the company to make even better returns on our investment. Because the amount of shares we could own in a given company was restricted, we were unable to capitalize on prime investments. It also felt prejudicial in some ways because this restriction was only because we were foreigners. Had we been Japanese, there would have been no restrictions on the amounts we could have invested and we would have made much, much more than we did. We also would not have run into the trouble that we eventually ran into in the late 1970s.

By the summer of 1971, my friends and I had acquired 11 million shares in a company called Japan Line. As with most of our other investments, we became interested in it due to its latent assets and strong potential. When we originally bought the stock, the purchase price was an average of ¥70 per share. However, Nikko Securities started to ask me to sell the shares. Although I was puzzled, we decided to sell them. They had treated us well, and perhaps they were concerned about some aspect of the company that we were as yet unaware of and were looking out for our best interest. After all, a securities house is supposed to provide its clients with accurate and reliable advice. Thus, we sold all the shares at about cost, with Nikko handling most of the sales.

However, the price of Japan Line shares soared after we parted with them. In October of the following year, 1972, it had reached ¥730 per share. Five months later, in February of 1973, it again surged, this time to ¥935, which was fourteen times our original purchase price. By selling the shares when we did, we ended up losing ¥9,515,000,000 (roughly $83 million) in lost opportunity.

So much for good investment advice.

Sanko Steamship, as well as all the other investors in Japan who bought the shares that we'd parted with, made a huge profit. Sanko Steamship especially benefited because it was well known that they had bought up about 40% of the shares in Japan Line.

While it might be easy to pass this off to the fact that everyone makes investment mistakes or takes bad advice, Japan Line was not the only transaction like this. Daiwa also came forward and asked us to sell our shares of Kao Soap and Ajinomoto. I didn't want to let go of these companies either, but because of Daiwa's earnest entreaties, I relented.

The Ajinomoto sale began with a telephone call from President Yamanaka of Daiwa Hong Kong saying that Vice President Chino of Daiwa Securities had received a request from President Bunzo Watanabe of Ajinomoto saying that they would like me to sell the shares. At that time, I was in America staying at a hotel in St. Louis. Since I had made the investment together with my friends, I avoided giving an immediate reply. As it was, despite the fact that the day I got back to Hong Kong was a Sunday, Mr. Yamanaka came to visit me and earnestly entreated me to sell the Ajinomoto shares. Overcome by such zeal, I did so.

Again, to my detriment, the price of Ajinomoto shares increased from my sale price of ¥535 to a high price of ¥4,350—although in reality, it may be more than that because I have not followed Ajinomoto's history since I sold it and don't know if Ajinomoto has had any stock splits since then. After the Kao Soap stock sale, Kao's stock has since split several times and reached a high price at ¥3,940 since my sale at ¥600. Whoever bought my Kao Soap and Ajinomoto shares, if they haven't sold them, now holds about $4 billion in capital gains.

After I sold the Kao Soap shares and the Ajinomoto shares to Daiwa Securities, Vice President Chino of Daiwa Securities made a point of visiting my office in Hong Kong, accompanied by President Yamanaka of Daiwa Hong Kong. At that time, Mr. Chino presented me with a woodblock print by Hiroshige out of deep gratitude for my selling the shares.

Such was our extremely cordial relationship with the Japanese securities firms. We followed their advice, and they were happy to have us as their customers.

But it was not to last.

Chapter Three

It Starts with a Phone Call

In January 1977, two people from the research division of Nomura recommended three corporations to me: Toho, Japan Paint, and Oji Paper Manufacturing. They recommended these companies because of their off-the-books assets and felt that the shares were undervalued. I took their recommendations and began to look into the companies.

Of the three, Oji Paper stood out. Oji Paper was Japan's largest wood pulp and paper manufacturing company, along the lines of Louisiana-Pacific and Weyerhaeuser in the U.S. So I hired a company to carefully investigate Oji Paper's assets over the next couple of months and, as time progressed, Oji Paper did indeed look promising.

In April 1977, Mr. Yamataka, a staff member of the Hong Kong Office of Nikko Securities rang me and very excitedly urged me to buy Oji Paper shares, believing it was an excellent buy and that it was due to start going up in the very near future. Combined with the research I'd done, I decided it was time to start buying some shares of Oji Paper. I was confident my purchase of Oji Paper would be a good one based on its latent assets. So over the next few weeks, I began to make cautious purchases of Oji Paper in blocks of several thousand shares.

Sometime later in April, while I was still purchasing Oji Paper, Vice President Yoshitoki Chino from the head office of Daiwa Securities in Japan and Ichiro Yamanaka, the president of Daiwa Hong Kong visited my office together. Mr. Chino presented me with an expensive woodblock print, accompanied with a card that read, "One Nishikie colored woodblock print: 'Tozuka Inn in the Tokaido Series.' Presented to Mr. Wang Tseng Hsiang to manifest my profound gratitude for your warm friendship." It was from the famous painter, Hiroshige Utagawa, and painted in 1843.

I thanked him for his kind gift and we talked politely for several minutes before the talk turned to investing.

"Incidentally," I said, "what do you think of Oji shares?"

Mr. Chino strongly recommended that I invest some more in Oji Paper Company and Mr. Yamanaka also recommended it, joking that the omens were good because the Chinese characters for "Oji" and "Oshi" (for "Mr. Wang" in Japanese) looked similar and were similar in pronunciation.

A few weeks later, Mr. Doi of Daiwa Securities, who later became the president of Daiwa, came to visit me at my Hong Kong office; several directors and executives accompanied him. He'd brought with him an expensive porcelain tea set as a present for me. I asked Mr. Doi's opinion about my investment in Oji Paper.

He gave me a very strong approval. "Oji Paper Manufacturing is the largest landowner in Japan. You've certainly made a good purchase," he said. "I once had to request the Aichi Prefect Police to conduct a search, because some of our staff members had gotten lost in the mountains. I subsequently learned that the mountains belonged to Tokai Pulp. If people can get lost in the mountains belonging to someone like Tokai Pulp, then the extent of the lands belonging to Oji Paper Company, Japan's biggest landlord, must be all the more impressive."

Again, in May, when Mr. Sengo Mizutani, the chief counselor at Nomura Research, and Mr. Masahiro Tsuchihashi, the general manager of the Hong Kong office of the same institute, came on a visit,

I asked them about Oji Paper Company. "With the future amendments in the Accounting Law, the latent assets of companies will be evaluated in terms of their market prices. Once this happens, Oji shares, which have substantial latent asset value, are a certainty to be aimed for."

They also said that the government of Japan was considering changing its printed money, which would mean substantial growth for all paper companies. Because of these factors, they agreed that Oji Paper Company was an excellent investment target.

Thereafter, Mr. Inoguchi of the Hong Kong branch of Wako Securities prepared a special survey report on Oji Paper Company and sent it to me. According to that report, the latent assets of Oji Paper Company were worth ¥1,421 per share for the land owned by the head office alone, and ¥2,561 per share when the land and the securities of its subsidiaries were included. At that time, the market price of Oji Paper Company was only ¥350 per share.

"Well," I thought, "this is it." All of these recommendations gave me more confidence, and the survey report especially made up my mind for me. So, having combined forces by now with four of my friends, who were all prominent business leaders in Hong Kong, we steadily began to increase our purchases in Oji Paper. Together we continued to purchase Oji Paper shares over the next couple of months until we'd purchased about 36 million shares.

According to the law in Japan at that time, there were restrictions in place on the number of shares that could be held by foreigners in a single company. One person, or one foreign company, could only hold up to 10% of a given stock, and the total investment by all foreigners combined could not exceed 25% in any Japanese corporation. The 36 million shares of Oji Paper that we had bought amounted to approximately 13% of the total number of shares issued. My own personal shareholding of Oji Paper was about 14 million shares or just a little more than 5%. These figures were far below the legal limits, which left us plenty of room to buy more shares of Oji Paper if we so desired.

Our investment in Oji, though, soon became a topic of conversation, and was picked up by the newspapers and magazines at the time. They weren't critical of our investment; to the contrary, people from Japan's securities houses without exception praised us for making a good investment.

I had a happy goal that as things progressed, I might be able to add to my purchases as much as possible, especially if the restrictions on the acquisition of shares by foreigners were abolished. I also hoped to even offer suggestions to the management on how they might even further improve their capital such as by making better uses of their land. After all, land development had been my business in Hong Kong so I felt I knew what I was talking about. One thing in particular I had noticed was that if one of Oji Paper's subsidiaries was to sell some of the land surplus to repay their lenders, some ¥10 billion in interest payments per year could be saved.

Around July 1977, Fumio Takehiro, who was the vice president of Yamaichi Securities, visited me in Hong Kong. He said he had come to Hong Kong at the request of President Tanaka of Oji Paper Company to ask me and the other Hong Kong investors to sell our shares in Oji Paper. Mr. Takehiro then asked that we sell the shares through Yamaichi.

This was not the first time we'd been asked to sell our shares in a given company, as was the case with Ajinomoto, Kao Soap, and others. However, this time, we felt we'd stumbled onto a really good investment and so we told him that we didn't want to sell the shares at this time. He left disappointed.

In early September, I had two more visitors. The president of Nomura Hong Kong and the president of Yamaichi Hong Kong visited me one after another, both asking me to sell the shares in Oji Paper. However, I again refused their requests to sell. These requests were not unusual but seemed rather odd. Yamaichi was obviously trying very hard to get me to sell if they had sent both the vice president of their Japanese office and the president of their Hong Kong office to ask me to sell the shares. Combined with the fact that the president of Nomura Hong Kong had also personally asked me to sell, all of this seemed especially strange. For whatever reason, they could not seem to understand that we believed this was a very good investment and we wanted to ride it out.

Around the middle of September, I was staying at my house in the U.S. when I received a call from Harry Merlo of Louisiana-Pacific. He wanted to come and visit me and talk to me about my investment in Oji Paper. I agreed to meet with him so he flew out on his private jet to meet me at my house in Bel Air and my second son, Kenneth, picked him up at the airport. We ate at my home and discussed the Oji investment for several hours before he left. Oji Paper was currently buying wood pulp from Louisiana-Pacific at the time and both Oji Paper and Louisiana-Pacific might mutually benefit if Louisiana-Pacific was to buy some of Oji Paper stock.

I wasn't overly interested in parting with my shares, especially since they were currently so undervalued, but felt that I might sell some if his offer was good enough. Besides, I was still interested in acquiring more shares and if he, another foreigner, bought some shares, then it would lower the amount of available shares for our Hong Kong investment group. After meeting with me, he also paid a visit to Oji Paper Company in Tokyo to sound out President Tanaka and to learn more about Oji Paper. He subsequently informed me by letter that he had decided that the deal was not in Louisiana-Pacific's best interest.

Toward the end of September I was back in Hong Kong when President Kato of Yamaichi Securities of Hong Kong called me and told me that something urgent had come up and that he wanted to meet me right away. I was in the middle of a meeting, so I apologized, saying I could not meet him just then. But consenting to his suggestion that a little later would be all right, I agreed to meet him at the Mandarin Hotel, a five-star hotel overlooking Victoria Harbor and set in the heart of the business and shopping district.

When I arrived, Mr. Takahashi, who was in charge of my account at Yamaichi, was there with President Kato. The urgent matter he had alluded to turned out to be yet another request to sell the Oji Paper shares.

"A decision has been made at the head office," President Kato said, "that they definitely want you to sell the Oji Paper stock at the yesterday's TSE closing price of ¥409 per share."

So now their head office was pushing more on this sale. This was the second time the president of Yamaichi Hong Kong had approached me.

However, I turned down this proposal too. I could not help but wonder what was going on. Our acquisition of Oji Paper was only 13%, which left quite a lot of room before the ceiling of 25% would be reached, so what was the matter?

About this same time, Mr. Kawakita, who was a Hong Kong representative of Nomura, asked me about the price at which I would be selling the Oji Paper shares. But I told him he was mistaken, that we had no intention to sell.

Shortly thereafter, around the first of October, when I put in another order for purchasing more of Oji Paper shares, the securities house declined to make the purchase for me. They didn't give me a reason; they just refused to make the purchase.

I had never heard of a securities firm—which makes their living by earning commissions on share dealings and which is usually only too eager to broker sale or buy orders—doing something like refusing purchase orders. Why would they do this? It made absolutely no sense. But if they didn't want my business, then I would just place the order with one of the other securities houses.

Puzzled, I called another securities house to place the buy order with them. But the next one turned me down also.

By now I thought there must be some mistake. Were there no more shares to be purchased? Had we reached the maximum limit allowed by law? That didn't seem possible.

However, the next securities house also turned me down, and the next, until all eight subsidiaries of the Japanese securities houses with a presence in Hong Kong had refused our orders. The local Hong Kong affiliates seemed baffled by it, too, but no matter how many times I tried to place orders, the answer was always the same: "Trading has been suspended."

The securities companies had decided to forcefully put an end to our purchases of Oji Paper.

I could not believe this. I was both bewildered and furious. I could not understand why they would choose to take this reckless course of action. Nevertheless, the result of their action was that we were unable to buy even a single share in Oji Paper. It was clear that we could sell them—which was their goal—but we would no longer be able to buy them even though there was no legal reason whatsoever for their actions. The matter was decided and that was that.

This, of course, didn't stop others from trading in Oji Paper. Other investors were still being allowed to buy shares, but not us. What if the price soared suddenly? We would have missed out on a large fortune by not being able to buy more shares in advance. The share price was still around ¥400 and the real value of the shares was nearly six times that.

Who did the securities companies think they were? They had no right to act this way. We had done nothing wrong and they were acting together to stop us from investing as we saw fit. There was a great deal of money to be made by investing in Oji Paper. Was this our money to invest or did the securities companies think our money was theirs to do with as they pleased? Who had ordered this and why? The more I thought about all of it, the angrier I became.

When I asked them why it had come to this, none of the securities companies could offer any explanation other than the action to stop buy orders was the wish of their head office in Japan.

That only angered me even more. This was not an answer at all. It didn't explain anything. I was furious, not only at the securities companies but also at a financial system that could allow such things. More than anything, though, I couldn't figure out why they would take this drastic action. It simply made no sense.

We discovered the reason on October 5, when the president of the Hong Kong subsidiary of Kangyo Kakumaru Securities (one of the smaller "quasi-major" securities houses) faxed me copy of an article from that morning's *Jiji Press*:

Investigation into the Contents of the Purchase/Sales of Oji Paper Manufacturing Shares: Tokyo Stock Exchange Pays Attention to Hong Kong Movements

The Tokyo Stock Exchange recently commenced an investigation into the details of trading in Oji Paper Company shares. Over 30 million shares have been bought up by Hong Kong parties and movements indicative of a subrogation of these shares have appeared, thus leading to an investigation for ascertaining whether or not there have been any violations of securities rules...

An examination of the movements up to now by the Hong Kong parties reveals that after amassing these shares, an approach was made to rival companies for a takeover and for exerting pressure on Oji Paper.

According to Article 59 of the Articles of Incorporation of the Tokyo Stock Exchange, "Collecting shares by purchase and using one's status as the owner of a large block of that stock in order to profit by persuading the concerned parties of the issuing company to buy them back against their will, or by buying or brokering the purchase of said stock in accordance with a direct or indirect commission from parties with aims similar thereto" is prohibited. In other words, such activities are regarded as an act of intimidation and blackmail.

Because of this, the stock exchange has requested all securities firms who are IEE members, to submit the names and addresses of clients who have traded in Oji Paper shares since May in order to ascertain whether there have been activities in violation of the above or whether a considerable number of orders at a uniform price have been placed recently are not for the purpose of paving the way for an advantageous takeover.

I could hardly believe what was being said and had to read it again. My friends and I were being accused of being blackmailers.

For three months the securities companies had been trying to get us to sell and, when that failed, they resorted to a smear campaign, accusing us of cornering, blackmailing, and subrogating. So now they wanted to force the sale of our rightfully purchased shares. Besides, if we really were blackmailers, then shouldn't they block both purchase and sell orders and not just purchase orders? Blackmailers would be trying to sell the stocks back at a premium, yet they were only interested in stopping us from buying any more stocks.

This was unbelievable. It was unbelievable that a simple investment would be causing this much trouble.

But it was far from over. *Jiji Press* ran another story dealing with this issue the very next day, which was also faxed to me:

According to a statement made by concerned parties on the 5th, various securities companies have decided to refrain from brokering purchases of Oji Paper shares by a Hong Kong group. Because of this, for all intents and purposes it has become impossible for the said group, reputed to have bought up nearly thirteen percent of the shares in Oji Paper up to now, to purchase any more of Oji Paper.

Whispers about the purchase of shares in Oji Paper Company in the stock market by the Hong Kong circle started to be heard at the end of May and, according to concerned parties, the number of Oji Paper shares purchased by the group during the period from then up to September reportedly reached more than 32 million. Oji Paper stock skyrocketed as a result, and shares that used to be no more than ¥300 have now risen to around ¥400.

Essentially, investment by foreigners in Japanese shares is welcomed by the Ministry of Finance and by Japan's securities houses, but the Hong Kong group's purpose is not to participate in the management of the business by buying up shares; it is strictly focused on large-scale speculation. The year before last, after the Hong Kong group had bought large blocks of shares in Kao Soap, Snow Brand Milk Products Co., Ltd., and Meiji Milk Products Co., Ltd., Japanese securities companies acted as mediators to absorb them by sharing them out, and this time they were aiming at the same effect again. However, the securities firms have started exercising self-restraint, judging that the practice of buying up shares to boost the price before selling them off not only damaged the interests of domestic investors, but also had an unfavorable impact on the market.

Owing to the Tokyo Stock Exchange's comments and actions— especially to submit the names and addresses of clients who had traded in Oji Paper shares since May in order to ascertain whether there have been "violations" of any securities laws—ordinary investors rushed to rid themselves of Oji Paper shares. Not surprisingly, Oji Paper's trading volume plummeted. In August 1977, two months before the start of the self-restraint program, 24.5 million Oji Paper shares had traded hands. The next month, share trading in Oji Paper reached a high for the year at just over 26 million shares.

However, after the announcement of the self-restraint program in early October 1977, it dropped to a mere 6,043,000 shares for the month, less than one-quarter its volume from the previous month. The average investor was obviously avoiding Oji Paper.

At this point, I should briefly explain some details about the Japanese financial markets, especially since Japan has a financial system that is unique to itself, especially in comparison to the other modern nations of the world. Chapter Five will deal in much greater detail with the Japanese system.

For now, what is very important to understand is that the Japanese securities market was—and to this day continues to be—dominated by an oligopoly for the benefit of insiders. Furthermore, the Japanese securities market was and is enmeshed in a complex web of reciprocal relationships. Although outsiders—like private investors and even U.S. pension funds—can survive in and potentially even profit in such a "market," their investments are substantially at risk to "rules of the game" that are unclear and tilted toward insiders.

The Japanese like to claim to the world that their system is an open one and one that is open to foreigners. Even today this is not quite true but it was especially untrue in 1977 when all of this started. At that time, there was a limit on the amount of investment by foreigners, which I alluded to earlier. The cap on foreign investment in any one company could not exceed 25% and no single foreign person or entity could hold more than 10% of a Japanese company. Legally speaking, if one held more than 3% or more of a company, then they had the right to present proposals at the General Meeting of Shareholders and the right to convene Extraordinary General Meetings, so that at 3%, a legal "right of voice," or "right to present proposals" came into play.

This "right of voice" doesn't necessarily mean anything, which will become clear in later chapters. For now, suffice it to say that the 25% and 10% per individual restrictions that were in place at the time were important for another reason because it is only when a person or entity holds more than 33% or more of a company that they could exercise a right of veto against special resolutions at the General Meeting of Shareholders.

This meant that due to the restrictions of 25% and 10%, there was no possible way that foreigners could take over a Japanese company. It also meant that foreigners had no true voice in the operation of a Japanese company because they could never attain the 33%

threshold. However, there was no domestic cap on the amount that Japanese citizens or companies could invest in foreign companies, which meant that the Japanese could take over companies in other nations but their own companies risked no true takeover.

All of this fit well with the Japanese view of investing, meaning that the Japanese welcomed foreign investment in their domestic companies but did not want the consequences of that investment. In other words, they would gladly take and use our money but not allow us any say in how that money should be used or how it could be used better in order to improve the company.

As for the October 5th and 6th articles, I could not yet understand why the Tokyo Stock Exchange would spread this false report about us in *Jiji Press*. What seemed especially malicious was that the Tokyo Stock Exchange had requested that the securities firms submit the names and addresses of clients dealing in Oji Paper shares. This amounted to share-price manipulation by the Tokyo Stock Exchange by scaring away the average investor. It would be the same as if the NYSE suddenly announced that anyone who invested in Intel might come under suspicion. One can easily imagine the effect that would have on Intel's share prices.

Ensuing reports in Japan's mass media saddled us with a bad reputation as a group of riggers who bought shares to boost the price and then greenmail the issuing company into buying them back at a premium. This, of course, was completely untrue and logically ridiculous. At that time, the Hong Kong investors who were investing in Oji Paper consisted of five persons and all of us were prominent businessmen. Wouldn't it be completely illogical for people like us— who owned assets valued in hundreds of billions of yen—to band together to engage in illegal activities for such a comparatively small sum?

This had gone far enough and I asked for a meeting between the Hong Kong representatives of the Big Four and the Hong Kong investors. We held a private meeting on October 8, 1977, in the conference room of Sun Hung Kai Securities head office. We wanted an explanation for the actions of the securities companies and the Tokyo Stock Exchange. We also wanted a chance to explain why we had purchased Oji Paper in the first place and to express our anger at being portrayed as villains in the Japanese media.

After we had sat down at the table, I explained how two people from Nomura Research, a Mr. Nagamine and Mr. Tsuchibashi, had first contacted me in January 1977 and had recommended the three companies to me based on the companies' assets. I also talked about how there had been requests for sales from both Yamaichi and Nomura in July and September but that we turned these down because we wanted to hang on to them for the long term.

One of my friends said that it was regrettable that this had happened just as we were becoming more familiar with Japanese stocks, because this set a bad precedent and certainly was not encouraging our group to make any other investments.

"One is free to buy or sell any listed shares," another of my friends said, "and there is no telling whether one will gain or lose by dealing in the stock market. In the past there were times when we missed the opportunity to make money and there were also times when money was lost. But I cannot understand why we are being told not to buy Oji."

I agreed and told the Big Four representatives that our purchases were totally legitimate. We had not violated any laws and we should therefore have access to the market.

Unfortunately, not one of the representatives was able to give us any clear reason behind the move by their parent companies. One and all, they insisted that these actions came from their headquarters and were not being decided at the local level. Chief Yamanaka from Daiwa said that it was regrettable that things had developed to the present situation. He went on to say that "Legal issues are currently being investigated in Tokyo but that such concentrated purchases in large volumes is considered to be cornering in Japan and is thought to be a bad thing."

Deputy Chief Komatsu of Nomura agreed with him and said, "Such cornering is thought to be bad and as such, misunderstanding can arise and has great effects."

Deputy Chief Suzuki of Nikko agreed with Nomura's position.

This seemed ridiculous on their part and was not an excuse or reason at all. Weren't they the very ones who encouraged us to buy in large volumes?

Deputy Chief Saito of Yamaichi said that before any of them did anything else, they should wait to hear from their head offices. "Since matters have become aggravated," he asked us, "is there any intention to quit by selling the shares you're holding?"

We told him we did not intend to sell. Obviously, the Big Four were hoping that we would sell the shares now that they had brought some pressure on us through the media and had displayed their power by shutting us out.

Unfortunately, nothing was resolved at this meeting. The representatives from the Big Four said they would "make good discussions about this" and that they would discuss the matter with their home offices, and we expressed our desire to settle the issue smoothly without it becoming any more complicated.

But things would not go smoothly.

On October 14th 1977, the *Nihon Keizai Shimbun* published another article on this affair. What especially got my attention, though, were some extremely interesting comments by concerned parties that appeared at the end of that article. They are as follows:

> "The Ministry of Finance is not telling securities companies to stop or refrain from brokering purchases by the Hong Kong circle. However, since we have concluded that the Hong Kong group's share dealings are ambiguous and unclear, and that the impact exerted on the market price is considerable, we have called in the persons in charge at the

eight securities houses with branches or subsidiaries in Hong Kong to interrogate them and to give them forewarnings."

—Mr. Yoshida, Securities Bureau Distribution Market
Section Chief, Ministry of Finance

"They came for an explanation of the circumstances regarding the accumulation of shares from Oji Paper Company by the Hong Kong circle, but the TSE has adopted the position that it cannot become involved in the relationship between securities firms and their clients, although it would be a different matter if there were a problem with market price manipulation or share price formation. However, we are taking an interest because there are reports with regard to the accumulation of shares by the Hong Kong circle that tangible and intangible pressures are being exerted on the issuing company at the time of transfer."

—Mr. Yamashita, Managing Director of the TSE

"The acquisition of shares in our company by the Hong Kong circle has reached 37,220,000 shares, accounting for 13.1% of the shares issued. Our company has absolutely no connection with the self-restraint from dealing pursuant to the statutes of the TSE, but there can be no mistaking the fact that the present type of accumulation is causing trouble to ordinary investors and is not desirable for the healthy development of the share market."

—Mr. Chiba, Director and Finance Division Head for
Oji Paper Company

From the comments of these three concerned parties, I finally grasped what was happening. It goes without saying that we had not contravened any securities law. However, merely because we foreigners had acquired a large block of shares in Oji Paper, those involved fearfully determined that we would try to take over the company.

As a result, Oji's management had submitted a false report to the TSE that we might commit illegal acts in order to protect themselves.

I found out later that the report that Oji Paper had submitted to the Tokyo Stock Exchange had said, "The Hong Kong group is attempting to pass the Oji Paper shares to rival companies overseas, and is trying to arrange for them to be bought back at a high price by exerting pressure on the issuing company." In other words, they accused us of being greenmailers and extortionists because we chose not to sell the shares when they had requested us to. I imagine, too, that not only our own investments made them worry but also the fact that Mr. Merlo from Louisiana Pacific, another foreigner, had come to call on them as well. Their fears and accusations were, of course, baseless—especially since I had not approached anyone and the fact that they were the ones who had first approached me to sell the shares in July and subsequently in September before Mr. Merlo had expressed an interest in Oji Paper or had flown to Tokyo to meet with President Tanaka.

In any event, the Tokyo Stock Exchange—without conducting any investigation whatsoever of its own to find out if there was any truth at all behind the accusations—had then leaked the story to the mass media at the same time that they were reporting it to the Ministry of Finance.

The Ministry of Finance received the reports from the TSE and Oji Paper, summoned the persons in charge at the eight securities houses, and gave them administrative guidance referred to in this article as "forewarning." This kept the Ministry of Finance's hands clean by not specifically telling the securities companies what to do. The eight securities firms had then unanimously adopted the "measure of self-restraint on buy orders" to prevent the Hong Kong investors from buying further shares in Oji Paper. It was a tremendous show of solidarity between the Ministry of Finance, the TSE, Oji Paper Company, and the securities companies to join forces against ordinary investors.

Granted that this is what happened, how transparent were the comments of these three parties? Section Chief Yoshida of the Ministry of Finance said that our "dealings are ambiguous and unclear" and that "the impact [was] considerable." This was rather ridiculous. The rise in the share price from July—when they had first started asking me to sell—was a mere ten percent or so. A ten percent level of variation in share prices is extremely common in share markets. To refer to that as "considerable impact" was an outrageous exaggeration.

Moreover, Yoshida's comment that the Ministry of Finance was "not telling securities companies to stop or refrain from brokering purchases by the Hong Kong circle" and that they had merely called them in to "give them forewarnings" was a cowardly evasion of responsibility by the Ministry of Finance bureaucrats. It also belied the true relationship between the Ministry of Finance and the securities companies. This is because in order to do business, securities companies must have a license, which is given by the Ministry of Finance. In practical terms, this means that securities companies have absolutely no choice but to follow the Ministry's orders; otherwise, the Ministry of Finance will simply pull their license, which would have shut them down completely. In essence, the eight securities firms had no choice but to embark on the self-restraint program. Regarded in this light, the securities firms were also victims of the powers-that-be.

Even if Section Chief Yoshida of the Ministry of Finance did not specifically tell the securities houses to "stop" or to "exercise self-restraint," it was an extraordinary measure for a branch of the government to advise securities houses to put a stop to the ordinary investing of an individual or investment group. Imagine for a moment if the SEC told the major securities houses in the U.S. to halt investment by Warren Buffet. However, in order for Yoshida not to commit himself or the Ministry of Finance, he may not have actually used the words "stop" or "exercise self-restraint." It would not be necessary in any case because everyone knew what was implied. Japan's bureaucrats can be truly cunning in this way.

In his comments in this article, Director Chiba of Oji Paper Company had stated, "…there can be no mistaking the fact that the present type of accumulation is causing trouble to ordinary investors and is not desirable for the healthy development of the share market." He really had a lot of nerve to say that. Although we had been making normal investments, Oji Paper was fabricating vicious rumors. It is precisely the activities of Oji Paper Company that were "not desirable for the healthy development of the share market" and not the activities of normal investors. Such false statements could only lead to investors of all levels losing faith in the market, which would certainly be unhealthy for the market. There is a phrase "flattering to deceive," a description that applied perfectly to Managing Director Chiba who prettily dressed up his words to dupe people.

At the time I thought, "What must Oji Paper think of its shareholders?" A limited company is one that is run by the directors, to whom the shareholders have entrusted its management. In particular, if it is a publicly listed company, then the directors are answerable to the shareholders. It was inexcusable for them to defame or slander the shareholders of their own company.

I couldn't help but remember the nice note I received from Kao Soap. When I became their top shareholder, I received a polite letter of thanks from Kao Soap's President Maruta saying, "Thank you very much for investing in our company. We are striving to achieve further improvement in our results, and hope for your support in the future."

What a difference from Oji Paper!

Also, if we really were greenmailers, as they claimed we were, then why did they wait three whole months to report the issue to the Ministry of Finance? If they were truly concerned for the welfare of their company or their other shareholders, then shouldn't they have warned the Ministry of Finance in July when we first turned them down rather than approach us "culprits" with further requests to sell our shares two months later?

Ordinarily, in Japanese circles, the Oji side would have engaged in a frantic scramble to buy shares as a defense measure. But had they done so, their actions would have leaked out and resulted in a sudden rise in the share price, thus exposing them to the risk of being faced with exorbitantly high defensive-battle costs.

This is merely a guess on my part, but could it have been that, in order to avoid such a wasteful expenditure, Oji conspired with the Big Four to re-purchase the shares from us and then allot them to their own shareholding group? It could certainly explain their actions.

Finally, the comment by Managing Director Yamashita of the Tokyo Stock Exchange was plausible at first glance, but in fact he *did* involve the TSE in our transactions by framing us as villains via the false report submitted by Oji Paper Company. Besides, if it really was not the policy of the TSE to become involved with the securities firms and their clients, then why would he take the action of asking the securities houses for the names and addresses of the investors buying shares in Oji Paper?

Obviously, what Managing Director Yamashita said was pure nonsense and contradictory.

If the TSE had simply checked the authenticity of the report submitted by Oji Paper Company, then none of this would have ever occurred. Isn't it just commonsense to check the reliability of such an accusation? But it is obvious that from the very beginning the TSE had no real intention of checking the authenticity of the report. Rather, they became an active partner in the conspiracy.

Although in some respects the securities companies were victims in this, some of the blame also lies with them. When they had been approached by Oji Paper to ask us to sell our shares, the securities houses could have told Oji Paper that we were not aggressive buyers with ulterior motives and that they should not worry about our investment but instead be happy for it. After all, isn't looking out for the interests of their investors one of the fundamental responsibilities of a brokerage house? In this sense, the securities houses betrayed us. They didn't look out for our interests at all and instead sided with those against us. They didn't even warn us what was happening behind the scenes or tell us the truth once all of this started.

The End of the Self-Restraint Program

As time went on, we didn't receive any response from the securities houses after they supposedly checked with their home offices, so I decided to write them and ask for a written reply. I wrote the letter through my attorney, C. Y. Kwan, and sent it off on October 27th, asking them to fully explain their actions in all of this. After some time and after I had not received any written responses, I wrote another letter on November 7th, saying that if I did not hear from them soon, I would have no choice but to seek legal action against them.

All kinds of replies came. Daiwa Securities wrote, "the reason is a matter of the Tokyo Stock Exchange's custom," while Nikko Securities said that their orders placed with their Hong Kong office were passed on to their Tokyo office, which was "subject to the various laws and regulations in Japan." Yamaichi merely replied that they had already talked with me by phone and thereby didn't put anything in writing.

In addition to saying their headquarters was "subject to the various laws and regulations in Japan," Nikko said some other interesting things. They said, "The recent buying orders here for Oji Paper shares were not only very big in volume compared with the usual volume of orders for the shares of one company in Japan but were also quite continual. Therefore, many Japanese investors and other people were given a kind of special impression as if there might be some specific purpose behind these orders." They also denied that they had acted in collusion with the other securities companies by saying, "Needless to say, our refraining from accepting orders was not 'together' with the other Japanese securities companies."

If that were true, then it was an unbelievably amazing set of coincidences that all of the securities houses (who, of course, had not been instructed by the Ministry of Finance) just happened to decide to no longer accept buy orders for Oji Paper on the exact same day.

Then it must also be highly coincidental that all four replies were written so closely together, even though I had written to them more than two weeks before. Two of the replies were written on November 10th, one on the 12th, and one on the 14th.

Likewise, although Nikko claimed they were not "together" with the other companies, by still another amazing coincidence all of them decided to once again start accepting buy orders for Oji Paper.

But most disturbing of all was the response from Nomura Securities, which stated, "it's up to the discretion of the company whether or not to accept orders." This was especially intimidating, and I am sure it was meant to be so. Nomura made it very clear that the self-restraint program could be implemented again at any time they wanted to in the future.

These were carefully crafted letters. Not a single one of them mentioned that they had been instructed to stop the buy orders at the instruction of the Ministry of Finance, even though the *Jiji Press* article clearly indicated that they had been.

The Intimidator

During this letter-writing campaign, I planned a press conference in Hong Kong on November 14, 1977 to address the self-restraint program that the eight Japanese securities companies had adopted.

I planned to explain the situation with the investments that the Hong Kong investors had made in Japanese stocks up to then and explain our side of the situation to the mass media in addition to trying to shed some light on some of Japan's stock trading practices. I also wanted to share some of our past experiences: for example, the fact that we had profited in the past but our losses were not small either; that we had done absolutely nothing to inflict losses on Japanese domestic investors; and that we had never pressured any issuing company by requesting a buyback at a premium since all our transactions had been conducted on a commercial basis.

I also wanted to say that the self-restraint program was entirely unfair and could only be presumed to have been a political measure implemented by someone influencing the Ministry of Finance and the Tokyo Stock Exchange so that the management of Oji Paper Company could serve its own self-interests while denying a profit to the Hong Kong investors, their legitimate shareholders. Finally, I wanted to say that the Hong Kong investors, depending on the circumstances, were considering the lodging of a lawsuit against the securities houses, Oji Paper, and even the Tokyo Stock Exchange.

I notified the press club in advance that I would hold a press conference regarding these matters, and the announcement had attracted strong and widespread interest.

However, before the event was actually held, the securities companies lifted the self-restraint program. Even so, I planned to go ahead with the press conference and address the other areas of concern, especially our past history with the Japanese markets and securities companies.

A couple days before the press conference, a man by the name of Mr. Akagi, who was the chairman of Juzenkai Hospital in Kyoto, arrived in Hong Kong, and started trying to arrange a meeting with me. His trip to Hong Kong had been arranged and/or requested by Nikko.

Mr. Yamataka of the Hong Kong branch of Nikko Asia, who had been handling my account at Nikko (and who had called me with the suggestion to buy Oji in the first place), was assigned to take care of Mr. Akagi. Although not directly connected to Nikko Securities and although Mr. Akagi was not an advisor to Nikko Asia, it was obvious that he had a close relationship with Nikko because during his stay in Hong Kong, Mr. Yamataka was constantly attending to Mr. Akagi and it seemed that all of the people at Nikko Asia turned out in full force to roll out the red carpet for him.

Late at night, on the eve of the press conference, Mr. Yamataka of Nikko Asia visited my home. His face was as white as a sheet and he trembled as he spoke. He told me about Mr. Akagi and his trip to Hong Kong and how he had been saying dangerous things during his stay, even making threats against my life.

I can assure you that reading in the newspaper or in a novel about someone's life being threatened and having your own life suddenly threatened are two very different things.

According to Mr. Yamataka, Akagi had said that my acquisition of Oji Paper shares had antagonized the Japanese government and that I'd thrown down the gauntlet, and, depending on how I played it, a situation could arise in which an attempt would be made on my life. Mr. Yamataka was supposed to set up the meeting between Akagi and myself but on hearing the threatening things that Akagi was saying, he didn't arrange it, even though he was under great pressure to do so. Mr. Akagi had given a message to Mr. Yamataka for me to call off the press conference and the lawsuit.

I could hardly believe what was being said but seeing Mr. Yamataka in my living room—pale and trembling and fearful not only of what he was saying but of the likely repercussions for going against his instructions—made me a believer.

At the time, I did not know who this Mr. Akagi was but I have since heard that he is a shadowy figure behind the scenes in the securities industry.

I immediately wanted to telephone the police. I picked up the phone and started to make the call to the police but Mr. Yamataka took the phone out of my hand and pleaded with me not to call them. I wavered for a moment, feeling deeply inside that I should report this to the police. It would demonstrate just how powerful the Japanese securities companies were and the lengths that they would go to in order to protect their power base, even criminal behavior.

In the end, I only decided against reporting the matter to the police in order to avoid the inevitable repercussions that would affect Mr. Yamataka. I knew he would already be in severe trouble for refusing to follow the instructions of his superiors and I wanted to spare this very brave man from as much trouble as I could.

Ever since, I have very much regretted not making that call.

I thanked Mr. Yamataka for warning me and he left, both of us very concerned for the future.

Even before this threat, I had already been harboring suspicions that the self-restraint program might be the result of pressure from Japanese politicians and the government. While I did not quite take the remarks of Mr. Akagi at face value (in that I had antagonized the Japanese government), I listened to them with foreboding. I began to fear that the powers in Japan might indeed do anything to eliminate someone who got in their way.

I held the press conference on the following day as planned, but because of what had happened, I had no choice but to exercise caution by leaving out some of the details in the explanation and by exercising restraint in the way I expressed myself.

What I also did not say was that after all that had happened, I had become perverse and determined then that I would never sell the shares, no matter what happened.

As it turned out, Mr. Yamataka nevertheless had to resign because his superiors constantly and harshly reprimanded him for failing to set the meeting between Akagi and myself and for failing to properly entertain Mr. Akagi. From this, and because of the red-carpet treatment they gave to him, it seems fairly obvious that Nikko had a particular interest in Mr. Akagi's meeting with me and may well have been privy to what Mr. Akagi wanted to say to me. One might even go so far as to assume that Mr. Akagi was trying to contact me at the behest of Nikko Securities.

As for Mr. Yamataka's phone call back in April that he believed the price would soon go up based on what he'd been told, his information never came to pass. Tragically, it seems that Mr. Yamataka, whose heart was very much in the right place in all of this, was also duped by those in power.

Chapter Four

The Forced Sale

Even though I had vowed not to sell the shares and the self-restraint program had been lifted, I was afraid to buy any more at this point. The threat from Nomura that they had the right to refuse to broker shares at their sole discretion was not lost on me and was meant to warn us that the securities companies could easily implement the self-restraint program (or some other such program) whenever they chose to do so. They may as well have stated openly that they were an entity whose very existence was incompatible with the underlying purpose and philosophy of a free market. They had set themselves above the law and did not even blink to tell me so.

Things were relatively quiet over the next couple of months. Perhaps it was an unspoken agreement between all of those concerned to have a cooling down period. For my part, I was still furious over the whole affair. Oji Paper and the securities companies had conspired with the stock market and the Japanese government itself to deny us one of the most basic and fundamental rights of an investor: to buy and sell one's shares of stock whenever one chooses to do so. If this were to be done to every investor, such practices would lead to the collapse of the entire market.

And yet it wasn't done to every investor. It was done to me personally and to my Hong Kong investor friends simply because we were foreigners. Even though I had grown up in Japan and considered it my second homeland, the Japanese would always view me as

Chinese and a foreigner. Had we been Japanese, they would not have been able to take the particular actions that they did, though even Japanese investors are open for abuse when they buck the system and don't follow orders. This was ugly—and painful—racial discrimination.

Unfortunately, racism is alive and well in Japan, even today. It may seem strange to say that the Japanese held racist attitudes toward us, who were fellow Orientals. Americans tend to think of all Asian people as "Asian," not realizing that to be Chinese is to be wholly foreign in the Japanese mindset.

The Ministry of Finance was the main culprit in this whole affair. They are supposed to be the governing body that oversees the market and financial system and yet their actions were directly counter to the principles of a free-market system.

What is especially telling about the Ministry of Finance's actions in this is that thirty Japanese companies saw large fluctuations in their share prices, some of which fell to a fraction of their original prices, causing serious damage to Japanese investors and foreigners alike. Yet for some reason, the Ministry of Finance never saw fit to "forewarn" the securities companies regarding these thirty companies. But with Oji Paper, which did not see any fluctuations in its price other than some ten percent, the Ministry of Finance decided to step in to shut us out.

I had also suffered the humiliation of being called a greenmailer in the Japanese media, which made me wonder how many of my other business associates that had known me in one capacity or another would read those reports and think badly of me. Perhaps the news was even spreading to financial circles abroad, like the U.S. I felt that those who truly knew me would know I was not a greenmailer but to be called one was still hurtful and made me feel my name had been dishonored, which angered me further.

Aside from these feelings, I felt very much betrayed by those companies I had done business with. They had earned fortunes in commissions off of my share trading only to treat me this way.

Additionally, there were all those "friends" of mine in the securities companies who had given me gifts and had been so happy to have my business—only to quickly look the other way when they could have helped me and stood up for what was right. So much for loyalty.

In December 1977, I decided to write a letter of complaint to Mr. Murayama, the Minister of Finance. In it I first apologized for my impertinence for writing to him directly and then said, "I have been investing in Japanese stocks and shares for the past ten years. But now I am very much astonished by the unjust discrimination against us foreign investors by the Japanese securities companies, government, and people."

I stated very plainly my reasons for investing in Oji Paper due to its latent assets and told him about the recent events, including the "political rascal," as I called him, that had been sent to Hong Kong to persuade me not to oppose those in power in Japan in respect to the Oji Paper shares or else I'd be in danger.

It was not only my friends and I who were affected, I pointed out, but also the other 47,000 shareholders of Oji Paper. Because of these events, the share price was being manipulated by those responsible.

In addition to explaining the facts of the case, I gave him further background information and gave voice to my suspicions about Oji Paper, including the fact that it was conspicuously excluded from Nomura's "Capital Fund." This was an investment list of lucrative companies that Nomura was pushing at the time and was made up of all the leading companies in their respective sectors—except for Oji Paper, even though Oji was the largest company in the paper industry. Ordinarily, it would have been an insult to Oji to not be included on this list.

Because of this, it was easy to presume that Nomura's intention was to keep Oji Paper's share price low. If Nomura had included Oji Paper in the fund, then—as with the other companies on this list—

their share price would have gone up as demand for their shares increased. This could have then forced Oji into an expensive defensive buyback, something Oji wanted to avoid.

I then went on to describe other suspicious incidents in the past where we had suffered unjust treatment at the hands of the securities companies. I mentioned our experiences with Japan Line and how, for reasons unknown to us, Nikko had asked us to sell our shares and how the shares had then increased nearly fourteen times after we had sold it, greatly profiting whatever unknown entity in Japan that had bought our shares.

Although I did not say it in my letter to the Minister, after our experiences with Oji Paper, it would not have been hard to believe that the securities companies' actions in these other dealings had been intentional. Had the securities companies used our money to build up a company and then, once a profit was going to materialize, they pushed us out of the way in order to give the profits to the Japanese rather than allow me and my friends to profit from our own investments? Perhaps it was a paranoid thought, but one that was not unreasonable.

I then went on to describe the current situation in more detail and our subsequent protests to the Big Four, and quoted Nomura's reply to him, in that they had absolute discretion over buying and selling shares. "If this is so," I said, "securities companies have even more power than the Japanese government.

> It is the belief of the Hong Kong investors, that the above unhappy and unjust incidents were caused by political pressure. If true, it is very regrettable and will definitely affect the honor, prestige, and the good name of Japan in international financial circles. I hope that similar incidents will not occur again and shall be much obliged if you will give me a reply after the completion of your investigation.

I had finished a draft of the letter but before I sent it, Mr. Yamanaka, the then president of Daiwa Hong Kong came to visit me at my office. Mr. Yamanaka was also the person who had taken the minutes during the October meeting held between the Hong Kong investors and the representatives of the Big Four Japanese security firms. I told him what I was up to and let him read the letter to the Minister of Finance. After he finished reading it, he offered to help me revise it.

He not only helped me revise the letter and correct my Japanese grammar but was also the author of many of the most strongly worded sentences in my letter and was extremely critical of the actions of Japanese securities companies. I felt at the time, and still do, that Mr. Yamanaka's conduct was evidence of Daiwa's unwillingness or reluctance in taking part in the self-restraint program and that Daiwa was somehow acting under pressure to do so. I remembered, too, that during the October meeting he had expressed his regret that "things had developed to the present situation" and that even in his written response, he'd said, "The reason is a matter of the Tokyo Stock Exchange's custom," which could be a subtle indication that the problem lay with the Tokyo Stock Exchange and not with the securities companies. Perhaps they felt as betrayed and manipulated as we did. When it comes to the Japanese people, there are many subtleties involved and that they are sometimes very indirect in their speech and in their dealings. It is often what is left unsaid that is most important.

Although Mr. Yamanaka was sympathetic, he was also president of Daiwa Hong Kong and therefore I knew he could never openly take a stance that was different from that of his company in the official reply that he made on behalf of Daiwa securities to my lawyers and could only say that it was a matter of custom with the Tokyo Stock Exchange. It is also not the way with most Japanese to come forward and state their personal opinions and so it would not be like him to state clearly what he felt or believed. But his actions spoke much louder than his words—spoken or unspoken.

I felt very grateful and touched by Mr. Yamanaka and his effort. I, of course, did not mention his name in the letter to the Minister nor his involvement with the revising it so he would not get into any trouble with his home office. Mr. Yamanaka, in fact, was later promoted to the head office in Japan and I was glad for him.

My letter to the Minister went unanswered.

What my experience with Oji Paper taught me was that in the Japanese securities market, there was no such thing as freedom of access to the market, which was and is one of the most fundamental market rules common to the securities markets in the rest of the world.

Japan was obviously very behind the times and was relying, instead, on incestuous business practices that were designed to protect the establishment and those in power. It is not just a matter of what they did as being right or wrong, but that the very foundation on which the Japanese market was based was seriously undermined.

Their proclamation that they were above the law and that they could re-institute the self-restraint program at any time could not have existed in any other market. Imagine for a moment if Merrill Lynch were to suddenly decide that they could restrict their customers' access to the market at their own discretion. I am sure the SEC would have something to say about it. Granted, there are certain, rare, exceptional circumstances under which securities companies in the U.S. can decline buy orders but these restrictions are only if the broker believes the client to be irrational and not acting in their own best interests. Such safeguards are designed to protect people (such as senile investors) but are never to be used as weapons against their own clients.

Nomura's proclamation indicated that the securities firms involved in the self-restraint program believed that they hadn't implemented an emergency measure but were merely exercising a right and power that they believed they had.

As time went on and the year turned to January and then approached February—and still I had not received any reply to my letter to the Minister of Finance or any indication that the situation would improve—I naturally began to fear the worst. Nomura's threat was weighing heavily on me during this time.

It did not help, either, that in January the price of Oji Paper shares dropped to a 52-week low of ¥272 from its high of ¥440 the previous November. Because of all of this, I began to wonder if, in a worst-case scenario, whether I might be forced to sell the Oji Paper shares at below my actual cost. Not only would we have suffered the injustice of what had happened but also lose money on our investment on top of it all.

Fortunately, the price began to rise again and by the end of January it had shot up to ¥370 and then leveled off to remain between ¥370 and ¥385 for the entire month of February.

Perhaps the sudden rise and subsequent leveling off of Oji's price was what brought me a visitor sometime in early February. I was staying in my house in Los Angeles when the director of the International Department of Nikko Securities, Mr. Tadao Kobayashi, flew over to see me from Japan and met me at my home.

We talked politely for a while before he came to the point of his visit. He had come to find out whether we had the intention of finally selling our shares. He said that Nikko had judged that the threat of a forced buyback had disappeared and so they had sent him to press me for a sale through Nikko.

"Everybody knows how much you originally paid for your Oji Paper shares," he said, "so please sell them to us at a price that includes interest." He stated that the Hong Kong investors' purchase price for the Oji Paper shares was an average of ¥360 per share, and when normal interest was added to that, it came to ¥380 per share.

Now, I had bought these shares through eight different securities companies. Not only that, but they had been bought at varying times and prices.

So this is where I thought, "Aha, all the securities companies really are in collusion with each other and it is not just my imagination."

He should not have known how many shares we'd bought from which securities house and at what price, since securities firms have the obligation of maintaining confidentiality. It was even less likely that a securities company would accidentally leak details of their clients' transactions to a rival company. However, he was quite familiar with the details of our transactions, which could only mean that the Big Four had exchanged information about all our dealings.

I rejected his proposal, my worries replaced once again with anger and bitterness at their blatant collusion. Even so, since trading in shares is normally done by telephone, I couldn't help but think that he was under some special instructions from the management in his head office to have flown all the way to the U.S. to speak with me in person.

As if Kobayashi's words alone were not enough to be convincing of the Big Four's collusion, on the very same day that he had come to visit, President Kawakita of Nomura Hong Kong telephoned me at 3:00 a.m. and asked me to sell the Oji Paper shares. He roused me out of sleep and said, "I'm very sorry, but could you see your way to selling us even 5 million or 10 million of your shares?"

Since he had phoned me at such an ungodly hour, I knew he must be under extreme pressure from his head office and was therefore considerably flustered to not think of the time difference. However, I turned down his request as well, feeling there was no need to sell the shares and that our original investment goals had still not been met.

Subsequently, while still in Los Angeles, I received a telephone call from the vice president of Nomura Securities himself, Mr. Setsuya Tabuchi (he later became the chairman of Nomura). He, too, asked me to sell my Oji Paper shares but I again refused.

Even though I had refused their requests, I began to worry. I knew that Nomura's threat was meant to convey that they could not only prevent purchase orders but might also deny me the chance to sell the shares. This mean they could tie up our money and perhaps never let us get it back.

With the persistent phone calls, it was becoming painfully obvious that I could no longer continue my investment in Japanese stocks, despite my good intentions. Unless I accepted the securities firms' offer to sell the shares at cost plus interest while the offer was still open, I could be trapped and suffer a huge financial loss. I was no longer welcome in the land I considered a second home. Maybe it was true; maybe you really couldn't fight city hall—or at least not the financial markets.

Even so, I did not want to give up just yet. Maybe they would give up first and just allow us to hold on to the shares as we'd intended all along. Maybe Oji Paper would calm down and finally see that we had good intentions.

When I returned to Hong Kong, President Toida of Nikko Asia visited my office. "Mr. Wang," he said, "how much are you prepared to accept for your Oji shares?"

I refused, by now a little put off about the securities companies' stubbornness, appearing on my doorstep so soon after my return. "In any case," he said, "when you do decide to sell, please give first priority to Nikko, won't you?"

On the same day, General Manager Yamanaka of the Daiwa Hong Kong branch also visited me, begging me to "please sell your Oji shares to us."

On the following day, President Kawakita of Nomura Hong Kong followed up his phone call to me in the States with a personal visit to my Hong Kong office to again ask me to sell the shares. He turned up around 4:00 p.m., sat down, and refused to budge.

"Mr. Wang, help us, please," he said. "Please sell your Oji shares to us, whatever happens."

When I stood up to go to the restroom, he followed me there and waited for me outside the door. At 6:00 p.m., I tried to close up the office and go home but he was very reluctant to leave. It was painfully obvious that he was under very strong pressure from the head office to persuade me under any circumstance.

Then, on April 17th, Vice President Setsuya Tabuchi of Nomura also followed up his phone call to me with a personal visit. He had been in the middle of a business trip to the United States but went out of his way to come straight to Hong Kong to pay me a visit. He descended on my office like a bulldog and lingered for an hour and a half. Naturally, his business was a request for the sale of the Oji Paper shares.

"Mr. Wang, won't you please sell your Oji shares through Nomura?" he asked. "This whole problem of the Oji shares has now become a political issue. Under normal circumstances, I would have the authority to buy twenty or thirty million shares, but the whole position has become extremely complex now.

"The reason why I've come today in this manner to plead with you," he went on, "is because I have been asked to do so by Chairman Goro Koyama of the Mitsui Bank and President Fumio Tanaka of Oji."

He went on to say that the Mitsui Group, to which Oji Paper Company belonged, would take up all the shares we sold. Mr. Tabuchi made sure to identify the principals in the request because he wanted to impress upon me that very powerful forces in Japan were involved in the background. His attitude was deadly earnest. In fact, he was so earnest that he didn't even realize that the ash of the cigarette he was smoking had gotten so long that it was about to fall until I cautioned him about it.

Once again, though, I refused his request to sell the shares.

Apart from these two personal visits, I also received numerous requests from other people to sell—it was a great to-do. I was psychologically worn out by the high-pressure rapid-fire requests but I continued to refuse their requests to sell.

Nomura Securities came to me and proposed a sale price of ¥380 per share, which was the exact same amount as that proposed by Mr. Kobayashi from Nikko. Not only did all of them know the price we'd purchased at, but it was also obvious that the Big Four had jointly come up with the sale price of ¥380.

After Vice President Tabuchi of Nomura's visit to inform me of the power behind the offer and the two identical offers of ¥380 per share from both Nomura and Nikko, the pieces of the puzzle finally fit together. A joint conspiracy must have been hatched between President Fumio Tanaka of Oji Paper Company and the leader of the Mitsui Group—Mitsui Bank Chairman Goro Koyama—to buy back the shares from the Hong Kong investors at a cheap price, and the Big Four were helping them in this. By tying us up hand and foot so that we could neither buy nor sell Oji Paper shares, the Big Four collaborated to set a cheap price for the shares we held.

How ironic all of this was. We had been accused in the media of trying to force Oji Paper into a buyback and yet here were Oji Paper, the Mitsui Group, and the Big Four trying to force us to sell our shares—forcing us to do what they had accused us of.

I was in a huge dilemma about whether to sell out or to put the shares in cold storage and hold on. Everything the conspirators were doing was simply wrong. It was wrong of them to deny us the fundamental right of access. The offer of ¥380 was simply not a fair offer. When it was originally offered in February, it was barely current market value and was still only current market value (Oji shares hovered around an average of ¥380 for February, March, and April). Besides, the offer was far, far below our original goals and expectations. So once again, the securities houses were denying us the chance to make a true windfall.

Still, I clung to the hope that somehow this situation would be resolved in a fair and honest manner. So on May 2nd, I contacted Mr. Shiraishi, the Japanese consul who was designated by the Ministry of Finance to act as one of the consuls to handle financial business of the Consulate in Hong Kong. Since he was appointed by the Ministry of Finance, I doubted he would be fair or impartial but by this time I had already resigned myself to the fact that we would not be allowed to keep the shares for long-term investment, so I wanted to salvage what we could out of this. I proposed to him that the Japanese side buy at ¥415. But the consul did not offer me any help.

On May 25, 1978, an article appeared in *Nippon Keizai Shimbun* titled, "Effects of Soaring Yen and Poor Market Conditions Bring About Substantial Reduction in Oji's Ordinary Profit this Term." This article was not some financial reporter's conjecture based on his investigation; instead, it was based on a special press conference called for by Mr. Kawage, Oji Paper's own managing director.

Mr. Kawage was quoted as saying, "During the current term, the market conditions for craft paper worsened as a result of the increase of cheap imports brought about by the strong yen. Consequently, substantial reductions in profit will become inevitable."

This was surprising to read because all along I had expected—and even anticipated—that a stronger yen would actually be good for Oji Paper. I came to this conclusion since ninety percent of the raw materials for their paper products were imported from the U.S. or Canada. A stronger yen meant their supply costs for raw materials would go down and thereby enhance their profits.

Instead, here was their managing director saying that the domestic craft paper market was depressed because of the sudden increase of cheap imported products caused by the recent sharp appreciation of the Japanese yen. He also "revealed" that under the circumstances the company's annual earnings before taxes for the current fiscal year would decrease by thirty percent as compared to the previous year.

At the very end of the article, it mentioned, "the major shareholders continue to be the Hong Kong Group, headed by Mr. Tseng Hsiang Wang." It was rather conspicuous, almost thrown in, that they mentioned us at all, as though going out of their way to include us in an article that dealt with the company's so-called decline in profits. Were they putting us on notice? Were they insinuating the blame lay with the foreigners?

Judging from the common disclosure practice of Japanese public corporations, it was rather exceptional for a company like Oji Paper to spontaneously make a big public disclosure of such negative information—even calling a special news conference in order to do so. This was not a quarterly earnings report. Besides, they would ordinarily protect such negative information to protect themselves and to prevent investors from losing faith in them.

It seemed rather obvious this entire article was a message intended for me and the other Hong Kong investors. Oji Paper was deliberately releasing false information to suppress the price of its own shares and the message here was to tell me that if I continued to keep the shares, the chance would be remote for me to sell them at a profit in the future so they wanted to make doubly sure that I would sell.

Disseminating false information to manipulate share prices is, ostensibly, a criminal offense in Japan and punishable by substantial fines and imprisonment. But by now I firmly believed that all of these schemes were integral parts of one big carefully designed and orchestrated act and that the other side would go to any lengths to force the sale. If Oji Paper would go so far as to commit a criminal act, I realized that the danger of losing a huge amount of money was very real.

Naturally, the market price of Oji Paper stock started to decline immediately after the press announcement and the volume of shares traded dropped precipitously. For the whole of May, only 3,023,000 shares were traded, less than nine percent of the volume of 35,376,000 in May of the previous year.

I didn't know if the Japanese press and securities companies were in collusion with each other and rather doubted that the press would do such a thing. But they were—knowingly or not—being used by those in power. There would be little hope for me if I were to struggle against the whole country of Japan and at last I finally despaired of ever seeing a successful end to this after all of my struggle.

Totally fed up, on May 29, 1978, I rang Vice President Tabuchi of Nomura and told him I wished to sell. Angry and bitter, I imagined that he probably had a hard time not shouting for joy.

I again tried to sell for around ¥400 but he refused. "Impossible," he said, "Nothing more than ¥380 will do." When we couldn't come to an agreement, he indicated we should let things cool off for a time, while striving for a resolution.

The very next day, however, I received a phone call from President Toida of Nikko Asia "You won't be able to conclude a successful deal by talking to Mr. Tabuchi of Nomura," he said. "Everybody on this side knows about the contents of your talk with Mr. Tabuchi, you know. No matter how much you discuss the matter with Nomura, I must remind you that it's only Nikko, as the main managing underwriter, that can purchase the shares."

I was completely shocked. The other companies already knew what I had discussed only yesterday in a private conversation with Vice President Tabuchi. Any remaining doubts—some small part of me still wished that it was not true—that everybody in the securities circles was in collusion with each other disappeared completely.

I finally resigned myself to the inevitable. I spoke with my investor friends to tell them everything that had transpired and all but one of us agreed that we should sell. One of my friends refused to sell and wanted to hang on to the shares in hopes that they would rise as we had originally hoped.

The next day, I phoned Nikko Securities, asking to speak to Mr. Kobayashi. When he came on the phone, I cleared my throat.

"We wish to sell."

It was not unlike putting a dagger into my own heart. It had been a long, terrible struggle, and an exhausting one, and now we were giving up the fight. If there was one bit of comfort in it, it was that at least it would soon be over.

I told him that we would be selling 29.3 million shares of Oji Paper and requested he purchase them at his stated price of ¥380, which he'd quoted to me in Los Angeles.

"I never said that."

I was dumbfounded and went over our conversation again in my mind, recalling clearly what had been said, and knowing for sure that he'd said this because Nomura had offered the identical amount to me after I'd returned to Hong Kong.

"I'm sorry, but I am sure that is the price you'd offered to me."

"No, I never said so. If you're willing to accept ¥360 then we'll purchase."

How incredible. Now that I had finally decided to sell, they would make even this part difficult. We hung up, not having come to any resolution.

Over the next couple of weeks we were still unable to come to any resolution. On June 7, 1978, I received a call from Mr. Seiichi Kurihara, who had served as the first president of the Hong Kong subsidiary of Nomura Securities and thereafter became a managing director at the head office. I shared with him my sense of frustration and confusion over why even the end to this whole affair was causing so much trouble. I gave up and told him I was ready to sell.

"I'm exhausted," I told him. "I cannot figure out who is playing the leading role on the Japanese side. Now I want the Japanese side to arrange a deal, any deal. I think no one other than a team of Oji Paper, the Mitsui Group of Companies, Nomura, and Nikko can solve this problem. However we can get this done, I want a deal to be arranged with equal participation of Nomura and Nikko, except for the shares owned by my friend who has decided he won't sell. I will need only three hours in which to give the Japanese side my final reply as to whether any offer made by the Japanese side would be acceptable to my colleagues and me. We're hoping for net sales proceeds of at least ¥380 per share. I don't want to suffer any further losses."

He said he would see what he could do. Now that even at the end this had become such a long, drawn out battle I was still wavering on selling the shares. A few days later, I heard from Kobayashi of Nikko Securities, who had originally approached me back in February about selling the shares and they offered a price of between ¥360 and ¥370. I told him that the price simply was not fair.

Finally, on June 12, 1978, I received a call from Kobayashi. He wanted to have me sell the shares at a price that was based on the current price on the Tokyo Stock Exchange. There were then several phone calls back and forth and we agreed to sell the shares to Nikko for ¥380 net, after all commissions and taxes, the actual price being something like ¥382 or ¥383.

He told me he needed to report this to Vice President Haraigawa of the Tokyo headquarters, who was in charge of the transaction. He also said that rather than release the shares into the open market they would do it by *baikai* (a cross-trading transaction or private placement transaction outside the market) so that the Mitsui Group would obtain all the shares. They were concerned if the 29.3 million shares were sold in the open market that the Mitsui Group might not get all them. In theory, this was against the TSE regulations at the time, because such transactions have a negative affect on the formation of true fair-market share price value. Still, *baikai* were allowed as long as the transaction had the approval of the parties involved. By this time, I had thrown in the towel and I didn't care how the shares would be disposed of, although I am certain that Kobayashi was right and that had they been sold on the open market, then the Mitsui Group would not have been able to get all of them.

When fifteen minutes had passed, Mr. Kobayashi called again and told me that he had spoken with Vice President Haraigawa who felt that due to the size of the transaction that it would be split among the Big Four with 35% each for Nikko and Nomura and 15% each for Daiwa and Yamaichi, and that the local Hong Kong subsidiaries had already been advised to that effect.

Once again, I couldn't believe what I was hearing. Why was Nikko not going to handle this by themselves? They were the ones I had finally come to an agreement with. Besides, who had ever heard of securities firms—whose aim was to earn commissions—sharing transactions with their rivals? And how, in fifteen minutes, could he have spoken with Vice President Haraigawa and also manage to confer with all of the Hong Kong affiliates in that short space of time?

Obviously, this has been settled in advance and that even the proportions of the shares had been previously determined.

Regardless, I told him this sounded good and that we should go ahead. I was very tired of the whole affair and was glad now that it was over at last. I was tired of the collusion, tired of fighting unseen forces, tired of the treachery and betrayal. I was worn down and just wanted it finished.

At last, it was over.

Some three months after the conclusion of this affair, on September 29, 1978, a news article appeared in *Nippon Keizai Shimbun*.

Oji Profit to Increase
as a Result of Rationalization and Cheap Raw
Materials Bought with Strong Yen.

It seems certain that the total ordinary profit will increase to ¥7,500,000,000, a 3% increase over the previous term. The market conditions for craft paper continue to be unfavorable but rationalization and the strong yen, which makes it possible to purchase raw materials at a low price, brought about the increase in profit...

The strong yen has brought about a 5% drop in the price of imported raw materials and a 20% drop in the price of heavy oil as compared with the previous term, and all these contributed to the increase in income...

As a result...the after-tax profit will be ¥3,500,000,000 (26% higher than the previous term).

Now Oji Paper was now claiming the exact opposite of what they had alleged four months ago in this very same paper. In May, they had declared a strong yen would hurt their profits in the upcoming term by some 30% but now they claimed a strong yen helped their profits and that their profits were actually up 3% for the June–September term and they are expecting a 26% increase in the coming term.

With this article, it was painfully clear that this had all been one big carefully designed and orchestrated plan to rid us of our shares. It felt as though Oji Paper and the others were dancing on my grave.

Once again, the securities companies had swindled us out of our chance for a profit. But not only had we lost money, we had lost faith in the Japanese system. In such a system, there was no freedom—we would never be able to do with our money as we saw fit. Imagine your bank telling you when you could or could not withdraw or deposit your own money. That was what had happened to us.

An article that later appeared in *All Toushi*, the magazine for Japanese stock investors, confirmed many of my suspicions about the powers behind all this. The article said that Mr. Koyama (a former chairman of Mitsui Bank, Ltd.) and Mr. Segawa (a former chairman of Nomura Securities who had strong connections among politicians, bureaucrats, and business executives) were the ones who had initiated the self-restraint program. Neither Mr. Koyama nor Mr. Segawa ever filed a lawsuit for defamation of character against the author of the article. They didn't even demand the magazine print a retraction or seek so much as an apology from the author. Could this be construed as a silent admission of guilt? I certainly took it as such.

As for my one friend who did not sell his shares with the rest of us, he held on for one more year. It was a year after his sale that the start of Japan's bubble economy began to hit and the Oji Paper shares truly took off as we had expected them to. If I had been able to hold on to the shares, and then sold them in 1989 when they reached their highest level of ¥2,160, I would have made a profit of over ¥50 billion.

Even after the forced sale of my Oji Paper shares, the Big Four acted as if nothing had ever happened and immediately started making approaches to me again. On one occasion, Mr. Yoshio Haraikawa, Vice President of Nikko came straight to my office from the airport, bringing with him a present of a *noh* mask that he'd specifically sent for from Kumamoto, Japan.

"*Noh* masks are a symbol of peace in Japan," he said.

At the time, I thought he must have been joking. The Big Four had been the ones who persistently sowed the seeds of discord and they shouldn't forget that.

All throughout the negotiations for selling the Oji Paper shares, I had expressed my frustration over this whole mess numerous times to the securities companies. They reassured me that if I would just sell the shares this time then they would be able to make it up to me and they promised over and over that nothing like this would happen ever again.

That remained to be seen.

Chapter Five

Notes on Japan

The Japanese, even today, like to pretend that they have an open and free economy. Those who have dealt with the Japanese know that this is not the case.

This does not mean, though, that the entire country conspires together to thwart foreign investment, nor do all Japanese corporations look at foreign investment in an unfavorable light. Even so, the rules of the game have been and continue to be slanted toward insiders whether one is a foreign investor or even a Japanese citizen.

The simple truth of the matter is that there are many "rules" that one is forced to play by or the system can quickly shut out anyone it deems to be an outsider. Fortunately, this doesn't mean that everyone in Japan falls in line with the orders from above and not everyone has lost their common sense. Or their honor.

And it is true, too, that not all of the media thought favorably of the Japanese side during the Oji Paper affair. An editorial appeared in the Economic Observations section of the *Mainichi Shibun*—a Japanese pharmaceutical newspaper—that was decidedly against the actions of the Japanese:

Hong Kong Dollar

I wonder how the extent of internationalization is measured?

As a recent example, it is said that all eight local securities companies turned down a purchase order for Oji Paper by the Wang Group, which is owned by a very rich businessman in Hong Kong. The securities companies said, "No, we didn't turn him down: we were just imposing self-discipline on ourselves and refrained from engaging in any further brokering business." This explanation is only a game of words.

It is common sense that a broker is only too happy to execute any order from a customer as long as the order is not illegal. In this case, neither the limit of 25% imposed on foreigners nor the limit of 10% per individual had been exceeded.

Perhaps they didn't like the idea of foreigners holding a large number of shares. I wonder if any securities company turned down anybody when the commercial firms, shipping companies, and bearing companies were buying and selling shares in a big way?

They said, "we weren't particularly told to turn down purchase orders" and this is probably not a lie. However, when a Japanese executive is summoned by the supervising authorities to "arouse their attention," his reaction is predictable.

I am not saying that this measure is wrong, but using foreigners as a tool for bolstering up shares when it is convenient by yelling, "the Hong Kong dollar has come to buy" and stopping things when the authorities utter a word is really a shame. Perhaps worshipping foreigners and rejecting them is one and the same thing.

Many years have, of course, passed since the Oji Paper affair and since I'd first encountered the antiquated and unfair practices of the Japanese financial system. The problem lies in that one is not only forced to fight city hall but that one must also fight a mindset that allows such practices to continue. This is evidenced by the following letter that was sent to me in August 1998:

I am pleased to reply to your esteemed letter.

The early summer rainy spell that has been unusually prolonged for our region this year has finally lifted, and the hot weather has arrived. Mr. Wang, please accept my best wishes that you will remain active and in good health.

I would like to offer you my sincere thanks for sending me the copy of your latest work *The Eve of the Financial and Securities Collapse* not long ago; I am deeply appreciative. I understand that you have sent it to persons from various circles in Japan, and I am grateful that you have gone to the trouble of sending it to me. I realize that you have a strong love for Japan and the Japanese people, that you are concerned about the country's future and that it is with the greatest reluctance that you have taken up the pen to write your work, which has moved me deeply. I have learned that you have gone to great effort and enormous expense over a long period and struggled alone on behalf of foreign investors and the mass of Japanese investors.

As is described in the sayings, "You can't fight city hall" and "If you have a scandal, put a lid on it," it is in the nature of the Japanese not to mention things despite being aware of them. You have displayed a resolute attitude in making many insightful proposals on behalf of such a silent mass of investors. Judging from their appearance, all of your proposals are logical. Moreover, you have fiercely pursued the problem areas in the Ministry of Finance, the Tokyo Stock Exchange, and the judiciary, and I admire you for your splendid courageous attitude.

As you have indicated, the abuses inherent in the Japanese-style system will be obsolete in the twenty-first century. If we simply let them go on, won't Japan be left out of the world economy? The fabled Japanese-style system, which has occasionally functioned successfully in a period of intense economic growth, has revealed numerous defects and weaknesses under the global economy after the collapse of the bubble economy. When everything is going smoothly, negative aspects are liable to be papered over, and there is little pressure for their reform, which would be accompanied by pain and friction. Now in this time of adversity, I believe that we have come to a period of crisis in which politicians, bureaucrats, businessmen, and the people must all sincerely reflect, reform themselves, surmount all difficulties, and establish a self-responsibility system. I firmly believe that your timely book will cause a stir not only among investors but among the general public as well.

Above all, I hope you will forgive me for taking the liberty of thanking you in this letter.

Sincerely yours,

Koji Saeki
President, College of
Distribution Economics

Understanding Japan

At this point, I would like to step away from the Oji Paper affair and attempt to explain in more detail about the Japanese system of finance—in brief, of course, since understanding the Japanese mindset and financial system could be a book (or two) in itself.

In many respects, the Japanese financial system is interconnected with the Japanese culture and mindset. On the surface, that statement may seem a bit bold until one realizes that the same statement—that a country's financial system is largely a reflection of the culture out of which it sprang—could apply in many respects to the American financial system and other systems throughout the world. In the U.S., individuality is prized and therefore the average U.S. citizen would never tolerate an oppressive system that told them how they should (or must) invest their money or when to withdraw it or when they must leave it in the market at their own peril. In the West, we believe that an individual's money is their own to do with as they please—to invest it, save it, spend it, lose it, or capitalize on it.

In the U.S., democracy is fully ingrained in the American way of life and so when investors invest in a company, they expect to have some say in the governance of that company. Granted, smaller investors that hold only a several dozen (or fewer) shares of stock do not have as much voice as those with several thousands, but that is acceptable because we realize that one share equals one vote, so those with more shares have more votes. It goes without saying that anyone who holds shares of a company is welcome to attend the annual shareholders meeting and that should the management perform badly, then the shareholders—the true owners of the company—would vote them out.

However, this concept of shared corporate governance and responsibility of the management to the shareholders is almost wholly lost on the average Japanese investor, to say nothing of the majority of Japanese corporations, which actually discourage shareholders from speaking out at shareholders meetings. Those who do speak out in a shareholders meeting are looked down upon as some sort of radical or villain. In fact, speaking out at shareholders meetings can earn one the label of being a *sokaiya*, a term that is actually intended to be applied to extortionists who would threaten to disrupt or prolong the general shareholders meetings (*sokai*).

In Japan, the management of the company is simply not to be questioned. While shareholders meetings in the U.S. or Europe can last an entire day or even several days, shareholders meetings in Japan are opened, speeches given on the health of the company, and the meeting closed, all usually within the span of thirty minutes.

Bear in mind that when I speak of Japanese or American companies, I am speaking in general. Not all Japanese companies, especially newer ones, share the viewpoints of their older, more-established corporate brothers; nor, for that matter, are all American companies democratic in nature and may have their own idiosyncrasies that rival those of their Japanese counterparts. However, the business practices I am speaking about apply to the majority of companies.

Investors in the U.S. are generally welcomed by companies and made to feel like what they are—part owners of the company. True, for some corporations this may only be lip service, but they would never dare to assert openly that a shareholder was not an owner of the company. investors have entrusted their own hard-earned money to a company and therefore expect—and deserve—some say in how the company handles its affairs. They are, in fact, guaranteed these rights under the securities laws of the U.S. If the company does well, then investors will receive the rewards of dividends from the company, rise in share prices, stock splits, and so forth. If the company does poorly, then shareholders will expect the board of directors and executives to right the sinking ship. Failing that, the investors will expect the management to resign and the company will then hire other managers; alternately, the investors will simply remove their money to invest in other companies—sometimes even putting their money with the company's rivals.

Such actions by Japanese investors, on the other hand, would be considered shocking, even traitorous to the company.

Whereas U.S. investors expect performance and a return on their investment, the majority of investment in Japan is done for wholly different reasons and is often more for social reasons and less for economic ones. In fact, the traditional market concept of shareholding as an ownership right does not apply in the Japanese mindset. In Japan, share ownership can be a key to unlock social doors. While some of the motivation is economic in nature (for example, by opening new social doors, the investment can help them further their ambitions and thereby increase their economic situation), investment has many levels attached to it that are not readily understood. Share ownership can serve as the cement in business relationships, means to raise funds for campaigning, collateral for bank loans, a favor to fellow group members and so on. In other words, Japanese share ownership serves various roles that have few, if any, counterparts in a purely free-market context.

A Brief History

While the Japanese financial system is as old as Japan itself, the roots of Japan's modern financial system first began to take shape during the Meiji Restoration Period (1868–1912), which saw the power of the government returned to the imperial family, which had lost power some 250 years earlier. The Meiji Restoration was initiated by a small group of samurai who had been growing discontent with the ruling shogun. Government financial problems had led to cuts in the income of the samurai, which only added to their growing dissatisfaction with Japan's rigid social structure that prevented them from rising to better stations in life. The revolutionaries also disapproved of the unbalanced trade treaties with the U.S. initiated by Commodore Matthew Perry, and wanted to increase Japan's security and well-being in what the revolutionaries considered a dangerous and competitive world.

The samurai who had deposed the ruling shogun in the name of the emperor created a strong centralized government and set in motion the ability for private ownership—facilitated by the emergence of banks—and dramatic economic growth ensued. (Private ownership had existed before this time, but it had been mainly small enterprises.) Ownership of businesses slowly began to pass from the state to individuals; land ownership became negotiable and mortgages came into existence. Economic rights that Western civilization had seen as fundamental since the end of the Middle Ages became suddenly available to the Japanese. In our modern age it is almost hard to fathom that the Japanese have had these rights for less than 150 years.

During this period, the Japanese people accepted capitalism without hesitation and Japan began an ambitious program of economic development, investing in coal mines, textile mills, shipyards, military industries, and many other modern enterprises. National wealth soared in the late 19th century, not only from the surge from building up Japan's military but also from the manufacture of everyday items such as bicycles, farm chemicals, light bulbs, and so on.

By 1872, companies had begun issuing shares—a remarkable leap forward since only a decade before the very concept of a "company" had not even existed in the daily life of the Japanese. The shares issued were not so much to raise capital, but to divide ownership. At this time, companies used bank loans rather than stock offerings as their primary source of capital. Thus, for roughly the next hundred years, banks, and not stock markets, fostered the growth of the private sector.

Nonetheless, trading and speculation did exist and by 1878, exchanges were established in Tokyo and Osaka to handle securities, including gold, silver, and bonds.

Stock market trading during this period, however, was largely regarded as a form of gambling since banking was considered the only proper financial profession. In the 1880s, the government began selling its government-owned industries to private family-run "corporations," or groups, known as *zaibatsu*. A family patriarch (usually a man of samurai descent) dominated every *zaibatsu* house. Central to each *zaibatsu* was the family bank (which funded the family enterprises), as well as the family trading firm, various enterprises and holdings, along with subsidiary companies that benefited the main family business.

Some of these companies—such as the Mitsui and Sumitomo groups—to which the government began selling its state-run industries, were old merchant houses that had been established since the 1600s, while others, such as the Mitsubishi group, sprang up after the Meiji Restoration.

By 1894, private industries were accelerating and corporate shares were traded actively. A true stock market began to emerge for trading in stocks, futures, and bonds, although banks continued to remain the primary source for capital.

In 1904, Japan declared war on Russia and almost immediately after Russia's defeat in 1905 the stock market began to boom. Japan instantly became a military and industrial giant. However, two years later, in 1907, Japan's market suffered one of the most dramatic declines in its history. Still, there were not those without success during this bear market (just as there were those who met with success during America's stock market crash in 1929).

For example, during this period, Tokushichi Nomura made some $60 million in today's money and became legendary. He wisely came to understand that it was the industry that stocks and bonds could build that made securities houses so important, which was why New York banks willingly funded brokers rather than deriding them as they did in Japan. Tokushichi went to New York and London to study their markets and went on to found Nomura Securities, which would later become one of the Big Four.

When World War I broke out in 1914, it sent average Japanese investors into a panic, but the burgeoning securities companies cleverly understood that war would have important implications for Japan. They believed that if the war were to last long enough, there would be increasing demands for Japanese goods and the stock market would soar. The securities companies therefore began buying heavily in textiles, shipping, and steel and eventually Japan's exports began rising faster than her imports. Money became plentiful.

Throughout the 1910s and 1920s, the great *zaibatsu* institutions, rather than the securities companies, were the real powerbrokers and continued to grow in wealth and power. The *zaibatsu* were to Japan what Rockefeller, Vanderbilt, Carnegie, and so forth were to America. However, instead of one or two firms controlling one particular segment of business, as was the case in America, four or five *zaibatsu* presided over the entire Japanese economy. At the start of World War II, five of these dynasties ruled Japanese business: Mitsui, Mitsubishi, Sumitomo, Yasuda, and Suzuki.

Wealth is viewed differently in Japan. In Japan, it is not just the fact that a person accumulates wealth; it is the manner in which he accumulates it that is important. At this time, if a person made his fortune through the stock market during the war, it would be seen as doubly shameful in the Japanese mind because his fortune was made through investing in companies that profited during the war. Essentially it would have been viewed both as "gambling" and "blood money." Because of the disrespectability of the stock market during the 1930s, the real power and prestige continued to remain with banks, which themselves were not a very old institution in Japan.

It was during World War II, however, that all of the securities companies flourished, generating large commission income as the Japanese government issued more and more bonds in order to finance the war effort. Also during the war, the securities companies, at the urging of the government that was desperately trying to raise funds for the war effort, guaranteed investors compensation for 20% of any losses they might suffer. This effectively removed the stigma of "gambling" from investment.

It was during the war that the foundation for the Big Four was laid. In the two years before the end of the war, the government seized greater and greater control of all facets of Japan in an all-out effort to win. In order to control stock trading and to try to help funnel money into the war effort, the government wiped out the smaller securities companies and consolidated them into larger groupings that it could more easily control, placing power in the hands of a few while the smaller brokers disappeared. Despite their efforts, the Japanese lost the war but their actions would have broad implications after the war.

As the war wound down, however, companies began to realize that Japan might lose the war and began to discreetly hide and protect their own assets and the companies would later ride out the post-war years with these hidden funds.

Japan's defeat in World War II brought foreign occupation to its shores for the first time. Under the direction of General Douglas MacArthur, the Allies carried out sweeping reforms inspired by American ideals while the Japanese government served only to carry out MacArthur's orders. The Japanese were stripped of their military, disarming the more than 5 million Japanese troops. The Allies tried twenty-five Japanese leaders for war crimes, seven of which, including former Prime Minister Tojo, were executed. The rest were imprisoned.

Unlike America, which fought its war for independence, the Japanese had democracy and capitalism thrust upon them and as such the idealism that would otherwise accompany such a movement was nonexistent. Instead, the old systems and ways of doing business continued but in new forms.

It is easy to assume that the Japanese should warmly embrace democracy and capitalism, but this is merely some sixty years since the beginning of democracy in Japan whereas in America, democracy evolved over the span of 173 years if one counts from the first permanent English settlement in Jamestown, Virginia, to the signing of the Declaration of Independence. And democracy as we know it then evolved slowly over the next 200 years to include women and all races.

Post-war Japan was one of hardship for the average Japanese citizen. Allied bombing had destroyed many of the nation's primary factories and nearly leveled most large cities—including Tokyo, which had suffered 60% damage. Many Japanese citizens were forced out of work with much of the population living in dire conditions in small rural villages, depending on relatives, friends, or neighbors just to survive. Food became scarce and harsh rationing was instituted. During the immediate post-war period, scavengers, barely clothed, roamed the streets, and those too proud to beg died of starvation.

In addition to losing the war and recovering psychologically from it, the Japanese had to deal with the occupation of their country. Even though the Allies were not villainous, the occupation was generally harmonious, and America provided financial assistance to Japan, the Americans also had their own agenda for what post-war Japan should be like.

One of the foremost goals of the Allies was to remove power from those that held it by promoting a plan of widespread ownership of corporate Japan. Defeat, therefore, seemed to spell the end of the insurmountable, omniscient power that the ten wealthiest families in Japan had exercised. By 1945, these ten families controlled more than 75% of all industry, finance, and commerce in Japan.

The redistribution of power meant the *zaibatsu* had to be broken up. This followed the democratic ideals of America, replacing the rule of the few with the rule of the many. MacArthur himself, in any case, believed that the *zaibatsu* had largely financed the Japanese war effort. MacArthur and his staff did not always see eye-to-eye, but one thing they all agreed on was that the Japanese economy was ruled by a tiny minority for the benefit of that minority and because of this the average Japanese—essentially working for slave wages—had little money left to buy consumer goods. The House of Mitsui alone employed over 3 million workers, perhaps the largest workforce ever in the history of the world.

Within four months from the end of the war, the Allied Forces stripped all the *zaibatsu* of their assets. In the summer of 1948, the Americans confiscated all the previously frozen shares of corporations and their subsidiaries with the intention of auctioning them off to the public—the goal once again being the promotion of the widespread ownership of corporate Japan.

Companies pleaded with the Americans against selling off Japan's oldest and proudest firms and, in the end, the Americans agreed to a plan to offer company employees the first option of purchasing shares. Since there was little danger that hard-pressed employees would be able to buy large blocks of ownership and because the plan seemed to follow the plan for promoting widespread ownership, the Americans agreed.

However, corporations—with the assistance of the securities companies—secretly loaned money to trusted employees so they could buy the shares and then sell them back to the company at a later date, ensuring that the company would not fall into unfriendly (or their competitors') hands.

As a result, family ownership was replaced by institutional cross-holdings in related firms, a practice that has become horribly entrenched even today. The various groups remained intact with their companies holding shares of each other's companies. For example, a securities company might own shares in a bank, which in turn held shares in that securities company.

Remnants of *zaibatsu* land were also secretly transferred into other *zaibatsu* corporations (such as construction companies) that had been set up towards the end of the war and survived as being a repository for *zaibatsu* wealth, and helped along as property values began to recover. Although on paper they were different companies, in reality, they remained under the same control as always.

These companies could also hold shares of the secret parent company or arrange for beneficial treatment of the parent company. Generally speaking, breaking up the *zaibatsu* was largely a wasted effort. When the Allies left Japan, the old *zaibatsu* simply reunited under different guises.

Because of the bleak economic conditions of post-war Japan, the Americans froze all bank deposits and issued a new currency. Although these draconian policies were devastating for the average citizen, advantageous loopholes existed for the securities companies. There were no laws against the transfer of bank savings to brokerage houses, which, in practical terms, meant that banks could transfer customer funds to brokers who would in turn buy stock for their clients who then sold the stock and collected new yen that they could redeposit in their bank. (Although the Tokyo Stock Exchange had been officially closed, an underground market had emerged). This, of course, meant fortunes for the securities companies who gained commissions off of these underground sales.

After the war, the Japanese government began to direct the nation's industries, forming the Ministry of International Trade and Industry to identify the key industries that needed to be developed in order to rebuild Japan. Once identified, the Ministry of Finance directed investment funds toward these enterprises. This further strengthened the ties between government entities and corporations.

In 1947, a law called the Securities and Exchange Law had dissolved the Japan Securities Exchange and established separate stock exchanges in Tokyo, Osaka, and Nagoya. In 1949, open trading was resumed when the Tokyo Stock Exchange in its modern form began trading again. The significant difference when trading resumed was that stocks, rather than bonds, were the focus as shares of individually owned companies—ostensibly stripped of *zaibatsu* control—were now traded. The fact that Japan was forced to renounce militarism meant that it would have to spend only a minimal amount on defense, about one percent of its GNP. Therefore the government could and did invest much more of its public funds into programs for developing the nation's industries, rather than into a vast defense fund.

Japan's Economy Today

From the discussion so far, it can be clearly seen that the basis of Japanese economics is firmly rooted in its culture. Lurking behind the economy and financial system is a network of interdependent relationships that work in a form of group mentality to protect and benefit one's collective. This mindset is largely the foundation upon which the Japanese economy is based and moves forward. It can be said that these relationships—sometimes hidden, sometimes not—are for the benefit of one's own collective primarily, those companies

that are beneficial to the group secondarily, and all others coinciden-
tally.

This web of cross-holdings poses significant obstacles to outsiders and to foreign investment. What have further emerged are the
concepts of stable shareholding and *keiretsu* relationships.

Simply defined, stable shareholders are individuals or corporations (companies, banks, etc.) that will hold shares of a given company indefinitely, regardless of the rise or fall—however dramatic—
of the company's share prices. This effectively keeps control safely in
the hands of entities who are favorable to the issuing company and
who will not question or dispute the issuing company's management.

Classical *keiretsu* are loose, largely informal, horizontal confederations of companies normally including a bank, a trading company,
and manufacturing companies. They are perceived widely as direct
descendants of the *zaibatsu*, the huge horizontal and vertical con-
glomerates of the pre-war era that dominated the Japanese economy.
Horizontal *keiretsu* relationships are created and held together by
cross-shareholdings and cooperative business ventures.

Stable Shareholding

As mentioned above, stable shareholders do not trade stocks in
their portfolios, but rather hold on to the shares for years or even
decades through both boom and bust cycles with little intention of
ever selling the shares unless it is to another member of the group.
This practice substantially reduces the number of shares in active
trading on the Tokyo Stock Exchange. Stable shareholders—a unique
Japanese phenomenon—hold some 60–70% of outstanding issues
on the TSE. Their motivation is neither dividends (which are minuscule for the Japanese market, averaging 0.4%) nor taking a profit
when the shares appreciate (because they rarely realize profits by sale
of securities).

Rather, stable shareholders are motivated by the opportunity to
create and nurture long-term business relationships, or the ability to

use appreciating stocks in their portfolios to secure loans with which to make other investments. In the case of Japanese banks, moreover, stable shareholding is attractive because they can utilize the unrealized appreciation of portfolio stocks as capital to meet international standards for bank capital.

Stable shareholders include banks cementing relationships with customers, insurers or pension funds seeking company accounts through their share purchases of that company, and suppliers fortifying relationships with their customers who are often leaders of modern *keiretsu* manufacturing groups.

Stable shareholding is made possible by the rules of the Tokyo Stock Exchange. On most exchanges, extensive concentration of shares or a low trading volume can lead to delisting as a publicly owned company. Japanese delisting standards are quite liberal, requiring delisting only when ten or fewer shareholders hold more than 70% of a company shares. The TSE also imposes no minimum shareholder requirement allowing company shares to remain listed with as few as 2,000 shareholders holding 120 million shares, or 60,000 shares per shareholder. The TSE therefore enables stable shareholding by allowing the concentration of shares in few hands and by failing to insist upon greater trading and wider ownership.

Among companies listed on the TSE, on average, the top twenty shareholders control 40.6% of outstanding shares with the top ten shareholders controlling 37.6%.

Stable shareholding largely prevents all but the friendliest of takeovers. The consent of stable shareholders—the acquisition target's banker, vendors, major customers, landlords, insurer or pension fund manager, as well as other shareholders without a commercial relationship with the company—is a prerequisite to a successful takeover. In short, the simple market-based approach used in United States for the acquisition of companies—allowing the owners of the company to decide—is not possible in the Japanese context.

Some observers argue that stable shareholding developed initially as an anti-takeover device. Japanese takeovers are performed differently than in the West because of these factors. One way in which the overvaluation burden is overcome is by exchanging equally overvalued stock. For example, Mitsui Bank acquired Taiyo Kobe Bank (to become one of the world's largest banks) through a share swap at an 8:10 ratio. The implied cost of the acquisition reportedly would have been a staggering ¥3.5 trillion (approximately $25 billion at 140 yen to the dollar). Needless to say, hostile takeovers are rare in Japan for these very reasons.

Keiretsu Relationships

The Tokyo Exchange is the arena in which Japanese corporations establish and nurture cooperative long-term relationships through reciprocal shareholding arrangements, stable shareholder relationships, and interlocking directorships. In many instances, these stable shareholding arrangements are between Japanese companies so interlinked to form a *keiretsu* of multiple securities in commercial arrangements. As defined above, classical *keiretsu* are loose, largely informal, horizontal confederations of companies normally including a bank, a trading company, manufacturing companies, along with the suppliers to and the dealer networks of the *keiretsu* leaders.

These relationships lead to collusion and conspiracy between companies that have joint interests to offer such things as highly discounted leases, special loan rates, preferential commercial arrangements for overhead and other items critical to doing business, along with other forms of cooperation to those inside their group but not available (or even known) to those outside their group. Obviously, such an arrangement gives the companies within the *keiretsu* an unfair advantage.

These relationships are especially relevant in the international markets, creating strong barriers to foreign investment in Japan, as well as placing obstacles to participation in corporate governance by foreign shareholders of Japanese corporations. The *keiretsu* relationships, in yielding unwritten preferences for *keiretsu* vendors, impede

American exports to Japan whether in the service or manufacturing sectors.

It also has tremendous implications in overseas markets, one of the most significant implications being the ability of major Japanese industrial companies—as market insiders—to raise capital at extremely low cost.

According to reports, Sony raised some $6.5 billion in new equity and equity-based bond issues between 1986 and 1990. During that period, Sony acquired Columbia Pictures and CBS Records for a reported $5.7 billion. Sony's cost of funds on these ventures reportedly was less than one percent. If major Japanese companies can raise cheap capital because of the structure and operation of Japan's capital and securities markets, then this has profound and far-reaching implications for competing American companies. Imagine what U.S. companies could do if they had the backing of a major bank that essentially printed money for them.

Structure

Structurally, the Big Four securities houses of Nomura, Daiwa, Yamaichi, and Nikko dominate the securities markets. These four brokers alone accounted for roughly forty percent of all equity transactions during the year. If their affiliates are included, their portion jumps to nearly sixty percent of total turnover.

This market power is actually down somewhat from the late 1980s due to an informal guideline from the Ministry of Finance directing each broker to limit its trading to no more than 30% of monthly trading volume.

The Big Four's dominance extends beyond traditional equities markets, enjoying similar influence in other markets like over-the-counter bond trading, convertible bond trading, equity underwriting, investment trusts, Eurodollar warrant-bonds, and stock/bonds futures. Even the smaller securities houses depend upon the Big Four for subcontracting.

The structural dominance by the Big Four is made possible by the practice of stable shareholding, which further enhances their market power. Stable shareholding results in active trading of only 30–40% of the total available number of issues on the TSE. Because stable shareholding distorts and reduces the true amount of shares available on the open market, it thereby enables the Big Four to exercise greater sway over the market than they might otherwise. Stable shareholding also means that all involved in the remaining market are dependent on the Big Four for liquidity and stability.

In Japan, this oligopoly is regarded as a necessary evil. Share issuers tolerate the Big Four because the Big Four can reliably distribute the issuing company's shares better, faster, and at a higher price than they might otherwise be able to obtain. Japanese investors follow the Big Four's advice and recommendations since they make a market liquid that otherwise has a tendency to stagnate due to the natural consequences of having such a large volume of shares that are locked in the vaults of the stable shareholders. Also, issuers and investors alike depend on the Big Four to stabilize the market when it becomes uncertain.

The Big Four also use their market power to drive the market. Anecdotal and other evidence has emerged that the Big Four churn customer accounts, drive the market through fictitious or exaggerated rationales (so called "market themes") to induce purchases of their current stock picks. The market is ramped upward through these devices for varying reasons. They may do it to earn commission revenues generated by market movements, to benefit politicians who have been given advance tips on favored stocks, to benefit new issuers hoping to maximize subscriptions, or to help selected customers who have incurred losses on stocks recommended by a broker.

Japanese securities companies have plenty of incentive to churn the accounts (much as they did in my own case when they asked me to sell our shares of Kao Soap and Ajinomoto or would ask me to make purchases of other companies). Brokerage fees are set by the Ministry of Finance and are fixed at relatively high levels. The average for equity brokerage commissions is around 38% of the Big Four's total yearly revenue. By U.S. standards, that is exorbitant. According to the *New York Times*, Japanese investors pay commissions thirty-five times higher than American investors.

In order to perpetuate commission revenues, Japanese securities companies use "market themes" to stimulate trading. These themes, whether buying or selling, are based on whatever stocks the Big Four are promoting at any given moment rather than the actual economic fundamentals of the favored companies. In other words, a company could be failing and on the verge of bankruptcy, but the Big Four would still promote it in order to push the company and generate revenue. The Big Four's reasons for promoting the company are not always realistic and the ensuing buying frenzy—and their support of the company—might last only a few days and sometimes only a few hours.

These market themes are successfully used to push certain stocks, often with the hint of "inside information" or an "exclusive" stock tip. For example, a Nomura "pick of the day," Mochida Pharmaceutical, had reportedly discovered a cure for cancer and its stock price soared from ¥1,100 in the summer of 1984 to ¥4,450 per share by the following February.

I have witnessed this myself. I had invested in Ishikawa-Harima Heavy Industries (IHI). IHI was heavily in debt and as a result, I decided to sell. Because of this heavy debt, I fully expected that IHI's share prices would decline or, at best, remain stable.

Contrary to these fundamental business indicators, IHI's share price began to rise. From less than ¥200 in 1986 to ¥700 by the first half of 1987 and to a peak of ¥1,150 in July 1988—all of this despite the fact that during this same time period IHI had net losses of ¥19.2 billion. IHI was ramped upward by Nomura Securities by the use of market themes and by including it in the somewhat notorious "Tokyo Bayfront Redevelopment."

Nomura repeatedly recommended IHI because of the alleged latent value of its real-estate assets, one of which was the "hidden value" of the land of one of IHI's factories—even though the factory remained in operation and the only possible way to realize the alleged latent value was to liquidate the plant. In addition, Nomura also treated the factory as though it lay within the redevelopment project then being undertaken by the Tokyo municipal government, even though official documents placed the factory outside the redevelopment zone.

Not only did Nomura ramp up the price using their various market themes, but also purchased 4.9 billion IHI shares between August 1986 and July 1988, selling 4.5 billion of them. The total number of IHI shares traded (purchased or sold) during the period was 11.4 billion, meaning that Nomura itself accounted for roughly 82% of these transactions.

This demonstrates the enormous power of the Big Four to drive the market when they so choose. It also shows the plight of outsiders—foreign investors, disfavored speculators, or small investors not privy to the information—who are left at the mercy of the "market."

Another example of the Big Four's market power and also of the preferential treatment accorded to favored customers is their practice of guarantees to investors against losses.

The Loss Guarantee scandal erupted into an international scandal in June 1991. According to press accounts, the Big Four admitted to paying approximately $950 million in loss guarantees to some 231 preferred customers. Another thirteen smaller brokerage houses admitted to paying 386 favored customers another $320 million in loss guarantees.

The recipients of the special payments were so-called "*oh-guchi*" (literally, "big-mouth") investors numbering among Japan's industrial, political, and financial elites. Although the Loss Guarantee scandal was the subject of considerable controversy in the summer of

1991, the practice had been well known—in both Japan and the United States—for quite some time.

In the wake of the October 1987 market crash, the preferred investors reportedly had accrued losses amounting to ¥17 billion. Yamaichi apparently was able to reduce this loss substantially by virtue of agile trading, but the aggregate loss still totaled ¥11 billion. Mitsui Bank and Yamaichi Securities agreed to compensate these preferred customers for their losses and each paid ¥5.5 billion (some $40 million) to these customers.

The loss guarantees only became known after the Japanese tax authorities questioned the companies' treatments of the payments. Yamaichi reportedly had claimed that the payments constituted a type of entertainment expense, while Mitsui Bank treated its share as an expense for "unknown use."

Naturally, such loss guarantees can easily distort a market. When investors receive loss-guarantee commitments, or at least have an expectation that their brokers will cover any losses, their investment decisions are quite different. A significant element of risk is eliminated, and investors will more readily purchase securities in larger amounts. The market is then distorted to appear more "bullish" than would be determined by the fundamental and natural indicators of stock value. Stock prices are therefore inflated beyond their underlying values by a risk-free mentality.

The securities houses can also use loss guarantees to enhance their ability to drive the market. For example, if investors are assured they will not lose any money, then the securities companies can insure broad subscription to new share issues underwritten by the Big Four by comforting subscribers that, if the stock price were to fall following its issue, their losses would be reimbursed. Because they have a ready and willing source of capital at hand, this further enhances the ability of the Big Four to ramp the market.

Another market-distorting effect of loss guarantees stems from the manner in which they are paid. Although market guarantees can be paid in cash, investors are often given "ambulance shares" that have been ramped up in value by the guarantor brokerage, or by over-payment for bonds or securities in the recipient's portfolio. One example that emerged from the Loss Guarantee scandal was the overpayment for warrants (i.e., separable conversion rights on bonds) on London markets, which raised the ominous question of how much of the international markets have also been distorted through Japanese loss guarantee payments.

Corporate Governance

It is not difficult to imagine that corporate governance is done by the few rather than by the many. Although shareholders technically have rights in the governance of the company, in reality they are actu-ally prevented in a number of ways from exercising their property rights, from participating meaningfully in the governance of the cor-poration they ostensibly own, and from protecting the value of their stock investment. Japanese corporate managers are not genuinely accountable to the shareholders, who are the supposed owners of the company. Additionally, the number of potential critics is reduced by stable shareholding, further limiting the potential for questioning the management.

For example, during the Recruit affair, which scandalized Japan in December 1991, Nomura had very few complaints at its sharehold-ers meetings, even though it was heavily involved with the entire Recruit affair. Few gripes were voiced about its involvement in the scandal, and, in fact, there were expressions of some support for Chairman Tabuchi who was forced to resign because of the scandal. By contrast, when the Enron scandal broke, the board and share-holders of Enron took action to remove the CEO and bring in new management. In the light of what happened with Enron, can one even imagine Enron's shareholders praising the company? Yet this was what happened with Chairman Tabuchi.

But this type of corporation-shareholder relationship goes beyond mere custom or tradition.

To stifle the few potential shareholder critics, Japanese management often resort to gangster-style organizations termed "*sokaiya*." Professional extortionists had been around since the late 19th century but it was not until the 1960s that they became problematic. The 1960s saw the rise of honest shareholders who actually began to speak out at shareholders meetings, demanding explanations for poor performance, reimbursement for faulty products, and so forth. Originally, the *sokaiya* had been hired by shareholders as a way to put pressure on management and to help shareholders who wanted to raise legitimate problems. Instead, borrowing a page from politicians who used shadowy underworld figures to hush opposition, the management of companies began actively hiring *sokaiya* thugs to intimidate shareholders who dared to oppose the management by shouting down, threatening, and using other means of intimidation. The *sokaiya*, realizing there was more money to be had by supporting the management changed allegiances but it was not long before the *sokaiya* began extorting a "fee" from management in exchange for keeping themselves and everyone else quiet. Soon, they became an accepted part of corporate Japan.

Shareholders meetings became a travesty. The ownership structure provided no incentive or reason to raise questions or issues and the Japanese were culturally reluctant in any event to voice their own opinions, especially to those they see as their superiors. Meanwhile, lines of *sokaiya* formed outside companies, waiting to be registered on the company's official lists to the point that most companies hired a manager whose job was to handle the pay offs. Such "registered" thugs were paid substantial sums per year for their service.

In 1982, a law was passed forbidding payments to the *sokaiya* and the Japanese police began cracking down on them. But even the new laws that were passed were not enough of a deterrent and the only way management is able to rid themselves of them is to continue to make payments. The surviving *sokaiya* groups simply have become more sophisticated by setting up fronts for their organizations and remain a potent deterrent to the development of an effective share-holder rights movement.

Beyond any effect that the *sokaiya* have, Japanese management does not appear to feel any sense of genuine responsibility toward shareholders. One observer argues that, in terms of any sense of duty manifested by corporate managers, Japanese corporations are truly "owned" by their employees rather than by the shareholders. Japanese shareholders have acquiesced in that relationship in part because of custom and for ulterior long-term commercial purposes, but also because during the 1980s, the seemingly endless upward trend in Japanese equities prices reduced pressure on management to declare dividends or improve short-term profits. So long as the share prices continued to escalate, the average shareholder had no com-plaints.

Granted, many companies in the West pay only lip service to investors, who often are only important when the company is in dan-ger of a being taken over, but investors do have the right of free expression and the right to complain, to raise issues, and to be heard. They also have the ability to sue the company should the company misuse corporate funds. Such practices in Japan are almost unheard of. Unfortunately, it is this intrinsic idea of ownership that is so often lost on Japanese ears.

The only persons that Japanese corporate managers truly display a sense of responsibility to are themselves and their counterparts in government, politics, finance, the bureaucracy, and other elements of "the system." This apparent lack of responsibility to corporate own-ers (the shareholders) originally stems from the *zaibatsu* family own-ers' practice of hiring professional managers. These professional managers became entrenched and bureaucratized during the wartime mobilization, and became further separated from owners when the American occupation forces broke up the *zaibatsu*. Postwar govern-ment policies that funneled money to companies it had targeted as necessary for the rebuilding of Japan also liberated managers from the need to court new shareholders (owners) to raise capital.

When Japanese corporate managers returned to equity markets in the 1980s, their power was entrenched and accepted, and their ability to raise capital was dependent more on the promise of capital gains in the endlessly appreciating stock market than on the returns available from actual corporate performance.

Due to such entrenched powers, Japanese corporations can use insider dealings, the acquiescence of stable shareholders, thin trading, and lax regulation to fend off outsiders, no matter how benign. Japanese companies that are threatened by an outsider can suddenly issue new shares to corporations within the "family," stable shareholders, or similarly friendly hands to dilute the outsider's voting power, thereby raising the costs of acquisition and placing the necessary voting power beyond the outsider's reach.

The costs incurred by the insiders to implement this sort of dilution strategy is also less than those incurred by the outside interests, at the ultimate expense of outside shareholders. To maintain position following a dilution, an outsider would be forced to pay higher, "market" price for stock—if any were available. In essence, whenever the insiders need more votes to retain power, they pull them out of thin air, quickly stuffing the ballot box by putting the votes in friendly hands.

All of this is done with little regard to the company's original shareholders who would then number among the losers as well because the value of their interests would now be diluted without any kind of compensating benefit to the company, such as a capital infusion reflecting the true value of the stock. The sole beneficiaries are the insiders, who not only help to perpetuate their own control but also receive valuable stock at a fraction of the true price or underlying value.

Obviously, this goes completely against fundamental free-market principles.

Securities companies can also play a role in this aspect of corporate governance. In a free market, the only fair way to distribute newly issued shares at market price is by drawing lots. Instead, securities companies can decide to make shares unavailable to the general public (or undesirable outside investors). For example, during the listing of Mitsubishi Automobile Industry, any public investor who approached the counter of a securities company seeking to buy Mitsubishi was turned away on the grounds that these shares were all sold out. None of the public was able to buy them. The securities companies only allocated them to parties with which they had a direct interest. I can personally attest to this type of offering because on several occasions the securities companies have approached me with the offer of receiving newly issued shares—provided that I agree to various other matters.

Land costs provide perhaps the most significant illustration of the unfair practices of corporate governance and *keiretsu* arrangements. The high cost of real estate in Japan is legendary. According to one widely-used proof of high Japanese real estate costs, the aggregate market of Japan's real estate is four times that of the United States, while Japan is four percent of the United States in total land mass. If these costs were born equally by Japanese companies and foreign companies seeking to locate in Japan, they would have the same competitive implications, establishing fixed costs for Japanese-owned and foreign-owned businesses alike. But they are not. Through cooperative relationships, Japanese companies are able to secure preferential, discounted rates on commercial leases.

For example, attracted by its underlying real estate assets (which were being held at original cost) we Hong Kong investors acquired a modest stake in Japan Wool Textile. Japan Wool Textile was a corporation whose principal business purposes were the manufacture, processing, and sale of woolen yarns, wool, and other textile products. In 1982, Japan Wool announced plans to develop a shopping center in its unutilized Nakayama plant. In 1983, a major Japanese supermarket chain—Daiei—acquired more than 2 million shares of Japan Wool. That stake represented nearly five percent of Japan Wool's outstanding shares and made Daiei the third-largest shareholder in

Japan Wool. Japan Wool and Daiei then entered into a protocol in which each would hold some 2 million of each other's shares.

Japan Wool then "decided" to lease Daiei 26,000 square meters, making Daiei the shopping center's prime tenant. The lease rate was at a ridiculously low level. We calculated that the land on which the Nakayama shopping center was placed was worth ¥240 billion, while Japan Wool announced that the development costs would amount to ¥14 billion. This represented a value of ¥254 billion. Yet Japan Wool projected a total lease of ¥2.0 billion per year—including its prime tenant, Daiei—a return of only 0.8%. At that rate, it would take almost 125 years for Japan Wool to recover the capital at stake in the project—hardly a profitable venture. Besides, the idea of using Daiei as a tenant was not a good business decision because it would be difficult for Japan Wool to replace it as a tenant. Obviously, these preferential lease terms were based not on economic reasons but upon the close inter-corporate relationship between Daiei and Japan Wool.

We sought an explanation from Japan Wool to reveal the reason behind their lease rates, but they refused to reveal their reasons. This attitude alone was sufficient to suggest that there were rather dubious circumstances in selecting Daiei and determining their conditions. But it was painfully obvious that under these circumstances, Japan Wool would cause a huge loss to its shareholders, violating not only commonsense but also constituting a violation of the faithful obligations of the directors on behalf of the shareholders. As such, two other plaintiffs and I sought an injunction to prevent the lease. Combined, we were the biggest shareholder.

Despite the obvious collusion between the two corporations, however, the injunction was denied.

By first unilaterally acquiring a significant stake, and by then entering into a long-term, cross-shareholding relationship, Daiei was able to secure lease rates unavailable to outsiders—to the detriment of Japan Wool's shareholders. Even so, these types of arrangements that are detrimental to the health of the company are the very ones that shareholders are discouraged from bringing up at shareholders meetings, let alone sue the company over such loss of income.

Needless to say, an American supermarket chain attempting to enter the Japanese market would not receive the discounted rate, but would instead be forced to pay the higher rate dictated by the fundamental economics of the shopping center project. This practice impedes foreign competition in Japan by imposing higher fixed costs on foreigners than on preferred Japanese companies, thereby reducing the ability of foreign entrepreneurs attempting to penetrate the Japanese market.

Politicians and the Securities Companies

In addition to all of their other influence, the Big Four also allegedly make indirect contributions to politicians by providing them with advance information and liberal credit to allow them to profit quickly from the stock being "ramped" upward. Indeed, Japanese politicians reportedly have developed a heavy reliance on the stock market as a source of campaign funds.

Government ministers and other members of the Diet (Japan's legislature) lack adequate official funds to run their offices, campaign for reelection, and build support with other "Dietmen." A moderately successful member of the Diet requires roughly $1.8 million to run his office and campaign during an election year. Of that, only about $200,000 can normally be secured through the Diet member's salary or through funds from his political party.

Diet members frequently make up this shortfall by contributions from lobbyists but also through stock speculation. Diet members, especially government ministers, receive campaign contributions from the industry lobbyists with which they affiliate and govern. To further make up the shortfall, the practice of providing advance stock tips—essentially, insider information, which is technically illegal under Japanese law—to politicians is reportedly widespread and accepted in Japan.

The notorious Recruit and Kotani scandals, in which former Prime Minister Nakasone and others became embroiled, provide examples of this. The Nakasone and Takeshita factions, as well as other political figures, reportedly received unlisted Recruit shares as part of a widespread "influence-buying" scheme by Recruit. Aides of former Prime Minister Nakasone were accused of purchasing shares of Kokusai Kogyo from stock speculator Mitsuhiro Kotani, who was ultimately tried for securities laws violations.

In 1987, Miss Ota, who was then called "Nakasone's treasurer," and Mitsuhiro Kotani, a representative of Koshin (Koorin, at the time) traded 100,000 shares of Kokusai Kogyo Co., Ltd., and made ¥120 million in just one month. Upon request by Mr. Nakasone, Mr. Togo (who was the president of Shokusan Jutaku Sogo Co., Ltd. at the time) asked Mr. Koyama, the president of the Mitsui Bank Ltd. to provide him a loan. Mr. Togo made use of these funds to trade his company's own stock and made ¥1.3 billion. Out of these profits, ¥500 million went to Mr. Nakasone's secretary's bank account.

The former Prime Minister was never prosecuted for the illegal dealings.

Politicians, although not as powerful as bureaucrats and industrialists in Japanese society, nevertheless can lobby the government and the bureaucracy effectively on behalf of their "contributors." Politicians can also prevent statutory reform of a mutually beneficial system. Given their desperate need for additional funds—whether to run for their own reelection, to build a faction by helping other politicians, or to rise in another's faction—Japanese politicians see the ever-expanding Japanese securities markets to be an easy and important source of funds with the right advance information.

All happily provided to them by the right contacts.

Conclusions

The issues that have been raised in this chapter point to several obvious and disturbing conclusions. Japanese securities markets do

not operate as free markets that are determined by the forces of supply and demand nor the fundamental indicators underlying a stock's
value. Instead, Japan's securities markets are dominated by a brokerage oligopoly, whose power is enhanced by the practice of stable
shareholding and such liberal exchange rules. Additionally, the dom-
inant forces are permitted and even fostered by the regulatory
regime. The Big Four then use their market power to drive the market for their own varied purposes, ranging from increasing their own
income through brokerage commissions, to indirectly making political contributions, to reimbursing favored customers for past losses.

Taken together, these manifestations lead inescapably to the conclusion that insiders dominate the Japanese securities markets for the
benefit of those who are enmeshed in their complex network of
reciprocal relationships. Although outsiders—like American pension
funds—can survive and even profit in such a "market," their investments will always be at risk due to the opaque "rules of the game."

All of this raises the question whether Japan is truly a market
economy, as we in the West understand that concept.

During the 1980s, Japan emerged as a leading creditor nation,
injecting essential liquidity into the international system. Japan helped
finance the United States' transformation from a creditor to a debtor
nation through Japan's purchases of U.S. public debt, direct investment, and portfolio investment. Since Japan has emerged as the pre-
eminent creditor nation, the health of its economy has serious, even
dire, implications for the U.S. and the rest of the world. If its economy continues to deflate or even burst, it will most certainly wreak
havoc on international financial markets.

U.S. investors, especially large institutional investors like pension
funds, have placed billions of dollars in risky Japanese securities.
Because the Japanese markets are dominated and controlled by an
oligopoly closed to outsiders, those investments—and the pensioners' savings they reflect—are in jeopardy. We have seen how quickly
pension plans—once believed to be safe—can dissipate in the wake

of the Enron scandal. But Enron is merely one company; imagine what can happen if an entire economy were to fail.

Most disturbing of all is that Japan is unlikely to address these ills on its own. Unfortunately, the institutions that are in the best position to provide leadership toward reform are actually those with the strongest interests in perpetuating the current system. Japanese politicians rely heavily on the current system to keep themselves in power. The Ministry of Finance, which regulates both securities and banking, has intimate and mutually beneficial relationships with the very industries it purports to regulate. Also, the banking and securities industries have surged to global prominence under this regime, and appear unlikely to tamper with their prescription for success. Prime Minster Junichiro Koizumi, though he is espousing reform, is making little headway in a system that is designed to prevent it.

The foregoing discussion, which merely skims the surface of the history, practices, and structure of Japanese securities markets, also no doubt makes one wonder whether the Japanese have any securities laws at all. They do. However, it should not be difficult for one to imagine that although they have laws in place, they are rarely enforced and they are usually only enforced on those that the system wishes to punish.

In my own case, the TSE's leak of information was a violation of its own rules and regulations, in addition to the Japanese Securities Code, and was punishable under the Japanese criminal code. Oji Paper's allegations that we were greenmailers and accusations to the Tokyo Stock Exchange constituted defamation, in violation of Japan's Criminal Code No. 230. The abuse of powers by the Ministry of Finance violated Japan's Criminal Code No. 193. As one can see, there are laws established, it is just whether those in power choose to enforce them.

Essentially, the Japanese establish the rules but when they don't like the rules anymore—or when they find themselves in a corner—they simply choose not to follow the rules or only follow those that are beneficial to them. Failing that, they change the rules without any consideration of fair play. It is not unlike playing baseball with the schoolyard bully who makes up new rules as the game goes along or applies rules to just your team but not to his own. In such a situation, there is never any way to win.

In conclusion—lest you think I am alone in my opinions—I would like to offer the letter of Kazuo Noda, the president of Miyagi University, which he sent to me on July 15, 1998

Dear Mr. Wang,

Thank you very kindly for presenting me with your book, *The Eve of the Financial and Securities Collapse*. It was sent to my home in Tokyo, but I have been living in Sendai as president of Miyagi University (Prefectural) since April of last year. I read this book for the first time a few days ago when I returned to Tokyo and was deeply impressed. Given the above circumstances, I hope that you will forgive me for my belated thanks.

Now, with regard to the "Japanese-style system" that you have criticized in this book, citing specific examples, I do not possess the necessary qualifications to express my personal opinion as an "expert," but as a Japanese university professor specializing in industrial management, I cannot help but fully sympathize with your opinion. As I was born in 1927, I have personal experience of pre-war Japan, and despite the "democratization" carried out as a result of defeat in World War II, I feel that the special character of Japan's power struc- ture (the Japanese-style system) that has been formed in the post-war process of economic growth differs hardly at all in terms of substance from that before the war. Therefore, even though it may cause hardships for the Japanese people, includ- ing myself, I frankly believe that the collapse of the "Japanese- style system" would be desirable for the justice and prosperi- ty of international society. If you do not just stop at criticism of the "Japanese-style system," and moreover try to promote some activity or other directed toward its collapse, I as a Japanese person would be there to give my heartfelt encouragement. I too have long had it in mind to fight my own battle against Japan's power structure. I would like you to understand that not all Japanese have blindly followed this absurd system. If you have the opportunity to come to Japan, I would like to get in touch with you without fail. I look forward with great pleasure to being able to meet and speak with you.

Once again, please accept my apologies for the late reply.

Sincerely yours,

Kazuo Noda,
President of Miyagi University

Chapter Six

More Oji Paper Troubles

Though I would have problems with other Japanese companies over the years, the Oji Paper incident seemed to go away. As a matter of fact, during the 1980s, I had a lot of trouble with a company called Katakura that involved several high-profile lawsuits in addition to raising numerous complaints to the authorities. Little did I realize that Oji Paper was but a sleeping dragon during all of these other troubles.

In early 1989, I gave an interview to one of the members of the Stock Market Problems Reporters Group of one of the leading Japanese financial magazines, *Days Japan*. The reporter had come uninvited to Hong Kong to meet me specifically for the interview. The reporter's zeal to meet with me is a good example of the concern and interest of the media in Japan over the matters I was complaining about.

The interview was published in great detail and in it I talked frankly about the collusion by the Japanese securities companies in the Oji Paper and Katakura affairs. I also spoke particularly about Nomura's involvement in the purchase and manipulation of the share prices of Ishikawa-Harima Heavy Industries (IHI), which was making a lot of headlines in those days. As you'll recall, Nomura had been ramping up IHI's shares by touting it as being part of the bayfront project when, in reality, it was not.

Below is an extract of this rather lengthy interview in *Days Japan*:

Tseng Hsiang Wang Hurls a Letter of Protest from Hong Kong Against the Four Leading Securities Companies

There is probably nobody in the Japanese stock trading circles who has not heard of the name of the individual investor of Hong Kong, Mr. Tseng Hsiang Wang. Why is Mr. Wang such an "important character"? This is easily understood once we see the extraordinary vast sums of money he has used in his tradings. It is this very Mr. Wang who is about to part with the Japanese securities trading circles. What replies will the [securities companies] have to his shocking statements?

— There is a rumor in some parts of Japan that you purchased and amassed shares and then unloaded them at high prices to the issuing companies and profited from the same.

Wang: Yes, cornering, taking over, or subrogating—I've been called a blackguard and a scoundrel many times. That's why, you see, I thought I must fight for my good name—I can't just die like this... I've never done any of those things. The only thing is, once a company offers its shares for purchasing on the open market, it may very well be for the purpose of raising funds, but at the same time, it must realize that it leaves itself open to the risk of having the shares cornered by somebody and eventually being taken over. However, certain companies in Japan have a habit of once their shares are purchased, they immediately say their company is being taken over and try to publicize this as if it were a crime. This is totally unwarranted in the world of today. As far as I myself am concerned, I have no intention whatsoever of managing a company, so naturally there was no question of my feeling that I wanted to take it over too.

— Up to now, you have filed a number of complaints against the irrational ways the [publicly listed] companies of Japan conduct their business; what do you consider the most unfair thing among all your personal experiences?

I gave the reporter a detailed account of the Oji Paper affair and the collusion by the securities companies, which you have already read about.

— You mean to say that it's the public investors who are suffering losses?

Wang: Yes, I do. There was the incident when a lot of fuss was made about the Miyaji Iron Industry shares—I believe it was sometime around 1980. Mr. Kato and his Seibi Group purchased up to 70% of these shares with the result that the price of about ¥200 jumped up to ¥2,900. By that time, most of the majority shareholders had already disposed of their holdings. At that point, the then chairman of the Tokyo Stock Exchange, Mr. Tanimura issued the so-called Tanimura Notification. It stated that the price of the Miyaji shares were too high, that securities circles should exercise caution in trading them, and that problems would arise if these shares were to be used as security for obtaining loans. As soon as this notification was issued, the price tumbled rapidly. As a result of this, the Seibi Group sacrificed the shares at ¥180...In the long run, it was the general public who suffered a loss from the deal—there were about 4,000 shareholders involved—while the financial circles were the ones that really profited from this... [Now we see shares being] used for amassing political funds or for generating hidden money. [All of] these practices must be stopped; otherwise, Japan will never to able to become an advanced nation in the true sense of the word.

— Is that the reason why you stopped investing in Japanese shares?

Wang: Well, I thought so at first, but there's much more to the story.

I then told the interviewer about my problems with Katakura and the subsequent troubles that arose, which I will give in greater detail in later chapters.

— From your point of view, what do you regard as the cause for such irregularities occurring?

Wang: It's because the Japanese society moves in collusion... The president and other board members of a company that issue shares must do well in business operations, and if they don't, then it's only natural that they should assume liability in the light of the shareholders' demands and be dismissed. In Japan, however, this is not so. Since the so-called stable shareholders, which are usually banks and financial institutions, hold the majority of the shares; as long as their interests coincide [with the issuing company], they don't compel the management to take responsibility for poor administration. So therefore, it's always the individual shareholders that suffer.

— How do you think this can be improved?

Wang: The only alternative as I see it is to adopt a system like the Securities and Exchange Commission of America. The SEC is an independent commission approved by the senate, and is granted wide power of authority based on the Securities Trading Act for protecting the rights of investors and ensuring fair trade practices on the stock market. There is a staff of 1,400 exclusively assigned to it. They go into every problem thoroughly and clarify all points of doubt. In the long run, I believe this system is the only answer... Don't misunderstand me, please. I like Japan, you see, and I want her to become a better country. And I'm also doing this because I hope the day will come when individual investors will be able to engage in sound share trading. Now, however, I'm really fed up. I shall never buy any more Japanese shares.

— You'll be cutting ties with Japan for the time being, at least?

Wang: Yes. But all the same, I take full responsibility for my words. So if you think what I said is a mistake, you're perfectly free to sue for defamation of character. I'm prepared to accept the challenge any time.

Even though I was prepared to accept any suit for defamation of character, none ever followed.

I gave a similar interview to *Shukan Bunshun* on May 2nd and 9th, 1991 in the Golden Week Special Issue whose reporter also came uninvited to meet me in Hong Kong. I stand by every word I said in both of those interviews.

The Interview that Caused a Fire

It was not long after this interview that I read an interview in *Nikkei Sangyo Shimbun* with President Tanaka of Oji Paper Company that made my blood boil. Even now, I still recall being overcome by blazing anger when I read it.

Testifying to the History of Industry in the Showa Era
Narrated by Fumio Tanaka

— On its foreign investment, there are all sorts of stories from the paper and pulp industry that haven't surfaced yet...

Tanaka: Around the spring of 1977, T. H. Wang and one other person bought up 20 to 30 million shares in Oji, and became first on the list of shareholders (with a shareholding ratio of approximately 10%) and asked us to buy back the shares through Nikko Securities. I believe that the share price was around ¥200 at that time. They first asked us to take them back at ¥250, and then ¥230, but I firmly refused. I should say that if Mr. Goro Koyama of Mitsui Bank (the chairman at the time) had supported a major proposal presented at the General Meeting of Shareholders on a merger or the like it would have been troublesome, but failing that, we could let things be. If the Mitsui group stuck it out, the other side would never gain control of a majority of the shares, and when we asked Mitsui to stick it out, they did. With that, the other side finally lost patience and sold out. At the time, the T. H. Wang Group, as it was known, was busy buying up large volumes of shares in others [industries], and putting requests to their managements as well.

— How much were they bought for?

Tanaka: That was still a time when the yen was weak, and they were bought with dollars. The yen appreciated while all this was going on, and by the time the purchase was completed in June, 1978, we even earned a bit of profit. I suppose that the Hong Kong circle must have sold out at ¥180 to ¥200 a share. Since the Mitsui group underwrote all of that for us, the shares didn't go onto the market. We are indebted to Mr. Koyama for that. The companies that underwrote those shares for us are all pleased with themselves because the price per share has since gone to about ¥1,700 (laughs).

In this interview, President Tanaka deliberately distorted the facts and also outright lied. I absolutely did not pass a message regarding an Oji Paper Company buyback through Nikko Securities and as the instigator of the affair, he knew it. After all this time, when I had thought I had put the Oji Paper affair behind me. Yet here he was, deliberately accusing me of greenmail. I could not believe it.

On reading this article of lies, I immediately wrote to the Big Four through my lawyers, and asked the securities companies to confirm in writing whether I had ever asked Oji Paper to buy back the shares through them. I especially wanted to hear from Nikko Securities' International Business Department Head, Tadao Kobayashi, since President Tanaka had specifically said that I'd approached Oji about the greenmail attempt through Nikko.

While waiting for their reply, I worried that they would not confirm the truth of the matter. I was worried not only because of what had happened during the Oji Paper affair, but also the other problems I'd had in the intervening years.

When their responses came a few days later, all of them replied that there had never been such a request by our side. I was grateful for their honest reply.

As soon as I received the statements from the securities companies, I sent a letter through my attorney to President Fumio Tanaka of Oji Paper, demanding an explanation for his remarks. President Tanaka replied that since, at the time, various securities companies such as Nikko, Nomura, Daiwa, and Yamaichi were talking about a buyback of the shares and saying that a buyback price had been proposed, "Naturally I took it to be at the behest of Mr. T. H. Wang, and I didn't accept."

On hearing that, I immediately made inquiries to the various securities companies about the factual pattern, and all of them answered that Mr. Tanaka's assertions were not correct. I was again relieved and grateful for their honest answers. Afterwards, I again sought an explanation from President Tanaka, but this time there was no reply. Without the securities companies to back up his story, he had nowhere to go.

It would be nice to pass off his remarks in this interview as the foolish blustering of a senile old man, but that wouldn't do. First, there was my reputation to consider and he had accused me in a very public interview of trying to greenmail his company. Secondly, from this interview, it was obvious that the party who was plotting the self-restraint program was none other than President Fumio Tanaka himself, even as he lurked in the background behind the securities houses, the Ministry of Finance and the Tokyo Stock Exchange. And since he named Mitsui Bank Chairman Goro Koyama as the overall leader of the Mitsui Group, he shouldn't be overlooked either.

I wrote to Mr. Koyama and also sought some answers from him. I said:

> President Tanaka has mentioned in [his] interview that you told him, "If the Mitsui group stuck it out, the other side would never gain control of a majority of the shares." This is an indication that you, as the supreme commander of the Mitsui Group, entertained the intention of maneuvering matters to obstruct me and the other Hong Kong investors in our acquisition of Oji shares.
>
> The reason for this is because the Mitsui Group's holdings of Oji shares at that time totaled less than 10% of the whole. As a result, it would hardly be possible to obstruct my colleagues and me from acquiring a majority holding if you were to resort to such a passive measure as refusing to sell your own holdings. Judging from your declaration, "the other side will never be able to take over a majority ratio of holdings," I cannot help but think that you were planning on taking full advantage of the tremendous influence the Mitsui Group has in the political, government, securities, and mass communication fields to obstruct the acquisition of Oji Paper stock by the Hong Kong investors and then put this plan into execution.

However, I did not receive any reasonable reply from the Mitsui Group.

The Suit Against Oji Paper

It was because of President Tanaka's interview and his assault on my name and honor that I lodged a lawsuit in Tokyo District Court on June 15, 1990, naming Oji Paper Company, its president, Fumio Tanaka, and the Big Four, Nikko, Nomura, Daiwa, and Yamaichi, who orchestrated the self-restraint program as the defendants. Although my goal was merely to recover my good name, the legal reason for bringing the suit was to seek compensation for the losses that I suffered because the self-restraint program left me with no choice but to sell off the shares in Oji Paper Company.

I began to build my case. I had been encouraged that the securities companies had responded to my request for a written reply as to whether I had ever asked them to have Oji Paper buy back the shares. Certainly, their letters would stand up to show that there had never been any greenmail attempt.

My attorneys informed me that the Tokyo Stock Exchange's leak of information, which led to the instruction by the TSE for all securities companies to get a list of names of investors might be a violation of securities law. Also, this move by the Tokyo Stock Exchange was an abuse of its power and was a direct violation of the confidentiality rule and thereby negatively affected the Oji paper share prices. This is was a violation of Japanese securities code (code No. 159) and punishable under criminal code No. 197, section 8. Also, the October 14th, 1977 article in the *Nihon Keizai Shimbun* in which Mr. Yamashita (the executive director of Tokyo Stock Exchange) stated that others had told him that the Hong Kong investors might directly or indirectly be pressuring Oji Paper to buy back their Oji Paper shares constituted defamation of reputation in violation of Japan's Criminal Code No. 230.

As my attorney put it, it was certainly the duties and obligations of the Ministry of Finance to control and regulate the activities of all securities companies and the Tokyo Stock Exchange and see to it that the laws are followed. Even so, the Ministry of Finance had not taken any action against the TSE or even tried to stop them or the securities companies from continuing the illegal activities. Additionally, the fact that the Ministry of Finance had given the securities companies "administrative guidance" was an abuse of power. Such abuses of power violated Japan's Criminal Code No. 193.

I felt we had a good case against them.

The Oji Paper Trials

At last, the trial of the Oji Paper case began in Tokyo District Court. However, midway through the case, a judge from the Tokyo High Court stepped down and became the chief judge in charge of this case. This is roughly the equivalent of a U.S. federal court of appeals judge stepping down to take the judgeship at a county court.

This judge was a former a lawyer and had been a junior partner in a law firm with eleven of the fifteen lawyers for Fumio Tanaka, Oji Paper Company, Nikko Securities, and Yamaichi Securities. Moreover, nearly all of these eleven lawyers had been the chief judge's senior colleagues.

In Japan's legal circles, the tradition of the relationship between senior and junior colleagues is a deeply rooted one. In such a senior-junior relationship, it is as though the junior is in a servant role and, in this case, the judge would look at himself almost as if he should be taking orders from his former senior partners rather than the other way around. Unfortunately, judges who had been junior colleagues to the lawyers they're hearing and then acting to suit them are frequent in Japan.

Such things put me in mind of the renowned Bao Zheng of China. He would never have tolerated this kind of behavior, to say nothing of the collusion of the Ministry of Finance, the securities companies, and Oji Paper. Had he been handling this case, he would have issued an order for all of them to be put to death. Bao Zheng, in case you're not familiar with the name, was a famous nobleman who was given special authority by the emperor. He toured regions where corruption was rife and executed many evil men, dishonest judges, and officials who banded together with corrupt merchants to plunder the assets of ordinary citizens. In Japan, there was a similar judge, Ooka of Echizen, who was famous for mercilessly punishing evildoers who plundered the property of innocent citizens. If only the judges who'd heard my cases could have been like Bao Zheng or

Ooka. Then those who'd conspired against the Hong Kong investors would have been given no mercy, and real justice would have ensued.

My lawyer obviously had doubts about the instructions of the chief judge in this suit. In fact, at one point the judge essentially told the defendants' lawyers that they would be given *carte blanche* by signaling them that if they claimed our witness applications weren't necessary, he would reject them and conclude the arguments.

A fair trial could not be expected with this kind of chief judge, so naturally I raised a challenge against the chief judge.

However, on July 15, 1993, the Tokyo District Court rejected the challenge. This came as no surprise, so I appealed to the Tokyo High Court. But here, too, the appeal was rejected. Once again, I lodged a special appeal, this time with the Supreme Court, but it was refused on the ground that it was not a constitutional issue. The decision of the Supreme Court was the proverbial shutting of the door and we would have no choice but to proceed with this judge.

Doesn't commonsense dictate that the circumstances here would prevent a fair trial? It seems rather obvious that fair judgments are impossible in a court system hedged in by personal relationships. Is the commonsense of ordinary people nonexistent in Japan's courts on any of its levels?

Despite this, we pressed forward with the case.

Not surprisingly, our request to call many witnesses in the Tokyo District Court was blocked and obstructed by the judge. Of the more than twenty witnesses my lawyers had proposed to call, the court allowed only one: Mr. Kobayashi of Nikko.

Betrayal

I'd had some hesitation about naming the securities companies as co-defendants. After all, they had sent me letters confirming that I had never asked them to request Oji Paper to buy back its own shares. But on the other hand, they'd also acted in collusion in the first place in the Oji Paper incident. They'd had the opportunity to stand up for what was right but they instead chose the Oji Paper side.

It really was quite sad since I'd had (I thought) such good relationships with all of them at one time. In addition to the Big Four, I'd also had a good relationship with one of the "quasi-major" houses, Kankaku Securities Company (formerly know as Kangyo Kakumaru Securities Company and now known as Mizu Ho Investors Securities Co., Ltd.). In fact, I was a major shareholder and director of Kankaku Hong Kong when it was first established. The board at the time was comprised of directors from both Hong Kong and the Tokyo head office, and I acted as the translator since I was the only director who was conversant in both Japanese and Chinese.

Kankaku had been the one who sent me the *Jiji Press* articles on October 5th and 6th, 1977, that had leaked the information about the administrative guidance and subsequent boycott by the securities companies. But despite the extremely close and cordial relationship between Kankaku and myself, Kankaku participated in the Oji Paper boycott for some reason.

Because of my past relationship I'd had with them, I believed that it was rather unlikely that they'd been a willing participant in the self-restraint program. I believed that they were probably under pressure from the authorities to take part in the unlawful and devious actions against my Hong Kong investor friends and me. As a result, I hoped that they would bear witness to this in the court hearings.

Wako Securities Company, another quasi-major securities companies, had been the ones that had prepared the report on Oji Paper that helped convince us to buy shares of Oji Paper. My relationship with Wako had also been a very close and cordial one. I was the first customer of Wako Hong Kong when they opened their Hong Kong office. Whenever the presidents or other high-ranking persons from their Tokyo office came to Hong Kong, they always visited me at my office to pay their respects.

Interestingly, after the Oji Paper affair had occurred, one of their executives, Mr. Inoguchi, told me that Oji Paper Company had reprimanded Wako for supplying the Oji Paper special report to us. Wako viewed this as a very serious matter that had to be remedied immediately and their Tokyo Headquarters president went with his friend, who was working in the Mitsui Group, to personally apologize to Oji Paper. But despite the apology, this was not the end of the matter. Mr. Inoguchi also later told me—which I subsequently verified through my own investigations—that when Oji Paper Company issued new corporate bonds that Oji penalized Wako by reducing Wako's percentage of the underwriting.

Despite the good relationship I'd had with the securities companies, for some reason all of them had betrayed me by participating in the self-restraint program with not one of them standing up to the authorities on my behalf. Their actions hurt very deeply. Still, there was a part of me that could understand their actions since the Ministry of Finance holds life and death power over the securities companies.

Perhaps the most astounding of all was that in the course of the Oji Paper court case, these same securities companies not only refused to take responsibility for their actions, but some of them even denied ever knowing me.

On February 12, 1991, Daiwa Securities alleged in court that before June 11, 1978, (the day before we sold the shares through the Big Four) they had no accounts with Newpis Hong Kong, Ltd. (my company) or myself. Daiwa also claimed that my original 4.395 million shares were not purchased directly from Daiwa and because I didn't purchase them through Daiwa that I'd had to physically bring the actual certificates to their offices. Daiwa also claimed that I had not purchased my original 4.395 million shares directly from them and because this, I'd had to physically bring the actual certificates to their offices.

This was nothing but an outright lie. First of all, I had a letter from Daiwa Securities dated September 3, 1981, in which Daiwa confirmed that my Kao Soap and Ajinomoto shares were transacted in June 1976 and March 1977. This invalidated Daiwa's claim that I had no account with them before June 11, 1978.

As for the allegation that I'd had to bring the certificates to their office, this was sheer nonsense. At the time, I had never known anyone who had actually seen a Japanese stock certificate.

This was because all Japanese stock transactions were done in Japan with the certificate remaining under the custody of Japan's securities houses. Normally, it took four days to settle a stock transaction and if the issuing company did not know a person, then it also took at least an additional week to authenticate a stock certificate. Therefore, investors left the certificates of any Japanese stock in the custody of the Japanese securities houses, who could act on the behalf of the investor since the securities houses did not require authentication due to their "trustworthiness" and being known to the issuing company.

Each certificate of Oji Paper represented 1,000 shares; therefore my 4.395 million shares would mean I had to be in possession of 4,395 copies of the original certificate. That's a lot of paper to have on hand, to say nothing of it being completely outside of normal business practices.

Besides, according to Daiwa's ridiculous story, it would take two days for me to transfer my Oji Paper certificate to the "newly opened account" at Daiwa Hong Kong. Since, according to Daiwa's claim, I hadn't had any business transactions with them before, it would take at least a week for them to authenticate my 4.395 million shares of Oji Paper. Thus, the fact that they paid for my 4.395 million shares on June 16, 1978—a mere four days after I supposedly opened my account on June 12, 1978—was inconsistent with business practices of the day.

Further, I had a certificate from the former president of Daiwa Hong Kong that specified the dates and quantities of Kao and Ajinomoto shares that I'd sold through them prior to the Oji Paper affair, which also proved Daiwa's lies. This certificate stated that my transactions with Daiwa Hong Kong involved a total of 38,304,350 shares with a total price of ¥15,853,450,000, and the commission earned by Daiwa Hong Kong was ¥96,000,000. All of which took place prior to June 12, 1978.

I wonder if Daiwa always "forgets" customers who earn them ¥96,000,000 in commissions?

Daiwa was not the only one. Nikko Securities also denied knowing me and denied ever having any previous dealings with my company or me personally prior to the Oji Paper affair. This perjury was proved beyond any reasonable doubt when Mr. Kobayashi testified in Tokyo District Court that on July 7th, 1974, Nikko Securities Hong Kong had solicited me to purchase $500,000 worth of the Wardley Nikko Asia Fund as they were not selling well at the time. I bought the fund reluctantly in order to help them, which was against Nikko's guarantee that it would earn an annual interest of 15.5%. This transaction guarantee was well documented and when Mr. Kobayashi was questioned about it in court he had to admit to it.

Once again, I was filled with the sickening and overwhelming sense of betrayal. I can't even begin to describe what a truly painful and shocking experience it is when people you had thought to be your friends and business associates not only betray you but also deny even knowing you.

No Justice in Court

In the interest of space, the court proceedings are summarized here in the running text. However, if you are interested in reading some of the actual testimony, expert analysis, and some additional comments on the testimony—please see Appendix A.

As you'll recall, the only witness that the judge allowed was Tadao Kobayashi, the head of Nikko Securities' International Business Department. Even though our requests to call other witnesses were denied, I felt Kobayashi was a key witness, especially since President Tanaka of Oji had specifically said that I'd approached Oji about the greenmail attempt through Nikko. He testified on two occasions, September 28 and December 1, 1992.

But in his testimony Mr. Kobayashi tried to avoid testifying, saying that he himself knew nothing. He said, "I [only] heard about [the development of the self-restraint program and the reasons for it] from the Trading Control Office." However, it is not possible that he didn't personally know since he was the person who had made a special trip to meet me in Los Angeles to ask about letting Nikko Securities handle the sale of the Oji Paper shares. Because the Big Four were already colluding together at that point to decide on the price of the Oji Paper shares they wanted to buy from me, he would have obviously been familiar with everything going on behind the scenes.

When it came to the crucial point of who was responsible for suspending buy orders, he said that the decision was entirely up to Vice President Haraigawa. However, Vice President Haraigawa had already passed away by the time of Kobayashi's testimony, so Haraigawa could not be called for testimony to confirm or deny this accusation. Since "dead men tell no tales," it is easy to see why Kobayashi put all the blame on Vice President Haraigawa, but it was still extremely contemptible to do so.

Moreover, when asked if there were ever any greenmail attempts, he answered, "I don't believe that there was anything like that." However, prior to that he had stated, "[The Hong Kong investors' large-scale purchases of shares in Oji Paper] indicate that there may have been such purposes." This is clearly contradictory testimony. Even though he admitted that there was no truth to the claim that I requested a buyback at a premium, he testified as if the measure of suspending the brokering of buy orders had been adopted because I had the intention of committing such illegal actions.

In his testimony, Mr. Kobayashi said that I broached the selling price, which was not true. I know he was the one who brought up the selling price because when he said he knew how much we'd bought the shares for, I clearly remember thinking, "Aha, all the securities companies really are in collusion with each other!" I knew they were, because there was no other way to explain how Kobayashi knew how many shares we had bought from which securities house and at what price, since securities firms have the obligation of maintaining confidentiality. However, he was intimately familiar with the details of our transactions.

Additionally, Mr. Kobayashi committed grave perjury. He testified that "[the shares (percentages) of the managing underwriters for Oji Paper Company] had been decided previously. This is something that varies, but when there has been an increase of capital just prior to or at the time of financing, if the share does not change, then it remains at the same level for a long time." He also said, "I was told by Vice President Haraigawa to make the allocation according to the manager's share, and since I am a salaryman, I did as I was ordered." As you'll recall—and which Kobayashi admitted in his testimony—the shares would be divided 35% each for Nikko and Nomura, and 15% each for Daiwa and Yamaichi. In his testimony, Kobayashi said that the managers' shares were decided by the immediately preceding increase of capital. However, on examining this matter, it became clear that the immediately previous increase of capital for Oji Paper Company was a publicly subscribed capital increase whose payment date was November 30, 1976, and that the managers' shares at that time were actually 40% for Nikko, 25% each for Yamaichi and Nomura, and 10% for Daiwa.

People like Vice President Haraigawa, who was a director, and Kobayashi, who was the head of the International Business Department of Nikko Securities would not make a mistake about the managers' shares for the most recent increase of capital. Further, Nikko Securities was the managing underwriter for Oji Paper Company, so it is impossible to think that the percentages of the lead managing underwriter Nikko Securities and of the underwriter Nomura Securities would somehow be mistaken to be the same. This was obviously deliberate perjury.

If we ask why he committed perjury, it would be to conceal the fact that Oji Paper Company was deeply involved. Oji Paper

Company admitted that Mr. Setsuya Tabuchi and others at Nomura Securities greatly contributed to this self-restraint program and to the buying back of the shares. As a reward for that, it increased Nomura Securities' percentage to 35%, the same as that for Nikko, the lead managing underwriter.

Although I suspected all of this during District Court the trial, other than my own recollections of the events, I had no proof. That would come later.

Judgment of the District Court

Things were not promising at the District Court level. There was a biased judge who had a strong personal relationship with the lawyers on the defendants' side and who had stepped down from his position at a higher court to direct the case in a manner favorable to the defendants. Combine that with our inability to call all of the witnesses that we had wanted to and witnesses who even lied about knowing me, and things looked grim. Still, even though it was only a slight chance, I held out hope that the chief judge might be able to see the facts of the case clearly and rely on his sense of fairness and justice. Perhaps he had stepped down to make the punishment of the other side as lenient as possible.

On October 11, 1994, the District Court issued its ruling. In the grounds for the judgment, the Tokyo District Court concluded: "There is no positive proof to support the proposition that there had been an intention on the part of the plaintiff's representative (T. H. Wang) to demand that Oji Paper Company, the issuing company, buy back the shares that he had bought; to the contrary, according to the evidence, it is proper to acknowledge that the plaintiff had no intention of forcing a buyback."

The Tokyo District Court also said the "administrative guidance" by the Ministry of Finance was given without any or any justifiable authority and that the Ministry of Finance had indeed issued its "forewarning" to the securities companies, but that the forewarning was not binding and did not justify imposition of the self-restraint measure by the securities companies.

Furthermore, the Tokyo District Court concluded that the self-restraint measure "could not ... be legally justified" and "constituted a violation of the obligation [by the securities companies]... to accept all purchase orders placed with them by their clients."

Additionally, the Tokyo District Court held that it "could easily presume that when [the Japanese securities companies] put the self-restraint program in operation, each of them undoubtedly shared with the others the common understanding that if it put the program into operation the others would also have followed suit." Otherwise, it would simply not work. This could only mean that the Tokyo District Court recognized that the Big Four and lesser securities companies were acting in concert with one another, which meant they were taking actions that would be illegal under the Anti-Trust Law.

Given such a conclusion, it would naturally follow that my lawsuit would be upheld.

However, the Tokyo District Court rejected all of my claims, stating: "Since the claim for compensation in this case involves losses sustained as a result of this sale (the differences between the market values at the time of the sale and May 31, 1989 or 1990), the ability to admit the claim would be restricted to cases in which it can be shown that there was a sufficient cause-and-effect relationship," and "In the final analysis, the sale of the Oji Paper shares by the plaintiff was a reasonable trading action made based on the free will and intention of the plaintiff's representative."

From a commonsense point of view, it is difficult to understand how the District Court could conclude that there was no cause-and-effect relationship between the self-restraint program and the sale. We had sold the shares in Oji Paper because the illegal self-restraint program had tied us into knots. Since we would have held on to the shares in Oji Paper until the price rose had there been no self-restraint program, it was natural to claim the loss for the difference in prices.

Essentially, what the Tokyo District Court was saying was that it had found that illegal activity had indeed taken place but did not believe that such illegal activities had any direct or even indirect effects on my claim for damages. On one hand this might be considered reasonable, since it is hard to judge what someone *might* do if something hadn't happened to them. However, the securities companies were clearly denying us one of the most fundamental rights of a free market: the right of access. Given that, they should have ruled in our favor.

Incredibly, despite this finding, no one was punished. This is unheard of. How many times does a court find that an illegal act has taken place and yet does nothing about it? If there is a court anywhere else in the world that can conclude the law has been broken and yet not punish the guilty, I'd like to know about it. If the rest of the world's courts were to follow this plan, then Heaven help the victims of violent crimes whose attackers go unpunished even though the court finds them guilty.

From a commonsense point of view, it is difficult to understand how the District Court could conclude that there was absolutely no cause-and-effect relationship whatsoever between the self-restraint program and the sale. We had sold the shares in Oji Paper because the illegal self-restraint program had tied us into knots. The securities companies had pointed out to us that the self-restraint program could be reinstated at their discretion, which was a very real (though implied) threat. Because of this, it was abundantly clear to us that we would not be allowed to profit from the shares. Since we would have otherwise held on to the Oji Paper shares until the price rose had there not been any self-restraint program, it was natural to claim the loss for the difference in prices.

What was also strange was that the Tokyo District Court had said that it had found that illegal activity had indeed taken place but did not believe that such illegal activities had any direct or even any indirect effects on my claim for damages. Incredibly, despite this finding of illegal behavior, no one was punished. This is unheard of. How many times does a court find that an illegal act has taken place and yet does nothing about it? If there is a court anywhere else in the world that can conclude the law has been broken and yet not punish the guilty, I'd like to know about it. If the rest of the world's courts were to follow this plan, then Heaven help the victims of violent crimes whose attackers go unpunished even though the court finds them guilty.

This, then, was the true failing of the court and the law. It recognized that an illegal activity—the threat and denial of our rights—had taken place, and yet it was powerless to punish the wrongdoer. It allowed the securities companies to comply technically with the law and yet completely go against the spirit of the law. The court, then, did not recognize the practical, day-to-day realities of business relationships nor of the realities of the threat.

I suppose that though they had denied my claim for damages, it was of some small comfort that the Tokyo District Court had found there had never been an attempt on our part of forcing a buyback as had been alleged by Oji Paper and the Ministry of Finance.

The Tokyo District Court was not the only one at fault here and not the only party who failed to punish wrongdoers. The Ministry of Finance also has within its authority to punish those who violate the law but it refused to do so. As such, it should also bear the burden of what happened. It is the duty, after all, of the Ministry of Finance to control and regulate the securities companies and also the Tokyo Stock Exchange. Yet no sanctions against the securities companies were ever implemented for their illegal self-restraint program. What is far worse is that they not only failed to punish those at fault but were, in fact, the main culprit behind the move.

The Tokyo Stock Exchange should have also borne responsibility. The TSE "leaked" information that the Hong Kong investors might be trying to greenmail Oji Paper and subsequently instructed all securities companies to submit a list of the names and addresses of any customer dealing in Oji Paper since May 1977. Japanese law experts have stated clearly that this move by the TSE had no legal basis and was intended to solely to deter and intimidate us. This act affected the share prices of Oji Paper. Manipulation of stock prices violates Japan's Securities Code No. 159, punishable under Criminal Code No. 197, Section 8, by up to three years in prison and fines of up to ¥3,000,000.

But what good are laws if they are never enforced?

Having lost the first round, we immediately appealed to the next court, the Tokyo High Court.

The Tokyo High Court

With the filing of the appeal in October 1994, we were able to obtain a new trial at the higher court. There were several additional witnesses, two of which were Tadaaki Yoshida and Tomio Miyanaga. For those interested in reading the actual court dialogue, portions of their testimonies, along with comments, can be found in Appendix B.

Tadaaki Yoshida was the chief of the Distribution Market Section of the Securities Bureau of the Ministry of Finance at the time of the Oji Paper matter. His examination was held on February 16, 1996, at the Tokyo High Court, and my attorney asked him many questions about the "administrative guidance" that the Ministry of Finance had ordered.

In his testimony, he said that the reason for implementing such strong administrative guidance was that, "The nature of investment in Hong Kong, [is one] that looks to quite short-term returns." Such a statement was nothing more than prejudice and discrimination based on race. First of all, there are indeed Japanese investors who invest for short-term results. Despite that, what would it matter if we were investing for the short term? How would that justify the Ministry of Finance's illegal actions?

What the Japanese side failed to grasp is the basic principle of investing that our money is *ours* to do with as we please. If we wanted to invest for only a few months or a year, then we could invest for a few months or a year. If we wanted to invest for a decade, then we could do that as well. These are *our* funds to do with as we see fit to allow us to gain money for ourselves. Perhaps it is this very concept of looking after one's own money that is so foreign to the Japanese mindset and which led to the Ministry of Finance to implement the self-restraint program.

There is no doubting the fact that Mr. Yoshida wanted to shut us Hong Kong investors out of the Japanese securities market from the outset. I heard from concerned parties within the securities houses that right from the outset Assistant Section Chief Yokota, who took charge of the interrogations, severely berated and intimidated the representatives from the securities companies whom he had summoned with his fierce, scowling expression. Scolded and intimidated, they were not even allowed to explain the circumstances. If honest interrogations had been conducted at this time, the Ministry of Finance would have learned that there was no danger that we would engage in illegal conduct, a fact that the lower court had confirmed.

The Oji Paper Company matter originated from the mistaken perception of a problem based on this type of racial discrimination on the part of Mr. Yoshida. Once he came to hold this mistaken perception, he judged that there was a danger that we might become greenmailers.

But in an effort to protect himself during his testimony, Mr. Yoshida declared, "With regard to [whether the Hong Kong investors had made overtures of greenmailing], I have no memory that there had [been such an attempt]." If there was no basis for any greenmail attempts, then why would he have judged that there was a danger of us becoming greenmailers and then implement the self-restraint program? The only logical explanation is that he'd predetermined to force us out of Japan's market.

Interestingly, he said that "[The self-restraint program was] probably the result of a certain degree of internal contact among the eight companies." In effect, Yoshida was acknowledging that the self-restraint program was a collaborative effort among the eight companies.

He also testified that he had taken no action to lift the self-restraint program even though he was aware of the boycott by the securities companies within days of its imposition and even had forewarning that it would occur. Despite the fact that he was directly responsible for regulating Japanese securities markets, the responsible section chief testified that he never even considered the legality of the self-restraint program. Incredibly, Mr. Yoshida stated "I didn't think that [the adoption of the self-restraint program by the eight securities companies] was a legal issue. Since it was a question of a business transaction between private parties, as an administrator, I felt that if it came to this stage, it was not a matter in which I should intervene."

Yoshida, who had official duties as the chief of the Distribution Market Section of the Securities Bureau of the Ministry of Finance, was in a position that *obliged* him to put a stop to the illegal self-restraint program being carried out in collaboration by the eight companies and yet he failed to do so. But by claiming, "As an administrator, I felt…it was not a matter in which I should intervene," was not merely irresponsible, but a total abdication of his duties.

This same section chief, in a 1991 interview to NHK-TV, entitled "Financial Scandal," admitted the implication of the self-restraint program and confirmed that he had given administrative guidance in the Oji Paper incident. In the television interview he said that the Ministry of Finance was in some sense anticipating that the various companies would adopt a self-restraint program and was leading them in that direction.

But in testimony, he disavowed this statement, saying when he agreed to do the interview that he wasn't prepared to talk about Hong Kong and that it took him by surprise. "When I was suddenly being interviewed," he said, "I indeed used an expression that no doubt has given rise to misunderstandings."

However, no matter how he tried to rationalize it, it was clear from his testimony that he was aware at the time that he had taken an exceptionally strong administrative action. This was an abuse of power by the servants of the state. Despite the fact that he had committed such a naked abuse of power, he felt no pangs of conscience at all. On the contrary, he retired, settled in nicely as the president of a private bank, and lived a life of quiet ease. Unfortunately, there is no way to call him to account in Japan. Not possessing the right of compulsory search, we cannot gather testimony or evidence to prove the guilt of bureaucrats. All we can do is grin and bear it.

Additionally, in the very last part of Mr. Yoshida's testimony, when asked if he had a close relationship with Nikko Securities director and head of the International Business Department, Tadao Kobayashi, he said, "I believe that we probably did meet each other once or twice in dinner groups or playing golf."

I could not suppress some slight surprise at this admission, because he was openly describing in court the real state of affairs about his close-knit relationship with businessmen. In particular, when he said, "in dinner groups or playing golf" shows that there were groups of businessmen entertaining Ministry of Finance bureaucrats with dinners and golf. In fact, in 1998—two years after this testimony—112 people from the Ministry of Finance were punished for accepting excessive gifts and entertainment.

The testimony of Mr. Yoshida did nothing but confirm my belief that he was guilty of abuse of the power vested in him and also guilty of failing to supervise or regulate the securities market to safeguard the interests of the general investing public. On the one hand he claimed I didn't ask Oji Paper Company to buy back the shares, but on the other hand he summoned the eight securities companies to give them "administrative guidance." Furthermore, despite his admitted duty and responsibility to supervise and regulate the securities market, after he became aware of the implementation of the Self Restraint Program, he took no action whatsoever to stop such an unlawful act.

Proof at Last

In February 1996, about the same time that Yoshida was testifying during the appeal trial at the Tokyo High Court, I came into the possession of a highly valuable document. It was the proof that confirmed the suspicions I'd had all along.

Mr. Kurihara—who had served as the first president of Nomura Securities Hong Kong and thereafter became the managing director at the head office—paid a visit to my office in Hong Kong. By this time, Mr. Kurihara had already retired as a director of Nomura Securities. Our various reminiscences naturally turned to the Oji Paper incident.

"I've put everything that happened at that time down in detail in my diary," he said. "If it would help, I'll send it to you."

True to his promise, he later sent me six pages from his diary. Vividly recorded therein were the facts involved in the sale negotiations in which the Big Four colluded at the behest of Oji Paper Company.

I immediately submitted it to the High Court and they subsequently recognized this Kurihara diary as authentic. Even Nomura Securities acknowledged that this diary was authentic, and had to make an admission with regard to the factual pattern recorded therein.

Let me introduce several excerpts from it:

> February 2, 1978. According to the message, Mr. Kobayashi of Nikko is in Hong Kong, and today met with Mr. Chan Tsang-hei. The outcome appears to have been disappointing. He (Mr. Kobayashi) left on the hop for Los Angeles.

From this, we can see that the activities and results of Tadao Kobayashi (the person who flew over to meet me in L.A. to request a sale of the Oji shares) were being conveyed immediately to Nomura Securities. How often do competing firms convey the whereabouts and activities of their employees to their direct competitors?

> May 2, 1978. There was a communication from Oji Paper that Mr. T. H. Wang requested the Japanese Consul in Hong Kong, Mr. Shiraishi, that the Japanese side buy at ¥415.

The details of what I said to Consul Shiraishi were likely passed on to Oji Paper through the Ministry of Finance—from which Mr. Shiraishi had been seconded. These details were then related by Oji Paper to Nomura Securities. From this single incident it appears that the buyback of shares plotted by Oji Paper Company was being implemented with the support of the Ministry of Finance.

> May 29, 1978. Telephone call from [Vice President] Tabuchi to Mr. Wang. ¥400 impossible. Nothing except ¥380 will do. From this point we will let things cool off for a time, while striving for a resolution.

The posture of Vice President Setsuya Tabuchi of Nomura Securities, Mr. Kurihara's superior, of sticking to ¥380 all the way through to the bitter end is now revealed. To me, this, more than anything else, shows that this was the price designated by Oji Paper Company.

> June 7, 1978. There was a telephone call from Oji Paper. Mr. Wang had told Nikko that he wanted to sell half of the shareholding at ¥380. Promptly called Mr. Wang...Conveyed message to that effect to Mr. Wang.

The message I gave to Nikko Securities—who, again, was a competitor of Nomura—was passed from Nikko Securities to Oji Paper Company and from Oji Paper to Nomura Securities.

> June 12, 1978, morning. There was a telephone call from Oji Paper. The ratios were set at 35: 35: 15: 15.

Recorded here are the ratios for allocating the Oji Paper shares that I had decided to sell to the four underwriters. Moreover, it is clear that the party that determined the allocation ratios was none other than Oji Paper Company.

In some ways, this diary came as a relief to me since it confirmed my fears and suspicions. When you think there is a conspiracy afoot, it is easy to doubt yourself and your suspicions but here was Kurihara's diary, which confirmed what I'd believed all along. Moreover, even the Ministry of Finance was implicated in this.

What this Kurihara diary made abundantly clear is the reality of the joint conspiracy in which Oji Paper Company and the Big Four colluded together in a scheme to buy back the Oji Paper shares from us at a bargain price. This diary was crucial evidence that established the cause-and-effect relationship between the self-restraint program and the sale of the shares—proof we did not have in the first trial.

Owing to the appearance of irrefutable evidence, I was confident that we would win this case.

Judgment of the Tokyo High Court

The judgment came out on March 27, 1997. The High Court confirmed the findings of the District Court, agreeing that the self-restraint program was illegal and that there was no evidence of greenmailing. Although they felt the self-restraint program was illegal, they, too, did not punish the offenders and found that the mere threat of a re-implementation of the self-restraint program was not enough to convince the Court to award damages. They again denied any causality between the self-restraint program and the sale of the Oji Paper shares and found that since I did make some money on the deal then I received a return on my investment, even if it wasn't what I wanted or as much as I wanted, and therefore I didn't suffer any damage since the basic purpose of my investment was fulfilled.

Specifically, the grounds for the judgment were as follows:

> The Appellant (T. H. Wang) contends that a situation essentially equivalent to a suspension of trading pertained even after the cancellation of the self-restraint program,

which lasted for approximately a month and a half. However, there is no evidence that can be discerned that the Defendants (the Big Four) specifically hindered securities transactions by the appellant after the above cancellation.

It cannot be said that the Appellant in this case became tired of continuing to hold shares in Oji Paper Company or of adding to his holdings or that his desire for investment was reduced as a result of the self-restraint program, and that consequently, as far as his own intention was concerned, he was even compelled to make the sale contrary to his intentions.

These grounds for the judgment placed a strict burden of proof on me and rejected my contentions by claiming that we had not met that burden of proof. I guess the court felt it was not obliged to take into account the very real threat of a re-implementation of the self-restraint program and the real-life effects of living under such a threat. While it is true that the securities companies did not specifically interfere with additional purchases after lifting the self-restraint program, the fact remains that we'd been warned that they could reinstate the program. Didn't our lack of action once the self-restraint program was lifted demonstrate this? We had purchased millions of shares up until that point and it would have been logical for us to buy more once we had the opportunity. Besides, even if we never bought another share after the self-restraint program, their actions were still illegal.

As a further reason for the judgment, it was stated:

The appellant contends that there was no reason to part with the Oji Paper shares even if there existed only a minimal marginal profit roughly equivalent to the normal interest for a period of less than a year because the investment by himself and the other Hong Kong investors was made with an eye toward the extensive land assets held by Oji Paper Company. However, in that case, the matter of concern to the appellant would be whether or not the share price rose, and it could be said that if the share price rose and the sale were made at a profit, then the purpose of the investment had at least been achieved. In other words, if a suitable profit were realized, the selling of the shares would be in line with the investment purpose. Therefore, granting that the sale in this case was within a year, that it was made at a profit, and that the profit equaled the amount of interest at the normal rate, it cannot be said that this sale was not in line with the investment purpose of the appellant, and therefore neither can it be said that it was not based on his free intention.

The court then concluded: "It is insufficient to acknowledge that a cause-and-effect relationship existed...between the self-restraint program and the loss owing to the sale in this case." It acquiesced in the judgment of the Tokyo District Court and rejected my appeal.

In this day and age, when financial markets are moving toward globalization, such a childish judgment isn't acceptable. The Tokyo High Court judges only demonstrated that they knew nothing about the free market concept that the laws of Japan had claimed to establish. In a free market, as long as one does not engage in illegal conduct, everyone may participate freely, and everyone has the right to be treated fairly. And is it not the law, is it not the administration of justice, that guarantees that right? In depriving us of our freedom to deal in the shares in Japan's free market, the Japanese courts trampled on our rights and the rights of every Japanese investor because now the courts had opened it up for more intimidation of anyone who questions the establishment and wants to invest their money as they see fit.

What surprised me most of all was the fact that the Kurihara diary, which was crucial evidence, was not even mentioned in the judgment. Why would the Tokyo High Court have completely ignored evidence in which the fact has been clearly recorded that Oji Paper Company and the Big Four securities firms hatched a conspiracy, and the Ministry of Finance participated in it? It is because if they had even mentioned the Kurihara diary then of course they would have had no choice but to acknowledge my contentions.

I was disgusted. Now, more than ever, it felt as though there was a secret intention from the outset to defeat me in the suit.

To Appeal or Not to Appeal

After my second defeat in the Oji Paper trials, I was in a quandary about whether I should lodge an appeal with the Supreme Court. Having thoroughly observed the process and results in the first and second trials, I had lost my energy for fighting against the intolerable irresponsibility of Japan's courts. I had expended a great deal of time, effort, and money, but the only thing I had to show for it was a distrust of Japan that would be very hard to cure.

As part of my debate, I sought legal advice from a number of sources. One of the sources I consulted was Professor Tatsuo Kamimura of Waseda University, who specializes in commercial and securities and exchange laws. He offered me his expert opinion on the Tokyo High Court's finding.

Professor Tatsuo Kamimura gave me an in-depth analysis, which provided keen and objective insights into the legal matters of the self-restraint program. Excerpts from his rather lengthy opinion (it ran to more than 15,000 words) are provided in Appendix C, though I will summarize them here.

His opinion focused mainly on his belief that the Court simply did not understand the implications of the self-restraint program and how such an action could have devastating affects on a free market system, to say nothing of how it was illegal. In failing to see a causal relation between the self-restraint program and the sale of the shares, Professor Kamimura said, "[it] seems as if the High Court is saying that it has totally abandoned making any findings with respect to any causality-related dispute cases or wrongful damage cases of the type peculiar to the stock market."

He also pointed out that the very basis for the formation of a fair market price assumes that securities companies absolutely must relay all buy and sell orders immediately to the market to reflect the fundamental principles of demand and availability in the share prices.

> Therefore, if securities firms were permitted to take any unauthorized arbitrary action on their part to prevent *bona fide* investment decisions made by their principals with respect to any particular issue from reaching the market in a timely manner, then the market mechanism would totally fail to function properly."

> What we can learn from this case, is that in the Japanese securities market there existed no such thing as freedom of access to the market, which was and is one of the most fundamental market rules common to the securities markets in the rest of the world. What is important here is not the right or wrong of the purposes underlying Appellant's investment in shares of Oji Paper Company, but the fact that [he] was totally denied the benefits arising out of the foundation upon which the securities market in this country was considered to have been based.

In Professor Kamimura's opinion, in order for the court to claim there was no causal relationship between the implementation of the self-restraint program and the sale of the shares, the Court would have had to make the rather broad assumption that the market had fully recovered from the effects of the implementation of the self-restraint program. But in order to say that the market had *fully* recovered, someone should have been punished for their actions in order to reassure the investing public that all was well with the market and that such illegal activities would not occur in the future.

> On the contrary, the four major securities firms dared to declare [that the self-restraint program was] a proper action for them to take; that [they] had the right to accept or reject

orders from their clients at their own discretion…In other words, they virtually publicly declared that they had a license to do illegal things and that the Tokyo Stock Exchange was a market where traditional illegal practices were still prevailing.

He agreed that it was only natural for me to assume that they might even deny me the chance to sell my shares in the future in a timely fashion, perhaps preventing me from even being able to recoup my initial investment. As he put it, "the only wise alternative left to Appellant was to leave the market as soon as possible."

In conclusion, he said, "when the High Court considered those conducts by [the securities companies], it should not have placed the primary focus on the self-restraint program alone, but should have considered all of them as a series of unlawful conducts designed to unlawfully prevent Appellant's legitimate investment activities and that as such they, as a whole, constitute one big tortuous act."

With such strong support of one of Japan's best legal minds, I felt very much encouraged. Besides, I reasoned, I had been fighting the case in order to recover my own good name and in hopes of rectifying the unjust practices of Japanese society. If I gave up at this point, I would be unable to achieve either of these purposes. Having thus reconsidered the matter, I went ahead with the appeal procedure and asked Professor Kamimura to re-draft his opinion so that I might append his written opinion to the reasons for the appeal. Part of his statement read:

> In an age when it is necessary to exclude administrative intervention before the fact and to arrange for the redress and remedy of private law after the fact, the expectations toward the Supreme Court are rising…In particular, Japan is a country in which not even one case of compensation for losses related to markets has been acknowledged. If compensation for losses is denied in such a case as this as well, the result can only be the lodging of civil claims for com-

pensation for losses in other even more complicated cases. For the sake of forming a fair and healthy corporate culture in the fullness of time, courageous decisions are to be asked of the Supreme Court.

His last sentence perfectly expresses my thoughts in my battle extending over twenty-five years. It is time for Japan to begin to make courageous decisions and to let go of the older ways that hold it back from joining the rest of the world and which has it poised on the brink of catastrophe.

The Judgment of the Supreme Court

The judgment of the Supreme Court was delivered on December 12, 1997. The full text is given below.

Judgment:

Appellant	Newpis Hong Kong Limited
Defendant	Fumio Tanaka
Defendant	Oji Paper Co., Ltd.
Defendant	Nikko Securities Co., Ltd.
Defendant	Nomura Securities Co., Ltd.
Defendant	Daiwa Securities Co., Ltd.
Defendant	Yamaichi Securities Co., Ltd.

The Appellant has lodged an appeal for partial nullification of the judgment of the Tokyo High Court delivered on March 27, 1997, in respect of Tokyo High Court Case (*Ne*) No. 4476 of 1994, a claim for compensation for losses between the above parties. Accordingly, this court hereby makes the following judgment:

Text of the Judgment

The appeal in the case is refused. The costs of the appeal shall be borne by the appellant.

Grounds

In Respect of the Grounds for the Appeal of the Appellant's Representative:

With regard to the points of the argument, the judgment of the findings of the original ruling reflect the evidentiary pattern of the original judgment and can be endorsed as correct, and there was no irregularity of argument in the proceedings. The point of the argument cannot be adopted.

Accordingly, judgment is made in accordance with the text by the unanimous opinion of the judges pursuant to Article 401, Article 95, and Article 89 of the Code of Civil Procedure.

Petty Bench of the Supreme Court

Chief Justice	Hiroshi Fukuda
Justice	Katsuya Onishi
Justice	Shigeharu Negishi
Justice	Shinichi Kawai

Appendices

Grounds for the Appeal of the Appellant's Representative (Omitted)

Attached Document — Opinion on the Grounds for the Appeal (Omitted)

The above is the original
This 12th day of December 1997
The Petty Bench of the Supreme Court
Court Secretary

Amazingly, this was entire text of the judgment. The grounds for their decision amounted to a so-called "divorce decree"—a mere three-and-a-half lines. I was left without a clue as to what the Supreme Court thought about the grounds for the appeal expounded by my lawyer, the valuable opinion of Professor Kamimura, or the Kurihara diary—which was irrefutable evidence. The judges, as part of their duty, should have at least explained how they arrived at their judgment instead of leaving us to guess. Instead, I received only a brusque conclusion that only said that no reply was necessary.

Perhaps the Supreme Court did not offer any insight into their judgment because there was no true defense that they could make. Instead, they bowed their heads to the collusion of bureaucrats, judges, and the financial sector. Justice is blind, but it is unfortunate when it turns a blind eye to the problem. The two previous courts had admitted that what the securities companies, Ministry of Finance, Tokyo Stock Exchange, and Oji Paper Company had done was wrong and yet neither court sought any punishment of the perpetrators. The Supreme Court had a chance to make a difference, to protect the rights of shareholders and to ensure the basic rights of a free-market system, but they decided to look the other way. In doing so, they had completely failed in their responsibility to uphold the law.

With a judgment like this from the Supreme Court, which is the very pinnacle of Japan's judiciary, where can people bring their cries for help? What can a person rely on if not the justice system? I pity anyone else who suffers a loss and looks to the courts for help.

After all of the struggle, after eight years of trials and appeals, I had lost the case. To this day, I am still angry and in disbelief that we lost. How can the judicial system in Japan be considered fair if it can allow such abuses of power by its own judges and not work to correct the problem but instead see it as a matter of being par for the course? How can there be any sense of "justice" if witnesses such as Yoshida admit on the one hand that there was no evidence of our forcing a buyback and yet implement the self-restraint program? It is talking out of both sides of one's mouth. How can clear and convincing evidence be completely ignored by the court?

Where was the justice?

Though I am still angry over the Supreme Court's final decision in the Oji Paper trial, before parting from it I would like to say that not all of Japan's judges are completely blind to what is happening in the corporate world. While many in the judicial system do lack a basic understanding of the corporate and financial sectors—to say nothing of the underlying fundamentals of a free-market system—there are some who do comprehend the dangers of what is happening. Unfortunately, they are a tiny minority.

A former Supreme Court Chief Justice, Ekizo Fujibayashi, organized a symposium at the Japan Law Society on June 27, 1983, entitled, "General Shareholders' Meetings and Special Shareholders." The informal comments of this former Supreme Court Chief Justice were later published in an article titled, "The Gap between Shareholders and Management" in October 1983.

What follows are excerpts from his published comments:

> It is my impression that it was not very long ago in our history that joint-stock companies came into being in Japan. Since no more than a hundred years have passed since then, I believe that at the outset, the company's management and capital were actually one and the same. You had the examples of Mitsui or Mitsubishi, and of individual companies as well, where it was the owner himself who ran the company… [Today, it is the opposite, where managers' actual holdings in their companies are actually quite small in comparison to the total holdings and shares of the company.]
>
> On examining an invitation [that I received] to a general meeting of shareholders, we can see that … there was a director with 3,000 shares [but] many people with 10,000 shares or fewer. How is it that this director was so simple that he didn't accumulate more money than this? I don't think that such a director will really take issues regarding the company's survival to heart.

Though he didn't actually come out and say it, the direction of the former judge's words naturally leads one to see how a manager—

since he holds almost no ownership of the company—would naturally put his energy into securing his position as manager rather than working to see the company grow and expand to the benefit of all shareholders. It is not difficult to imagine how the manager's primary focus will instead be on securing and retaining his position of manager, even if it means betraying the interest of the other shareholders, especially since any decisions that would adversely affect shareholders would have only a minimal effect on his own personal wealth.

> However, and perhaps it is because of this, they are still very aware of being the management. This is a strange thing. With the separation of management and capital, they will believe that the management had been entrusted to them. I feel that this is the place where the differences in attitude between today's shareholders and managers is critical...Recently, there has been a suit by a certain foreign shareholder [(a reference to my suit against Katakura)]...and because he is a foreign shareholder, it appears that there are all sorts of restrictions, but the management is paying hardly any heed to his demands and opinions as a [major shareholder].

> So long as such circumstances exist, whether it is ultimately because the companies are too prejudiced against shareholders, or that they treat shareholders who speak out [against management policies] as heretics, or that such things are a part of Japan's recent mentality, they cannot be eliminated from Japanese hearts.

If only more of Japan's judges were more educated in the ways of the entrenched management and how such managers will desperately do whatever it takes to keep themselves in a position of power. It was also especially good to see a former Supreme Court Chief Justice express concern for the shareholders and understand that it is the

shareholders who are the true owners of a company. It is unfortunate, however, that there are not more of Japan's judges who are
open to this concept.

In any event, the Supreme Court's judgment—if it can be called
such—only confirmed my belief that I would have to appeal to international opinion in order to correct Japan's unfair society. It was
obvious that Japan seemed wholly unable to address these ills on its
own.

Chapter Seven

Broken Promises

I have already alluded to Katakura several times in the preceding chapters and I would like to go back now and relate my experiences with them. This was in 1978, immediately on the heels of the forced sale of the Oji Paper shares.

While the forced sale was coming to a close, I became concerned about ever investing in Japan again. As I've said, this was doubly unfortunate, because I had seen these investments not only as financial investments but also ones of principle. I had begun to earn my fortune in Japan and I had family and friends there, so I felt it was a matter of social conscience to invest where I had strong feelings.

Throughout the Oji Paper affair, the other side had relied on intimidation: they had made overt statements about re-implementing the self-restraint program at any time; Mr. Akagi had made threats on my life; and they had used the media to communicate messages to us rather than to do so directly. In all of this they had sent a very clear message that although my friends and I had wealth, they had the power.

By the end of it, I was exhausted: mentally, physically, and emotionally. It had been nine months of struggle and worry. It didn't end the way I had wanted it to and I had once again lost the opportunity for a substantial return (the loss of over ¥50 billion as it would turn out), but at least it was over. It was an experience I didn't want to repeat, and I wanted nothing more than to put it behind me.

During the ending days of the Oji Paper affair, I received numerous promises from the securities companies. One of them was that if I would just give up, they would make it up to me by helping me to recover my losses and put my money into companies that could offer me a good gain on my money. The other promise was that what had happened in the Oji Paper affair would never be repeated.

It was of little comfort to me but I felt so exhausted over the whole incident that I took them at their word.

The Second Trap

In 1978, soon after the forced and humiliating sale of the Oji Paper shares, a representative of Yamaichi Hong Kong approached me and recommended we invest in Katakura Industries. Yamaichi had prepared for us a list of latent assets of Katakura and brought it along to show me.

"Katakura is a manufacturer of silk thread," the representative from Yamaichi said, "which is now regarded as a declining industry."

But this company, he stressed, had several hundred thousand *tsubo* (1 *tsubo* = 36 square feet) of land in the form of former factory sites that were located all over the country. The head office in Tokyo alone occupied a 2,000-*tsubo* site in Kyobashi.

"So while the share price may be low at present," he said, "the company has the potential of growing into a sound enterprise in the future."

Katakura Industries was an illustrious family enterprise boasting a century-long history of producing silk thread. Katakura's latent assets were truly enormous and although their mainstay, the silk thread industry, was in the doldrums, it seemed evident that if the land it owned were put to practical use in an efficient manner, their bottom line was bound to improve and could in fact be used to make its silk industry profitable again by paying off debt.

Our decision to invest in Katakura was made largely upon this presentation by Yamaichi. However, Yamaichi was not alone in their solicitation as Nikko Securities and Kankaku also approached me in the same manner and also highly recommended Katakura Industries.

They knew very well that I wanted to invest in a company where absolutely no problems would start cropping up and I reminded them once again of this before deciding whether to buy Katakura or put our money into other investments. "I have already had more than enough with the whole Oji Paper affair," I said. "So I want you to be very careful and ensure that no repetition of that this sort of trouble will occur."

They earnestly promised me that there would be no repetition of what had happened with Oji Paper Company so we began to invest based on the strength of their guarantee.

The Start of Trouble

Upon their recommendation, we acquired 3.5 million shares, roughly 10%, of Katakura. There were still restrictions at this time on the percentage that could be held by foreigners and over the next two years, we continued to increase our holdings until we owned 8.20 million shares, with an average purchase price of around ¥400.

At one time, the price had reached the ¥900 level but from there it started to drop and then stayed at around ¥400. It was disturbing that the share prices did not seem to rise very much but it was even more disturbing that the management of Katakura did not seem to be taking any actions to right Katakura's sinking ship. This was an investment that should be paying handsomely but it did not seem to be rising to meet our expectations. In the back of my mind, it seemed like a repetition of the same old trouble, so I began investigating what was going on.

I was shocked at what I found out.

A close examination revealed that even the selling off of approximately 300,000 *tsubo* (approximately 1,000,000 square meters) of land had failed to make a dent in Katakura's extraordinary debts of around ¥18.0 billion. The interest payments alone amounted to a huge sum. For the year 1977, interest payments totaled some ¥2.0 billion, as opposed to an operating profit of around ¥1.77 billion, while an operating profit of approximately ¥2.37 billion for the year 1978 was countered by interest payments of about ¥1.6 billion. In 1979, the operating profit of around ¥2.38 billion was largely offset by interest payments amounting to approximately ¥1.7 billion. Nearly all of the profits were being funneled off simply to pay the interest to Fuji Bank.

Katakura's living by selling off their land, and the structure of excessive debt itself was an indication to me of irresponsible management, and my investigations had indeed revealed that the company did have a very poor record of operation. I therefore was forced to conclude that without better management of their assets and debts, their outlook would not improve nor, for that matter, would the shares rise in value. So, relying on my rights as a shareholder, I wrote letters to the management and made some polite suggestions on how to improve their financial situation.

One suggestion was that they sell just enough of the land lying idle to cover their existing debts and that they should retain the rest and develop it rather than selling it. I suggested creating high-class residential blocks and other methods that would yield ongoing income rather than a one-time sale. I especially recommended that they should reorganize operations by arranging for the efficient use of the approximately 60,000 *tsubo* (around 200,000 square meters) of unused land in Omiya City in Saitama Prefecture. I also offered that should funds be required for that purpose, we Hong Kong investors, who were shareholders, would gladly provide the necessary financing.

Furthermore, one of my friends who had invested in Katakura Industries expressly paid a visit to inspect the land in Omiya City, bringing a Hong Kong architect along with him.

However, Katakura Industries rebuffed our proposals. When I received a reply it was to the effect that, "We are planning our own way, so leave us alone." They said that plans for using the land in Omiya City were already under way. They also pointed out that Fuji Bank was standing on the Omiya site and that they were planning to erect a shopping center there to be rented out to Ito-Yokado.

The 40,000-*tsubo* (133,333 square meters) shopping center that they planned to build was virtually in the center of the land. This land was the largest of the last assets remaining to Katakura Industries, which had only been hanging on by selling them off.

If Katakura rented away that central portion to Ito-Yokado on a forty-year lease as they intended to do, it would become impossible to plan for the intensive and overall efficient use of this land. Moreover, since there would only be a meager rent coming in, Katakura would lose the opportunity for improving their dilapidated financial structure.

They also declined our offer of financial assistance. Instead, the tenant, Ito-Yokado, would loan the more than ¥8 billion necessary for the project. In exchange for the loan, Katakura would offer the 40,000 tsubo of land and buildings on it as security.

This completely baffled me. Where in the world had anyone ever heard of a landlord offering their land and buildings as security to his tenant who was offering the landlord a loan? It was totally upside down. But it was also obvious what was happening: Ito-Yokado, which belonged to the same Fuji Bank Group, would be receiving a sweetheart deal on the lease, practically rent-free. This, of course, was actually detrimental to Katakura's profit margins, which in turn affected all the shareholders of the company. Once again it was obvious that the concept that a company belongs to the shareholders just had no meaning in Japan.

At this time, the last three presidents of Katakura Industries over a twenty-year period had formerly worked at the Katakura's main bank, Fuji Bank. These three presidents, making no attempt to improve the management, kept things going by selling off land that Katakura owned throughout the country. Obviously, the assets were being frittered away by these presidents, who did just as they were told to do by Fuji Bank, thereby causing great losses to Katakura shareholders.

Camouflage Shareholders

From the time that I started to offer suggestions in early 1980, Katakura Industries began to treat me—their leading shareholder— like a corporate raider. During this time, it was again alleged that I was a greenmailer. Allow me to give one example of how Japan's mass media spread malicious reports about me. *Evening Fuji* featured the following report:

Greenmail after Inflating Prices
—In his Fifties, True Face Unknown—
Secret Maneuvering in Buying up Oji Paper, Kao, Meiji Milk

Mr. T. H. Wang is said to be the man who rigged the Hong Kong Dollar. To date he has bought up shares in Meiji Milk, Kao Soap, Oji Paper, and other renowned family companies in order to have them bought back at high prices, causing the gnashing of teeth among the managers of Japan, Inc. This time he has set his sights on a family concern in the silk man- ufacturing field, Katakura Industries (Head office: Tokyo; Capital: ¥1.75 billion; president: Arita; Employees: 1,800), which is listed on Tokyo's first market…Owing to the buying up of the shares, it is being rumored that the company is in danger of being relegated to the Second Market.

This was sheer, unbridled nonsense. Even so, I sent my son to Japan to explain matters to the management of Katakura Industries, so that they would not be led astray by such irresponsible reports in the mass media and to let them know that I had only good intentions. However, despite such efforts on my part, it didn't do anything to soften them.

During 1979–1980, the share price remained at a depressed level of ¥400 for some time and didn't budge, which was why I began offering suggestions to the management to improve their lot. This depressed price naturally chased away many of the floating shareholders in Katakura Industries rather than any influence I might have had. Granted, I was buying shares during this time, but the restrictions of 10% and 25% were still in place and it was nonsense to say I was buying up all the shares from the other shareholders to the point that the company was in danger of being relegated to the Second Market.

Some explanation is needed here. There were regulations in place at the time that governed whether a publicly listed company was listed on the First or Second Market. Having a listing on the First Market was a matter of prestige for companies, roughly the equivalent of being part of the Dow Jones Industrial Average. According to the TSE regulations, Katakura, which had 35 million shares, needed to have 2,000 or more floating shareholders—those with between 500 and 50,000 shares. In addition, the number of floating shares had to equal at least 20% of the listed shares. However, the turnover and the number of shareholders had decreased and Katakura was dropped from the First Market.

The normal practice for increasing the number of shareholders was to have the large shareholders release some of their shares into the market. However, fearing that this would enable me to acquire them, the management of Katakura Industries opted to do something illegal.

The Katakura management (who, as I said, had formerly worked for Fuji Bank) conspired with the manager (also a former vice president of Fuji Bank) of Nihombashi Kogyo, which was in the same Fuji Bank *keiretsu*. Together, they carried out a camouflage operation in the shareholders register by saying that 1.60 million of the 1.64 million shares that were owned by Nihombashi Kogyo had been assigned to 160 employees of Katakura Industries, i.e., 10,000 shares for each person. Further, Taisei Construction (another member of the Fuji Bank *keiretsu*) and stable shareholder Ito-Yokado (the lessee from the shopping center) also collaborated in the creation of camouflage shareholders by employing the same type of artifice.

This was a clear violation of Article 58, No. 1 of the Securities and Exchange Act, which prohibits the adoption of illegal means, plans, or techniques in respect to securities trading and reporting. I gathered evidence of their illegal conduct and also courted the opinion of Professor of Law Yoshiro Kamizaki of Kobe University who clearly stated they had violated the law.

With this legal ammunition, I lodged a complaint against them with the Tokyo District Prosecutor's Office on August 4, 1980, for creating camouflage shareholders. However, the Tokyo District Public Prosecutor dropped the case on April 19, 1982, giving them a stay of prosecution. Amazingly, even though the prosecutor acknowledged the criminal act, he refused to investigate further. I then applied to the Tokyo District Court to appoint an auditor to investigate the affairs of the company but the judge said, "Since this has come to light without recourse to an audit, the appointment of an auditor is not necessary." I couldn't believe it. How many times does a prosecutor say, "It is true that a murder has been committed, but since the murderer was discovered without any investigation on the part of the police, there is no need for further investigation."

In Japan, a stay of prosecution is a disposition that finds that a crime has been committed, but since it is not "pernicious" enough to prosecute, the prosecution is suspended. In reality, it is equivalent to an acquittal. Had Katakura been found guilty, the legal punishment at the time under Article 197, No. 2 of the Securities and Exchange Act for their actions would have been "imprisonment for not more than three years or a fine of not more than ¥300,000." A crime that carried such heavy punishment was obviously not a minor offense.

Not surprisingly, when Katakura became aware that the case of false entries in their securities reports had been dropped, they showed no sign of contrition. Instead, they blatantly submitted securities reports featuring the same type of camouflaged shareholders for the following year and for the year after that. On the previous occasion, prosecution had been stayed on the grounds that their actions were not pernicious, but when the same type of criminal conduct is repeated over and over again, then one would think that it must now be characterized as such. I certainly thought so, and once again filed a charge with the Tokyo District Public Prosecutor's Office on July 1, 1982.

In January 1983, the Tokyo District Public Prosecutor disposed of my complaint by once again dropping the charges.

Apparently, the Japanese prosecutors don't consider securities reports to be very important. Perhaps every company should just make up whatever they want and put it in their security reports. But in reality, securities documents are *fundamental* to any country's economy because securities reports are far and away the most important factor when making investment decisions.

Securities Reports

As one might easily guess, such false entries in securities reports are an everyday occurrence in Japan and I'd like to take a moment to address this issue.

Recently, bankruptcies of listed companies in Japan have been occurring one after another. Most of these companies' failures have resulted from their inability to survive because they were carrying excessive liabilities owing to the bursting of the bubble economy. However, as far as one can tell on examining the securities reports immediately prior to the bankruptcies, there were no signs of impending failure because the securities reports seemed perfectly normal and indicated a strong, healthy company—clearly indicative that false entries had been made. This is why, when a listed company goes under, more and more hidden losses are discovered as authorities begin to look into the company's history. Here in America, the recent example of Enron is a perfect example of this same type of behavior as more and more begins to come to light.

The failure of major financial institutions such as the Long-Term Credit Bank of Japan and Nippon Credit Bank, caused a considerable shock not only in Japan's financial circles, but also in those throughout the world. In the case of the Long-Term Credit Bank of Japan, the president and three others were arrested on June 10, 1999, on suspicion of hiding losses of ¥310 billion in the closing accounts for March 1998, and of illegally distributing ¥7.1 billion in dividends to shareholders. The bank was carrying huge amounts of bad debts as a consequence of the bursting of the bubble economy, but the management set up subsidiaries to buy up the bad debts, thereby hiding the losses in these subsidiaries in order to avoid reporting them. Enron's similar actions of hiding debt didn't come as a surprise to those who were paying attention to Japan.

As for Nippon Credit Bank, the former chairman and the former president were arrested on July 23, 1999, for window-dressing the closing accounts. Since the former chairman hailed from the Ministry of Finance and the former president had been at the Bank of Japan, the arrest was considered a mistake in Japan, a society in which the judiciary and the bureaucracy collude to protect one another, and the prosecution was actually stopped.

The window-dressing of accounts was practiced not only by major financial institutions, but also by ordinary Japanese companies. Upon the bankruptcy of the internationally renowned photocopier manufacturer Mita Industries, it was learned that the final accounts had been dressed up. Mita Industries had used a simple trick that involved properly drawing up an in-house balance sheet and other documents, and then doctoring the figures before submitting the documents to the Tax Administration Agency and to their banks. This type of manipulation is impossible without the collusion of the auditor. Moreover, even though Mita knew that there was no profit to make it possible to distribute dividends, huge dividend distributions were made to the president and his relatives, who were shareholders. On October 13, 1998, as a result of the investigation, it was established that the president, the managing directors, and the certified public accountant had all conspired in the exercise and all six were arrested.

Even though illegal conduct was discovered in failed companies, it appears that there are quite a few other companies in Japan that have also dressed up their accounts in collusion with their auditors. Examples have therefore continued to crop up of companies going bankrupt where the company auditor must have stamped a big seal of approval on the various financial forms even though they were nothing but lies. Since there have been so many cases like this recently in Japan, cries are being raised to call the auditors to account. On December 1, 1999, shareholders whose holdings had all been rendered worthless by the bankruptcy of the Long-Term Credit Bank of Japan lodged a suit claiming compensation for losses against the president, the directors, and the auditor. Similar suits have been brought in the cases of Nippon Credit Bank and Yamaichi Securities as well.

Have Japan's public prosecutors now come to a realization of the importance of securities reports? Suddenly, they have started to strictly pursue the crime of making false entries in securities reports. If the Tokyo District Public Prosecutor's Office had dealt strictly with Katakura Industries for this crime in the early 1980s when I first raised the issue, perhaps other instances of corporate wrongdoing might have been prevented. Perhaps the other companies would have seen that they would not be able to get away with their crimes and Japan wouldn't have ended up by having its shame now exposed to the whole world. Instead, the lack of prosecution might have only encouraged these companies in their schemes.

Seeking More Shares

By early 1980, we held 23.5% of Katakura, which left an additional 1.5% of shares open to us. Although we still could not legally exceed 25%, we could at least acquire these remaining shares. Even though Katakura had problems, they were still a good buy due to their latent assets. There was also talk at this time—at the strong urging of the Carter administration in the U.S.—of opening up the Japanese markets to foreigners and of lifting the restrictions, which would allow us to increase our holdings even further.

In February 1980, we contacted the securities companies to seek more shares, however, our buy orders were refused. When I asked why, they said it was because the 25% restriction on foreign investment had already been reached. At least we hadn't been told it was because they said they could choose to stop taking buy orders, though you can imagine that my heart skipped a beat when I first heard they were refusing our buy orders.

Even so, this seemed incorrect. According to our figures and research, we had only 23.5%, so I asked the securities companies to buy shares as they became available. But whenever I inquired about their efforts over the next few months, I was told that none had become available yet.

Not trusting the securities companies, I contacted the Bank of Japan directly on August 29, 1980, to seek clarification and to double-check our figures. I informed them that we were being told that the limit had already been reached but that according to the 1980 edition of the *Japanese Company Handbook*, we had only acquired 23.5% of the available shares in Katakura Industries and that it then followed that it should be possible to acquire the remaining 1.5% of the shares. However, the Bank tried to sidestep our question and merely said that they did not know where we got our figures from because, according to their records, the 25% limit had been reached.

Not to be deterred, I wrote back through my attorney and asked for the exact percentage of shares being held by foreigners. On September 22, 1980, I received a reply from Section Chief Tetsuo Takeda of the Investment Section of the Foreign Bureau of the Bank of Japan. He wrote:

> Since 25% of the issued shares in Katakura Industries
> Co., Ltd. have been acquired by foreigners, as of February

1980 the Bank of Japan has halted the acceptance of applications for the acquisition of shares in Katakura Industries by foreign investors.

With regard to the statement in your letter that the percentage of shares held by foreigners in the aforesaid company is 23.5%, we regret to say that we do not know what your basis is for said calculation.

I regret to say that we are not in a position to disclose the ratio of foreigners' share holding of any individual company. When it becomes possible to resume receiving applications for acquisition of shares of any company, we will make it public at the headquarters of the Bank of Japan.

Essentially, the Bank artfully dodged the questions we'd asked and refused to answer or disclose the share rolling of any individual company. Nor did they make any additional shares available.

This dragged on for some time, and the securities companies continued to refuse our orders. In the meantime, I wrote to other people in positions of authority, such as the Commissioner for Securities in Hong Kong, to inform him about what was happening and also to seek his assistance, but I received none. Additionally, I wrote more than 1,000 letters to the other shareholders to inform them of what was happening with Katakura and to urge them to add their voices to my own. Unfortunately, I received only one or two replies. Everyone else, it seemed, was too timid to speak up against what was obviously poor management, despite the fact that it was their own money that Katakura was squandering.

The Japanese Government Takes a Hand

It was at this same time when we were contacting the Bank of Japan that the Japanese government finally decided to lift the 25% restriction on foreigners in an effort to encourage greater foreign investment. The new law was due to go into effect on December 1, 1980.

This was excellent news for all foreign investors and we Hong Kong investors certainly looked forward to now being able to expand our holdings in Katakura. Although we had no intention of running the company, increasing our holdings to more than 33% would mean that we could exercise a right of veto against special resolutions at the General Meeting of Shareholders. Katakura would finally be forced to listen to us.

But then something extraordinary happened.

A few weeks before the law was to go into effect, the Japanese government designated eleven companies as being important for the sake of "national security." These eleven companies would continue to have the 25% limit to prevent these strategic industries from falling into the control of foreigners. Among them, six were involved in the petroleum industry, two in the nuclear industry, one in aerospace, and one in the pharmaceutical industry.

The eleventh was Katakura. The government had declared that Katakura Industries—a medium-sized company involved in making and selling silk underwear—to be a company that was "vital" to Japan, and if it were to fall into foreigners' hands, it would pose grave difficulties to Japan's security and economic well being.

One can easily assume that Katakura's management panicked when the new law was slated to go into effect. I had already lodged a complaint against them with the Tokyo District Prosecutor's Office in early August 1980 for creating camouflage shareholders and sought to have an auditor appointed to investigate them, so they we were unhappy with their performance. If the new law was to be enacted, it would expose them and they might very well have been forced to resign. Their only course of action was to appeal to the government to protect them.

Katakura's designation led to public outcries both in Japan and overseas.

How could a company in the sunset industry of silk thread manufacturing be "indispensable" for Japan's security and economy?

Obviously, the designation was clearly a spoiling operation carried out by a joint conspiracy of Katakura, politicians, and bureaucrats aimed at excluding foreign investors and preventing us from buying more shares. (A later study in April 1981 that was printed in *Asian Banking* revealed that rather than having any relationship to national security, the factor that these designated companies all had in common was that they all already had high levels of foreign investment.)

The author Kyu Ei Kan ridiculed the decision in his newspaper column:

> When all is said and done, the biggest laughing stock in the world created by the recent abuse of the "Supplementary Provisions" would be the Ministry of Agriculture, Forestry, and Fisheries' transformation of Katakura Industries into a "designated company." When the so-called "Hong Kong Dollar" bought up 23% of Katakura Industries, the latter must have rushed to the Ministry of Agriculture, Forestry, and Fisheries for help; if a company that makes underpants and undershirts is deemed to be a key industry, then the only explanation can be that the Ministry of Agriculture and Fisheries was showing strong signs of concern over the popularity of "no pants" coffee shops.

A bit of explanation is required here. At this time, coffee shops whose waitresses wore no panties under their miniskirts were booming in Japan. Mr. Kyu is poking fun by saying that the Ministry of Agriculture and Fisheries designated Katakura Industries as a key industry out of fear that panty sales would fall.

An article appeared on November 18, 1980 in *Nihon Keizai Shimbun (Japan's Economic News)* entitled, "Advance Notice to Prevent Takeover." This article discussed the new law that would lift the 25% restriction by foreign investment with the exception of the "government-appointed enterprises." I found the following especially interesting:

Katakura Industries Company (silk maker) is also appointed, because of the strong purchase desire of Hong Kong investors... On the other hand, some enterprises (40 companies, at present), whose foreign stock purchases have been stopped because their foreign capital reached conventional limits, have not been "appointed" by the government according to the new law, and are free to sell more shares; thus, foreigners will again be able to buy their stocks actively.

It was nice to know we weren't alone and that even the media was openly stating that the only reason Katakura Industries came under this program was because of the Hong Kong investors. Katakura, much like Oji Paper before it, had run to the government for "protection."

But this designation went far beyond the simple manipulation of some bureaucrats at the Ministry of Finance. In this case, there were four government entities involved in the strategic designation: the Ministry of Finance, the Ministry of Agriculture, the Ministry of Trade, and the Ministry of Health.

Amazingly, Katakura had found a way to block us once again. Once again, a company didn't want to play by the rules so they simply changed the rules.

In February 1981, aggravated at what was happening, I took these government agencies to court to try to cancel Katakura's appointment as a so-called strategic company. The suit against them lasted from February 1981 to May 1984. I will deal with this suit in a moment.

We Seek an Injunction

On another course of action, in an attempt to exercise our rights as shareholders—and for the first time in Japanese corporate history—we Hong Kong investors filed an action in court in February 1981 to challenge the business judgment of Katakura's management of the company. We filed the motion to prevent Katakura from giving Ito-Yokado a ridiculously below-market lease agreement because it was detrimental to the company.

On October 29, 1981, the Tokyo District Court dismissed our petition for an injunction.

The court rejected a survey report by Mr. Sashijiku that I had submitted, which showed the potential income if the lands were to be used properly. As grounds for the dismissal of the petition, the Tokyo District Court declared that since Katakura's plans for the shopping center had been decided upon after a prudent in-house consideration of a concept from an outside professional organization more than ten years ago, "It can be inferred that it falls within the bounds of reasonability." The court also judged Katakura Industries' trial balance as reasonable, saying it could not accept that there would only be a minimal profit, as I had contended. The trial balance forecast a total net profit of approximately ¥1.8 billion in ten years' time, rising to around ¥6.3 billion after twenty years.

I was disappointed with the court and found their decision to be unreasonable, going against sound business principles. So I filed an appeal. However, due to the initial court's refusal to grant the injunction, and because the building was completed during my appeal, it was too late to do anything and I had to withdraw my appeal in May of 1983.

As time would tell, my projections proved to be accurate. Instead of the net profits that Katakura had predicted, the actual results by 1991, ten years later, showed a profit of only ¥735 million—less than half what they predicted. In fact, their profits declined each year thereafter, with the exception of 1993 when they exceeded their 1991 profits by a mere ¥1 million. To this day they are still not even close to their projections and, in 1998, they actually showed a loss of ¥172 million.

In the final analysis, the only ones that ended up making money were Ito-Yokado, the lessee, and Fuji Bank, which lent the funds for the construction. Moreover, Fuji Bank put up a building on the best spot on that land, and established a branch there.

A Letter Sheds Some Light

I received a letter dated April 30, 1981, from a Japanese citizen whose name I will withhold. There was a good deal of uproar in the mass media about Katakura's designation and the lawsuits that were being filed, and this person who had been following the stories closely finally decided to write to me.

There are many obscure points in connection with the adoption of designated shares on this occasion. There is also a strong impression that the company [Katakura] was plotting a scheme in conspiracy with the administration. In Japan, few people still attach any importance to silkworm farming. The general view is that this is a declining industry. Thus, most people consider the steps taken on this occasion improper. Action taken by the Ministry of Finance was highhanded and the company's disregard of its shareholders has also created a problem. The Stock Exchange's strict surveillance over the trading of Katakura shares has prevented people from getting near them. It seems that the securities companies have been turning down customers' buying orders...

In about 1973, a Mr. Akira Tatsumi came into the limelight after he acquired a large number of Katakura shares. He remained a major shareholder for a few years but he finally released his holdings because the management did not respect him as a major shareholder. It seems that the management always tries to reject shareholders that it does not like. This present case is no exception.

According to the information I have gathered from various quarters, Yamaichi was asked to dispose of Mr. Tatsumi's shares, and you, who were not familiar with the situation, were chosen as the target. Thus, it is not an exaggeration to say that it was Yamaichi who started this present unfortunate incident...

When things go sour, people will do anything. There are many such examples in the stock market in the past. How relentlessly the public investors have been sacrificed! …The Japanese economic circles would consider it a shame if a foreigner becomes the largest shareholder. They will never let it happen. I do not necessarily hope for such a thing to happen, but I think for the Japanese stock market to normalize itself, the shock treatment is a must.

I was very happy to receive this letter and others like it, and appreciated them very much. When placed in such stressful and unfair situations as the Oji Paper affair and now the problem with Katakura, such kindnesses are like gems. I did find it very interesting indeed that he'd mentioned Yamaichi's role in the whole incident, especially since he could not have known that it was Yamaichi that had first approached us with the false report to persuade us to buy Katakura shares.

The Japanese Government

No doubt it seems almost like fiction that the Japanese government and industries would work in such close collusion simply to thwart foreign investment. And it is true that in most western companies such actions would indeed be the stuff of fiction. However, as I mentioned in Chapter Five, Japanese politicians, bureaucrats, and businessmen have a long history of close-knit relationships. Evidence of this can be seen again and again in Japan.

The most prominent example of this phenomenon is the Recruit affair, which was briefly mentioned in Chapter Five but needs to be expanded on in order to see the levels to which these ties can go. This was an incident in 1988, in which a Japanese property company called Recruit Cosmos transferred shares to politicians, senior bureaucrats, and businessmen before they were offered to the public, thus presenting the beneficiaries with the profits resulting from the rise in the share price that immediately followed the public offering.

Among the politicians involved, there appeared the names of such prominent figures as then Prime Minister Noboru Takeshita, former Prime Minister Yasuhiro Nakasone, Minister of Finance Kiichi Miyazawa, Liberal Democratic Party (LDP) Secretary-General Shintaro Abe, and LDP Policy Research Committee Chairman Michio Watanabe. In all these cases, the transactions were carried out in the names of the individuals' secretaries or sons. Remarkably—or perhaps not surprisingly—the affair ended without a single influential politician being called to account. The only ones arrested were the chairman of the parent company, Recruit, and a few minor bureaucrats.

Before this matter came to light, I had been astonished to discover in the *Company Quarterly Report*, which records the results of all listed companies, that the outstanding loans to Recruit Cosmos (whose shares were sold over-the-counter) totaled something like ¥500 billion. I was surprised because the scale of indebtedness was around half of the total lending to Nippon Steel, which was the largest company in Japan in those days. I therefore assumed that it was just a typo. However, when this case became public, I realized that the figure had indeed been correct.

This method of gifting profits to politicians and bureaucrats adopted by Recruit Cosmos is practically an everyday occurrence in Japan. In fact, it is customary—as a matter of courtesy—for securities house or the issuing company to actually put up the funds for the initial "purchase" of the shares by the influential parties. In essence, the politician makes money with no actual investment of their own.

This fact alone should be enough to clarify the nature of the cozy relationship structures among politicians, bureaucrats, and businessmen, but the real events were even worse. The shares in question in the Recruit affair were never *actually transferred*, but rather merely *deemed* to have been transferred, and the payouts were to equal the difference in the value of the shares before and after the public offering. On paper, the VIPs were said to have duly purchased the shares, then sold them and received the inflated sale price. But the whole thing was nothing more than a scheme to enable influential politicians and bureaucrats to line their pockets without lifting a finger.

Managers of Japanese companies have been funneling profits like this to politicians and bureaucrats for a long time. And, although the approach is usually a little less blatant, corporate managers' contributions to politicians and their wining and dining of bureaucrats have been an everyday experience. In March 1998, an assistant section chief in the Securities Bureau of the Ministry of Finance was arrested on suspicion of accepting bribes in the guise of entertainment. According to the investigation, he was said to have accepted entertainment in the form of meals, drinks, and golf from Nomura Securities, Nikko Securities, and others in return for arranging benefits. With this as a lead, an investigation was launched in the Ministry of Finance. The prosecutor in charge of the matter observed, "The Ministry of Finance is wallowing in entertainment."

In response to the scathing criticism that erupted, an internal investigation was conducted in the Ministry of Finance, and 112 people who had received excessive entertainment were punished. I say punished, but they were just slapped on the wrist. The most serious punishment was a suspension for four months.

There is no doubt that such cozy relationships among politicians, bureaucrats, and businessmen have distorted the free market in Japan. Politicians and bureaucrats who have received such profits have intervened in the market, even to the extent of bending the law or creating new ones just to protect their corporate sponsors, such as the case with Katakura.

Regrettably, under such circumstances, it is not possible to invest in Japan with an easy heart. For Japan to get their market functioning in a healthy manner again, it will be critical to first eradicate the close-knit ties among politicians, bureaucrats, and businessmen.

Another Foreign Investor

Even though the government itself was now blocking us, the 1.5% was still available to us. We continued, however, to be stymied in our attempt to at least acquire the last remaining shares. Not believing that no shares at all were available to foreign investment, I came up with an idea. I asked one of my son's American friends to buy some shares in Katakura. In August 1981, after more than a year and a half of being told that no more shares were available to foreign investors—and six months after my filing a suit against the government for its designation of Katakura—he placed a purchase order for 10,000 shares in Katakura Industries with Nikko Securities in Los Angeles and they accepted it.

Not only did they accept his order but he was also able to buy 5,000 shares on the 6th of August; 2,000 shares on the 8th; and 3,000 shares on the 10th, all at ¥400 each. The Bank of Japan's answer back in September of the previous year—that there were no more shares available to foreigners—had been a complete lie. This was clear evidence that even Japan's central bank had joined with Katakura Industries and the securities companies to make it impossible for the Hong Kong investors to acquire shares in Katakura Industries.

However, when he subsequently placed a further order for 20,000 shares with Nikko Securities, the order was refused. When he asked for a reason, he was told that an instruction had come from the Tokyo head office not to accept orders from him. In the next few days, he placed orders for Katakura Industries shares by telephone with the Los Angeles branches of Nomura Securities and Daiwa Securities, but their answer was also that they could not respond to the orders.

When he raised complaints to the U.S. SEC, who then contacted the securities companies, Nomura said that they had the privilege of refusing buy orders; Nikko also believed that they could refuse orders at their discretion. The example Nikko gave was that there might be times when they viewed the shares as being extremely speculative or not suitable for the customer's investment aims. They also claimed to be entitled to refuse an order purely for business reasons. Daiwa, too, considered that the purchase of Katakura shares was extremely speculative and were not suitable for individual American investors. The SEC, unfortunately, took them at their word without digging any further into the matter.

While I knew the securities companies would come up with some sort of answer, this especially surprised me, as it was directly contrary to the recommendation of the securities companies that Katakura shares were a good and rewarding investment. These same shares were now somehow considered as "extremely speculative" or not "suitable for investment."

It is obvious from this how unfairly and fraudulently the Japanese public companies and brokers treat foreign investors. On one hand, they are advising American investors not to buy Katakura shares claiming it to be "highly speculative and volatile" while on the other hand they welcomed and urged my purchase of the very same stock in Hong Kong.

Perhaps, too, the Japanese Securities Companies knew that the U.S. would be able to bring much more pressure and exposure to Japan than could Hong Kong and the Hong Kong investors. As such, the Japanese securities companies used, literally, the Hong Kong investors to fund their corporate structures without allowing us any of the shareholders' privileges.

Court Battle Over Katakura's Designation

As I said earlier, I was frustrated by the conspiracy between Katakura and the government's designation ploy and filed an administrative lawsuit with the Tokyo District Court in February 1981. But the court rejected my suit. The reason for the rejection was very strange. It was:

> In the case in question, it cannot be held that there will be
> a direct effect on the rights and obligations of non-resident
> individuals who have acquired shares in a designated compa-

ny merely by virtue of the fact that the company has been designated, [but this is said to be] effective under private law, even if the shares are acquired in violation of the Foreign Exchange Act.

This was equivalent to saying that it would be all right for any Japanese, no matter whom, to buy shares in Katakura Industries on my behalf. Thus, the court was *endorsing* illegal conduct, saying it would have been all right for me to circumvent the law. Apparently, the court was making light of the entire purpose of the Foreign Exchange Act.

I immediately lodged an appeal with the Tokyo High Court to challenge this ridiculous ruling.

However, during the appeal process in May 1984—whether it was due to the embarrassing ruling by the lower court, or due to the pressure from outside the country, or for some other reason—the Japanese government suddenly canceled the special designations of all eleven companies. My suit obviously was no longer relevant. Now, their original reasons—which had had some merit to protect certain companies for national security reasons—were thrown out the window.

More Camouflage

When I was checking the minutes of the board of directors of Katakura Industries, quite by chance I discovered that the company had engaged in the illegal acquisition of their own shares. President Shinichi Funatsu conspired with Managing Director Mr. Haruo Yanagisawa to trade Katakura's own shares, and it became clear that a loss had been inflicted on the company. Trading in the company's own shares is a means of manipulating share prices, and at that time it was (and still is) prohibited by the Commercial Code because it incorporated the additional aspect of the company's own funds being used for the self-protection of the management.

What I discovered was shocking, even for the likes of Katakura Industries. I knew they had created camouflage shareholders and although it was not unusual for Japanese companies to "fudge" things a little, this was blatantly illegal.

Back in 1972—before I'd even invested in Katakura—the management of Katakura Industries arranged for 8 million of its shares that were then held by a company called Chugai Furnace Industries to go to companies that Katakura wanted to turn into stable shareholders. However, since there was no taker for 2 million of the shares, these were temporarily undertaken by Nihombashi Kogyo, an affiliate of Fuji Bank, until a buyer could be found. The following year, they used the Katakura's own funds to purchase those same 2 million shares along with the remaining 2 million owned by Chugai Furnace Industries. Perhaps some of this was the management's reaction to Mr. Tatsumi who, as you'll recall, had begun acquiring large blocks of Katakura in 1973.

Katakura Industries carried out some highly complicated manipulations in order to conceal this illegal self-dealing. They created a wholly-owned subsidiary, Gyosei Enterprise, strictly for the purpose of a concealment operation, and assigned Katakura's own shares to this fictitious company, which Gyosei Enterprise had "bought" at par value, along with shares in several banks to help cover up their scheme. According to the minutes of the board of directors, the securities that were assigned consisted of the aforementioned 4 million shares of Katakura, 10,000 shares of Mitsubishi Bank stock, 16,665 shares of Kyowa Bank stock, 19,740 shares of Saitama Bank stock, and 35,000 shares of Shin-Ei stock, for a total value of ¥2,375,901,759. Because of the involvement of the banks, this made for a very deep scandal indeed, with many people involved. Imagine, for a moment, if Enron, which employed similar tactics, had enlisted the help of Citibank, Chase Manhattan, and other banks to help give their fictitious corporations an air of legitimacy. You can imagine the outcry.

To make the deception even more complete, they also assigned roughly 10,000 *tsubo* of land and buildings that Katakura owned in the center of Seki City, Gifu Prefecture. These assets had a value of several billion yen, but they assigned them to the newly created Gyosei at a price that merely equaled the book value, which, according to the minutes of the board of directors, was only ¥3,476,260.

In order to make all of this look plausible on the books, they had Gyosei underwrite funds borrowed by Katakura Industries corresponding to the assignment value. According to the minutes of the board of directors, ¥1.184 billion was borrowed from Mitsui Bussan and ¥1.184 billion from Nihombashi Kogyo.

However, Gyosei Enterprise then sold the assigned shares in Katakura Industries to the other major shareholders at an undervalued price, incurring a loss of ¥730 million. In order to cover the deficit, Gyosei Enterprise sold some of the land in Seki City—which, of course, actually belonged to Katakura anyway. What is more, the management of Katakura Industries finally merged Gyosei Enterprise (the fictional subsidiary that still "owned" the remaining assets) with Nakagoe Nitto, an actual subsidiary of Katakura Industries.

By carrying out these complicated operations, the management of Katakura Industries made it difficult for the losses produced by their self-dealing in the company's shares to be brought to light. Meanwhile, the net result was that the extremely valuable land that the company owned in Seki City had been consumed in order to conceal the illegal conduct of the management.

Needless to say, this was disturbing and harmful to the company. The assets of a company belong to its shareholders not to the company's managers. But here was a case where company assets were being peddled off piecemeal through complicated means to cover losses of ¥730 million suffered in illegal self-dealing. It was unforgivable that the management had caused losses to the company and then pretended that nothing was wrong. What is more, Katakura

Industries—either out of foolishness or arrogance—left a record of their actions that had been taken in the minutes of the board of directors. This appeared to be a case in which all the members of the board, who attended the meetings and signed and sealed the minutes, could not escape being charged with a breach of trust.

I requested the Tokyo District Court to appoint an auditor in 1981 on the basis of Article 294 of the Commercial Code, which stipulates: "When there are serious grounds for suspecting that the law has been violated in regard to the conduct of a company's business, a shareholder owning 10% or more of the shares may request a court to appoint an auditor."

However, the Tokyo District Court rejected my request, saying that "The fact that the acquisition by Katakura Industries of its own shares is in violation of Article 210 of the Commercial Code constitutes a major fact showing that there has been a violation of the law referred to in Article 294 of the Commercial Code. However, since this has become evident without requiring examination by an auditor, the appointment of an auditor is not necessary."

I appealed this decision to the Tokyo High Court. However, the Tokyo High Court also rejected my appeal, giving the following statement among the reasons for its judgment:

> There is an extremely strong suspicion that the real motive in the request for the appointment of an auditor in this case is to cause the management of Katakura Industries distress for no good reason, and to profit by greenmailing Katakura Industries to take back the shares. It is clear that acknowledging this request would do nothing more than give further impetus to the quagmire of the dispute existing between the appellant (T. H. Wang) and Katakura Industries. The request in this case, which exceeds the bounds of the proper exercise of rights by a minority shareholder, constitutes an abuse of rights.

I had never heard of a judgment that was so unreasonable or so filled with prejudice and malice. As a shareholder, what was wrong with my action of lodging a lawsuit to correct mismanagement and to prevent them from further squandering the assets of the company? Is it not the responsibility of the management of a company to act in the best interests of the company, to protect it, and to foster its growth? Also, why should the exercise of shareholder rights in accordance with the Commercial Code constitute an abuse of rights? Wasn't the Commercial Code enacted to provide shareholders with exactly the kind of protection I was seeking? And is it not the expectation of the law that illegal conduct by major shareholders and the management be corrected and prevented, not by turning minority shareholder rights into a mere shell, but by having a number of shareholders putting them to practical use? Even now, while thinking about this decision, I still feel a great sense of anger, betrayal, and a deep sense of disappointment regarding "justice" in Japan.

Finally, the charge of being a greenmailer was outrageous and unjustified and to be specifically called one by the court itself seemed especially malicious. From the very beginning I had simply wanted a good investment that would not cause anyone any trouble. Apparently, such a wish was impossible in the system of Japan.

The charges of greenmail that Katakura brought up in this case stemmed from "evidence" that Katakura Industries submitted, which amounted to a letter in English that Mr. Mo—who was the responsible person at the local subsidiary in Hong Kong of Kankaku Securities—addressed to Mr. Takuji Matsuzawa, the chairman of Fuji Bank, which, of course, was part of Katakura's *keiretsu*. What should also be noted is that at the time, Fuji Bank was the leading shareholder of Kankaku Securities, which Mr. Mo worked for, and the two companies had a close relationship. Further, as I have previously stated, the last three presidents of Katakura Industries had come from Fuji Bank. A close-knit, incestuous relationship indeed.

Fuji Bank took this supposed letter from Mr. Mo and gave it to Katakura Industries, which translated it into Japanese and submitted it to the court. I quote the Japanese version here (translated back into English):

> July 1, 1980
> Dear Mr. Matsuzawa,
>
> A long time has passed since I last wrote to you. I believe that the past half-year has witnessed developments in regard to the Katakura case. It appears to me that I am an appropriate third party to handle a harmonious reconciliation of this issue. If I am appointed, I will extend my best efforts on behalf of both parties concerned. If I do not have your support, I believe that all my efforts will be fruitless.
>
> Once again, I would like to say that it is my earnest wish to come to Tokyo to see you any time to receive your instruction in this respect.

I did not even know about the existence of this letter, which is vague at best, and I was very surprised that it would be used as "evidence" in the trial. The Japanese version translated by Katakura Industries was fashioned to suit their own convenience, exhibiting the malicious intention of trying to give the impression that I was probably a greenmail artist. What was particularly insidious was that although the word *wakai* (reconciliation) was not used at all in the original English text, they deliberately inserted it into the Japanese translation in order to mislead the judge. In Japanese, *wakai* contains the nuance of "a transaction based on an out-of-court settlement." This suggested that I would make them buy back the shares I owned in Katakura Industries at a high price.

It was hard to believe that someone like the chairman of a major Japanese bank would pass this letter on to Katakura Industries. But it was obvious that the members of the *keiretsu* were banding together to protect one another, even if it meant fabricating evidence.

I sent a letter of protest to Mr. Mo, seeking an explanation. His answer came back promptly:

September 29, 1981
Dear Mr. Wang,

I refer to the set of documents that I received from you yesterday, which included a copy of my letter related to Katakura Industries dated July 1, 1980 addressed to Mr. Takuji Matsuzawa, the chairman of Fuji Bank, and a Japanese translation thereof.

I would like to expressly state that up to now I have never in any way broached this matter to you, nor have I in any way been appointed by you to function as your representative. This can be gathered from the aforesaid letter, in particular from the phrase 'If I am appointed...' I spontaneously offered my services for handling this case to Mr. Matsuzawa from the simple standpoint of increasing the volume of our company's transactions.

This came as a relief of sorts. Mr. Mo clearly stated that he had proposed mediation on his own initiative out of his desire for a commission, and that I was not involved at all. Enclosing Mr. Mo's letter and relevant documents from the trial in the same envelope, I sent a note to Chairman Matsuzawa of Fuji Bank saying, "The fact that even the chairman of Fuji Bank, one of the leaders of Japan's economy, took part in making me out as a greenmailer at any cost by arbitrarily construing a Japanese securities broker's conduct of business out of a desire for a commission to be something that I forced upon him is a worldwide disgrace. Such things will cost Japan its international credibility, and also give sensible Japanese a good laugh."

After more than a month passed, a brusque reply came in the name of Secretariat Head Yoshinaga of Fuji Bank.

According to your letter, this (Mr. Mo's letter dated July 1, 1980) was submitted to the court, but our bank is not a party to the suit, and it is not involved.

The fact that Mr. Mo's letter was translated into Japanese is something that we first learned from your letter. Please be advised that the pattern of facts is in accordance with the above.

We have advised you of the above by the order of Chairman Matsuzawa.

Although he passed Mr. Mo's letter to Katakura Industries and planned to frame me as a villain, Chairman Matsuzawa had the nerve to say that he was not involved. I was disgusted by them and by their actions. At the time, I thought, "With such contemptible persons as leaders in Japan's economic circles, what will Japan's future be like?" My premonition turned out to be accurate and, sure enough, some ten-odd years later, Japan met disaster in the form of the financial collapse, and many banks, both large and small, have failed. Even Fuji Bank had no choice but to combine with the Industrial Bank of Japan and Dai-Ichi Kangyo Bank.

Owing to this scheme between Katakura Industries and Fuji Bank, there is no doubt that the judge—likely already full of erroneous preconceptions that he'd read about me in the media—was given the impression that I was a greenmail practitioner.

Still More Lies

When the shares of Katakura had begun to level out and show no improvement, we investigated Katakura's business practices. The company was in debt and showed no signs of being able to climb out of its position on its own and so we'd offered to help only to be rebuffed. Worse, we'd discovered that they were selling their valuable assets simply to make interest payments in addition to using illegal methods to create camouflage shareholders. Unfortunately, as we continued to investigate, that was not the end of it.

In 1982, we made an appalling discovery. Although the report by Yamaichi Securities had said the land used for the head office in Kyobashi amounted to 2,000 *tsubo* (approximately 6,667 square meters), in fact it was only 300 *tsubo*. Incredibly, to make matters even worse, Katakura didn't even actually own the land—they rented it. Yamaichi Tokyo, who had been the sole underwriter of Katakura, would certainly have known this all along.

I could hardly believe that Yamaichi had the audacity to fraudulently misrepresent the Japanese government's *chika kooji* ("official prices"), which is published once a year by the government for real estate assessments. Yamaichi had simply invented official prices for properties that Katakura supposedly owned in order to calculate an inflated latent profit statement and present it to us.

Yamaichi knew that I was looking for companies with latent assets and knew that I would not question the government's official prices of the properties. I had not thought, in my wildest imagination, that Yamaichi would go as far as to invent government official prices to defraud me. Now, four years later, here we were holding around 8 million shares.

But this still was not the end of it.

It turns out that all of the "official prices" or "published land prices" of lands set out in Yamaichi's list were untrue, since none could be found in the Official Price publication, which was the document Yamaichi Tokyo had allegedly relied upon to establish the value of Katakura's assets. Additionally, they had used figures from the 1976 edition of the *"Zenkoku Kooji Tsuuran"* (a reference resource for all factories in Japan) and not the 1978 edition; as a result, a manufacturing plant that had been sold by Katakura in May 1977 was misrepresented as still being one of Katakura's properties in the list they'd given us. They had also overstated its size by a factor of ten. Finally, some of the addresses of properties given in the list as belonging to Katakura were simply false.

The report had been utter nonsense. The Japanese securities companies—when all I had wanted to do was to find a company that I could invest in safely and not have any trouble with—had deliberately lied to me.

Once the pack of lies about the latent asset value was revealed, the share price would drop and I would suffer serious losses.

The Attempt to Sell the Shares

In March of 1983, feeling like this was one big act of collusion and that there were too many people working against us, we decided to try to sell our shares. We approached the securities companies to sell the shares en masse, but they told us that there were no buyers for Katakura.

This astounded us. Repeating the past, the securities companies were working together to stymie legitimate business dealings. We also thought that Katakura—which had worked so hard to prevent us from obtaining any further shares—would jump at the chance to be rid of us. But apparently, they wished to punish us for daring to intrude on them. We continued to ask the securities companies to look for buyers, but they said they couldn't find any for such a large block of Katakura.

The whole situation was ridiculous. Originally, we were tired of Katakura's poor management that wasn't improving the company's performance, but now when we finally despaired and wanted to sell the shares, we couldn't get rid of them. Our only other resort was to replace the bad management but in order to do so we needed to purchase more shares, which, of course, we couldn't do because of the restrictions still in place at that time.

In June 1983, we then asked the securities companies to sell any portion of our holdings. Up until now, the share prices of Katakura had been continually lagging at around ¥400 for quite some time. They initially told us that they could find no buyers, which was an outright lie since one could easily look at the Tokyo Stock Exchange reports and see that shares of Katakura were still trading.

Once again, I asked for help from outside authorities and began to contact government regulating authorities in Hong Kong for any assistance they might provide. I included the facts of the case and even included the letters from the American investor to demonstrate the securities companies' collusion.

Mrs. Ada Yeung of the Hong Kong SEC wrote to me on September 29, 1983, regarding my requests for assistance. In reference to our allegations that nine Japanese brokers had concertedly refused to accept our selling order she said:

> This Office has spoken to these brokers on this matter respectively. All these brokers denied that they negotiated with each other in the incident. They claimed that they were merely unable to find any person who would be interested to make an offer to your holdings in the light of its considerably large size. They also explained that it was particularly difficult to find buyers at the moment since Katakura has just reported a substantial setback in their profits for the first half of 1983 and the outlook for the silk industry is gloomy. They said the shares were scarcely traded in Tokyo market recently and the market price as of September 27, 1983, was ¥440.
>
> These brokers further added that they would be too pleased to execute any firm selling order in a transactable amount for you on the Tokyo Stock Exchange. Should you wish to dispose of part of your holdings through this channel, please contact directly with your broker.

I appealed for more help by writing to the Hong Kong Commissioner for Securities for help, but here, too, received none. Mr. M.R. Surry, writing for the commissioner, wrote to me on October 7, 1983:

> My officers did make inquiries of some Japanese stockbrokers in Hong Kong and ascertained that there was only a nominal price quoted in Japan for Katakura shares. You may be able to confirm this by examining Japanese newspapers or an international publication.

No stockbroker is obliged to 'make you an offer' for your securities, which seemed to be the basis of your complaint. If you have a relationship with a particular firm you should be able to place an instruction to put a sell order onto the Tokyo market for all or part of your holding at a price specified by you can see if this attracts a buyer...

In short, if there is no buyer for a particular security, it cannot be sold. We have no jurisdiction over internal practices on the Tokyo Stock Exchange but to try to ensure that registered stockbrokers do not breach the Hong Kong Securities Ordinance.

Our inquiries have not revealed any such malpractice. I am afraid we're not able to entertain the matter any further.

It was unfortunate that the securities companies were able to convince the SEC of their innocence. I was and remain convinced that the only way to affect change is to bring external pressure on the Japanese. What the Hong Kong authorities failed to understand is that this was normal business practice for the Japanese. Of course I knew very well that I could not demand that the securities companies force someone to buy the shares if it was really true that *no one* was interested in buying them. The problem was that the securities companies were acting in concert to ensure that no one was interested. The Hong Kong authorities also overlooked the fact that they had pitched the shares to the Hong Kong investors with great effort and fanfare and now were telling others what a poor investment they were, that they were not safe for American investors, and that they were volatile—which in itself is a lie because how could the shares be volatile if no one was buying them? If a company's shares are volatile, by definition it means the price is fluctuating wildly as people sell and buy the shares rapidly. These obviously were not.

How typical of a bureaucracy to not take any action and to dismiss legitimate complaints with little thought. It felt as though the Japanese had invaded Hong Kong.

About the end of September and into early October, we attempted to sell just a small quantity of the shares and finally met with some success. It took the brokers over ten days to execute the sell orders and, suspiciously, all of our sell orders at the various brokers were executed on exactly the same day, October 12, 1983, and at exactly the same price of ¥388 per share.

The struggle with Katakura would continue over the next three years with no end in sight.

Still, I was not without hope, as you will see.

Chapter Eight

Efforts in the U.S.

I'd like to step away from Katakura for a moment to discuss my efforts in the U.S. to bring some pressure on the Japanese financial system. Perhaps up until now, you might have been wondering why— if the Japanese economy is so bad and if there really are such outrageous business practices going on—hasn't this met with more publicity in the U.S.?

It's a good question.

It's true that lately Japan is often overlooked—despite having the second-largest economy in the world. However, I'd like to remind you that during the 1980s, when Japan's economy was growing by leaps and bounds and the U.S. was lagging behind, Japan was very much in the forefront of the news during this time. When Japan's economic bubble burst and the U.S. economy began heating up, Japan slipped into the background where it has been ever since, even now when its economy is teetering on the brink of disaster. President George W. Bush, in his visit to Japan in February 2002, encouraged Prime Minister Koizumi in his efforts for reform and to encourage lawmakers to take care of the outrageous debt that the Japanese banks are carrying.

But efforts in the U.S. to bring attention to the Japanese problem have been going on for some time, since the early 1990s.

Congress Takes Notice

Mr. Speaker, imagine the outrage if the U.S. Treasury Department were to instruct Merrill Lynch or Goldman Sachs or other brokerage houses to stop trading in foreign stocks. No one in this House would stand for it. But indeed, that is exactly what has happened in recent years in Tokyo.

The Ministry of Finance in Japan instructed firms in Tokyo to stop trading through their offices in Hong Kong because Hong Kong investors were buying shares in paper companies in Japan.

Mr. Speaker, for a long time, the peculiar ethics of the markets in Japan were a Japanese problem. But today, when pension funds and mutual funds of American investors increasingly are used on the Tokyo markets, it is our problem.

Recently, I introduced H.R. 3283 asking the Treasury Department to do a study on the safety, the security, and the practices for funds used on the Tokyo markets. Soon that legislation will return to the House attached to Senate legislation. I ask my colleagues for the sake of the security of American investors to support it, to review it, and to lend it their vote.

— Representative Torricelli
October 1, 1992

Though it is tempting even now to disregard the problems in Japan as being a wholly Japanese situation, if Japan is unable to handle the difficulties it is facing, it will most certainly affect the U.S. and the rest of the world. It is logically impossible to assume that problems in the world's second-largest economy will not spill over to affect the other economies of the world. The Japanese consume vast quantities of American and foreign goods, own companies that are based on U.S. soil that employ U.S. workers, and supply raw materials and finished goods to American manufacturers. The list could go on and on.

If Japan is unable to change and instead collapses, then there will most certainly be dire consequences for the world economy. During the 1980s, Japan helped finance the United States' transformation from a creditor to a debtor nation and Japanese banks financed a good portion of America's multi-trillion dollar debt through the Japanese purchase of public debt, direct investment, and portfolio investment. With the current banking problems that Japan is facing and the difficulties the Japanese government will have in trying to rescue the ailing banks, one can easily imagine the consequences for the U.S. and the rest of the world.

In 1989, my son, Robert Wang, an American citizen, began to take up the fight against the Japanese. He owned stock in Saitama Bank, which had a branch in Los Angeles. However, this otherwise well-respected bank became involved in a stock scandal. He learned that Saitama Bank accepted inadequate stock collateral in its dealings with a Japanese stock speculator, Mitsuhiro Kotani, who was the owner of Korin Sangyo.

Mr. Kotani reportedly acquired a significant stake in Janome Sewing Machine at a price of ¥1,200 per share during the spring of 1987. Some of Janome's top officers had come from Saitama Bank, which was Janome Sewing Machine's primary banker, and Saitama Bank held a significant stake in the company. In April 1989, Saitama Bank (through an affiliate, TOA Finance) repurchased 10 million of those shares at ¥3,560 per share, a price that Robert believed was far above the stock's fair market value. Shortly thereafter, Saitama Bank, Janome, and affiliates accepted Mr. Kotani's remaining Janome shares as collateral for a loan, which he then used for stock specula-tion but borrowed the funds through Janome.

Robert filed a suit for damages and relief for breach of official and fiduciary duties in the Los Angeles courts in 1989. However, even though the Bank had a branch in the United States, the local courts did not pursue the case and turned it down, saying that they felt the jurisdiction lay wholly in Japan. It is unfortunate that the justice system took this view; not only did the U.S. justice system miss a chance to defend a U.S. citizen against scandalous behavior on the part of a company with bases of operation in the U.S., but taking the case could have brought a great deal of exposure to the many problems in the Japanese financial system that were all clearly demonstrated in this example.

When these revelations about the over-valuation of the Janome shares were made during Mr. Kotani's trial in December 1990, the reported closing price for Janome shares stood at ¥2,690 per share. If Mr. Kotani had defaulted at that time, Saitama Bank and Janome would have suffered a collateral shortfall on the order of ¥90 billion ($643 million at ¥140 to $1). Janome's share price continued to fall further, to between ¥500 and ¥600 per share in late 1991. In February of 2002, it further dropped to about ¥65 per share. At that price, the collateral shortfall would exceed $1.0 billion. The president of Kyowa Saitama Bank (Saitama Bank's successor) resigned as a result of the Kotani-Janome affair.

Pressure from the U.S.

If my family's experiences with Japan's convoluted financial and judicial system have taught me anything, it is that Japan seems incapable of making changes to its financial system on its own. Japan has effective laws on its books that are designed to prevent the very things that have happened to me and to other investors, and yet despite these very adequate laws, they are not enforced. Or, when they actually are enforced, it is on some lowly person who had very little to do with the actual crime, and not on the ringleaders who are truly responsible.

Starting in 1989, my son, Robert Wang, began to work with the U.S. government and to brief American policy makers on the implication of Japan's financial excesses. He began speaking with various representatives and senators about our belief that Japan was headed for tragedy if it did not change its ways.

In late 1991, Robert was invited by members of Congress to testify before the House Committee on Appropriations and Subcommittee on Treasury Postal Service and General Government Appropriations of the U.S. Congress.

Unlike their Japanese counterparts who bristled at the thought of an ordinary citizen making suggestions for reform, those who were in positions of power in government warmly welcomed our suggestions.

In a November 1991 letter to U.S. senators and representatives, my son Robert wrote:

> Historians may decide that the biggest financial scandal of the late 20th century was *not* the American savings and loan debacle, BCCI, or the Salomon government bond trading scandal, but rather the bursting of Japan's bubble economy. Yet that threat to global financial stability has received the least attention among American policy makers...
>
> [My family's] experiences also have led me to doubt Japan's ability to reform itself. The example of the Japanese stock market suggests that Japan may be run in a neo-feudal fashion, by an oligarchy of interests with a greater sense of responsibility toward one another than to Japanese society or to the international system from which Japan has profited so greatly. Only pressure from the international community, and particularly from the United States, has a chance of effectuating meaningful reforms that will benefit Japan as well as its trading partners.

As part of his testimony before Congress, Robert prepared a White Paper titled, "Japan's Financial Crisis: A Study of Japan's Capital and Securities Markets." In fact, much of the information in this chapter comes from the White Paper. Robert received many positive replies back and thanks from prominent senators and representatives for his testimony and for his White Paper. Among them were letters from Senator Tom Daschle and Congressmen Richard Gephardt, Robert Torricelli, and Tom Campbell.

Robert's 1991 testimony before Congress and his White Paper was preceded by the fall of the Japanese stock market, falling some 40% from its peak in late-1989. This precipitous drop, along with several scandals in Japan, caught the attention of international leaders. In the summer of 1991, there were revelations of loss guarantee payments totaling more than $1.2 billion by Japanese securities houses to preferred customers, which confirmed suspicions that the Japanese market was then, and continues to be, rigged toward market insiders. This means that American investments in Japanese securities are at grave risk, including the billions of dollars of American pensioners' savings invested on the Tokyo Exchange. Look at the huge losses sustained to retirement funds by Enron, a single U.S. company, and one can easily see how devastating the losses would be if Japan were to falter.

Japanese banks rely heavily on unrealized capital gains on their stock portfolios to meet international banking standards. As the stock values in their portfolios decline with the market, Japanese banks are facing significant capital shortfalls. This has had and will continue to have a cascading effect as banks decline and bankruptcies continue. In the bubble economy of the 1980s, Japanese banks loaned heavily and freely based on the ever-spiraling values of Japanese real estate. However, as the real estate markets decline, the banks' customers are facing bankruptcies. This has exposed the soft underbelly of the Japanese banking system, since they loaned money based on over-priced false collateral.

Worse, it has even brought to light the various banking scandals that were not based on faulty economics but rather on devious and fraudulent collateral schemes involving billions of dollars in loans.

As Robert told the congressional committees, Japan's securities markets are dominated by a brokerage oligopoly permitted and even fostered by Japan's regulatory regime. Japanese banks provide myriad services to their primary customers far beyond financial intermediation or the banks' self-interests. Because of my family's experiences in the Japanese market, it raises the question of whether Japan is truly a market economy, as those of us in the West understand it. Perhaps it was time for the U.S. to begin to wake up to this fact.

In his 1991 testimony before the U.S. Congress, Robert addressed these very points and the ability of Japan to correct these ills.

> In my experiences and those of my father, Japan is unlikely to address these ills on its own. Indeed, the institutions best positioned to provide leadership toward reform are among those with the strongest interests in perpetuating the current system...
>
> I believe that only the United States is capable of providing impetus for critical reform. Movement in that direction, originating both in the Executive Branch and in Congress, already has begun.
>
> In Congress, Representative Robert Torricelli (D-NJ), along with original co-sponsors Representatives Mike Synar (D-OK), Tom McMillen (D-MD), and James Inhofe (R-OK), introduced House Resolution 3283, the Foreign Capital and Securities Markets Study Act of 1991. This measure would call upon Treasury to conduct a yearlong study of the implications for the United States of the structure and operation of Japan's capital and securities markets. A Senate version of the bill, S. 1861, has been introduced by Senator Tom Daschle (D-SD).
>
> I applaud these efforts, as well as any steps that will illuminate the global ramifications of the structure and operation of Japan's financial sector... I hope that [this] will spark debate and serious consideration of these topics. Ultimately, I hope that my efforts, along with the efforts of other concerned citizens and policy makers, will help to stimulate reform in Japan—reform that will benefit Japan as well as the rest of the world.

Consequences for U.S. Investors

What is critical for Americans to understand is that U.S. investors—especially large institutional investors like pension funds—have placed *billions* of dollars in Japanese securities. Those investments—and the pensioners' savings they reflect—could be in jeopardy. Look at what has happened to pension plans across the U.S. with the collapse of Enron. The very same could happen with other pension funds that have invested heavily in Japanese stocks, because Japanese markets are dominated and controlled by insiders who do not have the best interests of investors at heart and only serve their own interests.

The structure and operation of Japan's securities and capital markets contribute in myriad ways as barriers to U.S. investment in Japan. Stable shareholding largely prevents all but the friendliest of takeovers, while the Japanese corporate practice of preventing meaningful participation in corporate governance prevents those American shareholders who have acquired an ownership stake in a Japanese company from maximizing the value of their investments. Questionable practices permitted by loose stock market regulation enable Japanese management to fend off outsiders. The preferential treatment attainable by Japanese companies through cooperative relationships forged in securities markets is not available to American investors, thus creating investment barriers in the guise of higher costs than to local competitors. Moreover, because the securities markets are the ground upon which cooperative relationships among Japanese companies are created and nurtured through cross-shareholdings, interlocking directors, or stable shareholding relationships, the U.S. companies are effectively locked out of these cooperative relationships. Such relationships, facilitated by the securities markets, are at the heart of the exclusionary structural trade barriers confronted by Americans attempting to do business in Japan.

The consequences for the United States extend far beyond securities matters. Due to the structure and operation of Japan's capital and securities markets, major Japanese companies can raise cheap capital at virtually no cost. As I mentioned in Chapter Five, Sony raised some $6.5 billion in new equity and equity-based bond issues between 1986 and 1990. During that same period, Sony acquired Columbia Pictures and CBS Records for a reported combined total of $5.7 billion and yet Sony's cost of funds on these two companies was less than one percent.

With such low capital costs, it is almost as though Japanese companies can print their own money. With the full cooperation of the banks and their trillions of yen behind them, Japanese companies have a huge advantage over their U.S. counterparts.

Needless to say, the differential in capital costs has profound implications for competing American companies.

Perhaps the greatest failing of the United States government in this regard is that the United States' trade and financial policy toward Japan has been predicated upon the assumption that both economies are more or less market-based: that prices are determined by supply and demand; that prices "clear" the market and achieve an efficient allocation of resources; and that transactions occur as a result of rational economic decisions about price and quantity—in short, the fundamentals of a textbook market economy. However evidence about Japan's capital and securities markets suggests that Japan simply does not operate in this fashion, and may not be a free market at all. If this is so, then all of the United States' international trade and finance policies throughout the postwar era have been based upon flawed assumptions.

Impact on U.S. Exports

Another ramification of the structure and operation of Japan's securities markets for U.S. competitors is its impact on trade. The close, cooperative relationships among Japanese manufacturers—created and fostered through, among other things, reciprocal stock arrangements—impede the efforts of foreign suppliers and foreign service-providers to do business in Japan.

This factor has been recognized by the U.S. government in the context of the Structural Impediments Initiative (SII). The U.S. government has taken the position that *keiretsu* relationships impede U.S. access to the Japanese market. The Final Report of the SII working group concluded that *keiretsu* relationships also promote preferential group trade, negatively affect foreign direct investment in Japan, and may give rise to anti-competitive business practices.

As mentioned elsewhere, the exclusionary effects of *keiretsu* relationships are frequently the result of cooperative business relationships established and nurtured in Japan's securities markets. In a *keiretsu* structure, non-price factors can enter into the buying decision for goods. These factors could range from stable shareholding to preferential commercial lease terms, and can effectively freeze out foreign suppliers no matter the quality or price of their products. American companies in fact must compete not only with the price and quality offered by their Japanese competitors—a formidable task in itself—but also with a history of wide-ranging reciprocating "favors."

The same barriers that manufacturing sectors encounter in Japan would also be encountered by foreign service-providers seeking to compete with Japanese competitors who have cemented business relationships through cross-shareholding, stable shareholding, and purchases of high-priced new issues.

This unfair advantage is not only against foreigners but also within Japan itself, where companies are forced to rely on relationships rather than their skills. To do any kind of business, one must learn "the system." I have cooperated with Japanese companies as much as possible and have had many personal experiences trying to work within the system.

Sadao Umeda, the president of Kajima Construction & Co., Ltd. (one of Japan's largest construction contractors) wrote to me in October 1997 to thank me for our company's consultation with the Marunouchi-Ichome Project and for helping set up meetings for him. His letter offers a clear demonstration of "the system":

Mr. Peter To, vice president of Pacific Century Ltd, is in charge of the present construction. Mr. To has always given us high marks for our performance and earthquake-proof techniques in this area. We have ourselves explained to him on various occasions about our superior ability.

However, some say that Obayashi Corp. and Takenaka Corp., who have long been on friendly terms with the chairman, Mr. Richard Li, have a little advantage among the actual competition of our three companies (Obayashi Corp., Takenaka Corp., and ourselves). Because the final nomination is not decided, we are now making even more efforts for this project. It is our hope that you review the attached paper that briefly summarizes the circumstances up to this point.

I am hoping to meet again with the chairman, Mr. Li, and discuss this with him once more, but I also think it is very important to gain the understanding from Mr. Li Ka-shing; therefore, I would appreciate it if you could give us your further kind assistance and support in this matter.

This is truly an unfortunate situation because here was a Japanese businessman who was forced to navigate a labyrinth of personal ties and relationships to obtain the project rather than obtaining based on his company's ample qualifications. It is a genuine pity for those who don't know someone to help them, because no matter how skilled they are, they will never be able to compete.

Illegal Bid-Rigging in Business Circles

In the Oji Paper affair, the unanimous refusal by the securities houses to broker buy orders for Oji Paper shares was rooted in a decision made through *dango* (literally, "consultations," but commonly used as a euphemism for "bid-rigging") held within the industry under the guidance of the Ministry of Finance. In this fashion, illegal "consultations" within industries have been repeated time after time in Japan. Such insider dealing obviously has enormous implications for competition.

In some areas in particular, such as bids for construction work on public projects, *dango* has come to mean a pernicious abuse in which the successful bidding prices are determined in advance by the businesses concerned, and the payments awarded for bids that are conducted purely for form's sake exceed the actual costs. Every time such illegal bid-rigging arrangements are revealed to the Fair Trade Commission, the construction industry says that it will not happen again, but every year it becomes clear that there are absolutely no second thoughts in the industry about a practice that refuses to go away.

During the bidding for the New Kansai International Airport in 1986, the U.S. government declared that unfair price-fixing practices in the Japanese market were preventing American companies from participating, and the United States Department of Justice launched an investigation. As a result, it was learned that 140 companies, including leading general construction companies, had predetermined which companies would get the orders, and even the tendered bids were controlled, proving that the criticisms by the American side were correct.

Another bid-rigging arrangement was exposed in 1988, in the construction contracts for the U.S. naval base at the city of Yokosuka in Kanagawa Prefecture. Around 100 companies, including leading general contractors such as Kajima Corporation, Shimizu Corporation, and Obayashi Corporation, were cited and punished with suspensions. Later, the American side even called for a "Prohibition on Bid-Rigging" to be set down in black-and-white in a revision of the Japanese-American Construction Agreement of 1990, and the Japanese government reluctantly agreed to include a provision on the "observation of the Antitrust Act" in the document.

Despite such developments, it was revealed to the Fair Trade Commission in 1991 that bid rigging had been involved in the procurement of telecommunications equipment and machinery for U.S. military bases in Japan, e.g., the U.S. Army base at Yokota. The three companies that had engaged in the bid rigging were ordered to pay fines totaling ¥275 million.

These examples of bid rigging are ones that only involve the United States. Cases where only Japanese companies are involved are simply too numerous to mention. Naturally, the practice is not limited to the construction field alone but occurs in a large variety of corporations, including trading houses and oil companies. Most of these consist of illegal pricing agreements referred to as "black" or unauthorized cartels.

Why hasn't bid rigging disappeared? The reason is found in the structure of close-knit relationships existing among business, political, and bureaucratic circles. One reason is that the place that bureaucrats from the Ministry of Construction often look to for re-employment opportunities after they retire or leave the ministry (where they hope to land after their "descents from Heaven") are the construction companies. The bureaucrats play a key role in obtaining information that is absolutely indispensable for fixing prices from their government offices. In short, they are able to get hold of confidential information that is normally unavailable.

Another reason is that the politicians play a key role in keeping bid-rigging alive. This is because they look forward to receiving the votes and political contributions that the construction industry commands at election time. This identity of interests on the part of politicians, bureaucrats, and businessmen has given birth to the bid rigging that is part and parcel of Japan's unique structure of close-knit relationships. It is no wonder that Japan is quite fairly referred to as a "country of cozy ties, collusion, and bid-rigging."

Japanese Banking Problems and the U.S.

Japanese banks have played a pivotal role in the industrial development of Japan and number among the world's largest financial

institutions. Paradoxically, Japanese banks succumbed to the excesses of the 1980s, and are now confronted with problems that could
have much wider consequences both in Japan and in the global community.

Japanese city banks especially have provided multifaceted support
to Japanese industry. The financial regulatory regime administered by
the Ministry of Finance, along with Japan's high savings rate, enabled
banks to lend at low interest rates during the formative postwar period (1960s and 1970s). Banks developed special and close relationships with their manufacturing customers and provided management, stable shareholding, interlocking shareholding, financial
reserves, and similar services. In fact, *keiretsu* banks reportedly supplied some 80% of the capital raised by *keiretsu* manufacturing com-
ponents until the 1970s. Japanese banks, following administrative
guidance, also apparently loaned funds to Japanese corporations in
excess of normal limits on a systematic basis during this period, and
even would prevent the bankruptcy of a favored manufacturing concern with the reassurance that the central bank would support the
assisting bank in the event the bail-out became too burdensome.

For example, in the Kotani scandal mentioned previously, Saitama
Bank—who had supplied Janome Sewing Machine's top two officers—held a significant stake in Janome equity, and acquired an even
larger stake to reduce stock speculator Mitsuhiro Kotani's influence
in Janome's affairs. Along these lines, Oji Paper publicly thanked
Mitsui Bank for "rescuing" Oji Paper from myself and my fellow
Hong Kong investors; Mitsui Bank and its affiliates maintained their
stable shareholdings when we began to accumulate shares, and
absorbed the shares when we sold our stake after being forced to by
the Big Four. Likewise, Fuji Bank provided three successive presidents of Katakura Industries during the 1970s and 1980s. These
instances of close ties (one might even say incestuous) between
banks and industry are not isolated, but rather typical of the relationship between banks and their industrial customers.

Buoyed by booms in the real estate and equities markets through the 1980s, Japanese banks engaged in credit, lending, and investment practices that would prove troublesome in the 1990s and continue to be so today. Credit was freely available in Japan for risky and speculative ventures during the 1980s boom. For example, stock speculator Mitsuhiro Kotani bragged of the ease with which he could secure funds from Sumitomo Bank, one of Japan's most prestigious city banks. Kotani allegedly borrowed some $175 million from Sumitomo Bank to speculate in shares of Fujita Sightseeing and Kokusai Kogyo, activities that led ultimately to criminal charges against Mr. Kotani and Akinori Yamashita, a Sumitomo Bank branch manager. The chairman of Sumitomo Bank, Ichiro Isoda, resigned over the scandal.

This frantic lending into the bubble real estate and securities markets sounds disturbingly reminiscent of the savings and loan industry scandals here in America. The collateral, usually real estate and securities, accepted by the banks funding these speculative ventures was equally speculative and even fraudulent in some cases.

Since 1991, a number of Japanese banks have admitted to accepting "faked" or "forged" certificates of deposit as collateral for a staggering amount of loans. The largest single incident involved Toyo Shinkin Bank, which was a regional credit union. A branch manager allegedly forged at least thirteen deposit receipts for Ms. Nui Onoue, an Osake restaurateur and stock speculator. Ms. Onoue apparently then used the fraudulent deposits as collateral for some ¥342 billion ($2.44 billion at 140 yen to the dollar) in loans from a number of Japanese financial institutions, among them Industrial Bank of Japan (IBJ). IBJ's chairman and three directors resigned in October 1991 to atone for IBJ's role in the scandal but did not face criminal prosecution.

This incident was not isolated. By September 1991, three of the world's "Top Twenty" banks—Fuji Bank (No. 5), Tokai Bank (No. 13), and Kyowa Saitama Bank (No. 20)—had admitted to similar scams. In the case of Fuji Bank, a deputy manager of a Tokyo branch reportedly issued forged deposit receipts to several real estate companies, who used the forged receipts as collateral for an aggregate ¥260 billion (or $1.9 billion at 140 yen to the dollar) in loans from Japanese finance companies. According to a September 14, 1991 article in *The Economist*, Japanese bankers "know of ¥2 trillion (or $14.3 billion) in phony certificates of deposit that have been issued as bogus collateral for loans." The chairman of Fuji Bank resigned in early October 1991 to take responsibility for Fuji Bank's role in this scandal.

Fraudulent collateral is not the only source of insufficient security for bank loans in Japan. Speculative and inadequate collateral, especially in the form of real estate or securities, could prove to be an equal if not greater problem. As stock, real estate, and other asset markets have fallen, defaults on loans extended on those assets have increased. Bankruptcies, especially in the real estate sector, have been rising precipitously; in January 1991 alone they totaled ¥400 billion (nearly $2.9 billion) in liabilities, which more than doubled the previous year's average monthly rate. During the first seven months of 1991, more than 5,600 companies went bankrupt, leaving ¥4.0 trillion ($28.6 billion) in bad debts. Another ¥15 trillion ($107 billion) in debt has been restructured. Bankruptcies and loan defaults have reached staggering proportions during the 1990s and the crisis facing Japan and the current government puts Japan at a true crossroads.

Incredibly, Japanese banks were completely unprepared for these looming defaults. One analyst estimated that Japanese financial institutions had lent ¥100 trillion ($714 billion) for property development. Given the use of hidden assets in the form of real estate by Japanese corporations to secure all sorts of borrowing, Japanese banks' exposure to falling real estate markets is probably far greater. Yet Japanese banks have woefully inadequate loan loss reserves, and heretofore have not acted to increase them. Japanese banks have outstanding loans of ¥448 trillion ($3.2 trillion). Aggregate loan loss reserves against that total, however, stand at only ¥3.0 trillion ($21.4 billion), or 0.1% of total loans.

Due to the massive losses and the falling values of "hidden assets" (unrealized gains on securities in bank portfolios) upon which Japanese banks rely heavily to meet international capital standards, these factors have led to bank failures and tighter credit, a scenario disturbingly familiar to American observers.

After a decade of banking scandals and failures, the Japanese government is now faced with a massive bailout program. If Japan does not act to stem the tide, then things will only get worse.

Concealment and Procrastination

One of the greatest tragedies of Japan's economy has been the concealment of bad debts held by financial institutions and the procrastination in dealing with them. As stated above, during the period of the bubble economy in the 1980s, financial institutions in Japan were all involved in lending out a veritable flood of funds to the real estate industry without obtaining collateral that corresponded to the amount of the financing, an illegal method that constituted a violation of the Commercial Code. Is it any wonder that land prices soared to abnormal levels? A flustered government tried to apply the brakes, but financial institutions continued to pour massive amounts of funds into the property industry via roundabout financing through housing finance companies that were set up under the sponsorship of the Ministry of Finance.

As a result, a surge in both share prices and land prices to an extent that was divorced from reality, and the failure to exercise proper control invited the bursting of the bubble economy. If the Ministry of Finance had taken hard, decisive action at this juncture and subjected the housing finance companies (*jusen*) to a strict accounting, the Japanese economy might have emerged without serious damage. However, since the Ministry of Finance dragged its feet on the "*jusen* issue," the bad loans being carried by the financial institutions subsequently ballooned to astronomical figures.

Both the Ministry of Finance and the financial institutions down-played the staggering size of the bad loans and tried to cover them up. For example, in the case of Hyogo Bank, which went bankrupt in the summer of 1995, the figure of ¥60.9 billion for bad loans announced prior to the collapse shot up to ¥1.5 trillion after bank-ruptcy was declared. The Ministry of Finance resuscitated it with the injection of ¥500 billion in public funds and changed its name to Midori Bank. However, it collapsed again in 1999—before even four years had passed—and was merged with Hanshin Bank, at which time a further injection of ¥1.56 trillion in public funds was made.

Why was a failed regional bank bailed out so many times? It turned out that its president had previously been the director gener-al of the Banking Bureau of the Ministry of Finance. Once again, the devious truth behind the scenes comes to light. Unfortunately, this action has cost the citizens of Japan more than ¥2 trillion. Perhaps even more surprisingly, this ever-failing bank has not been called to account for such an incredible waste of public funds.

The Japanese government has prepared as much as ¥60 trillion in public funds to deal with the financial crisis, and as of March 1999, it had injected ¥7.46 trillion of these funds into leading banks. It has been decided to inject public funds into regional banks in the future as well. Thanks to these therapeutic measures, financial uncertainty has receded for the moment, and it appears as if the first step has been taken toward restoring Japan's economic health. Under these circumstances, there is definitely a general perception that the gov-ernment's injection of public funds has been the right thing to do.

But it's a false hope. This type of rationale is simply not correct. This is because, with some exceptions, the parties who precipitated the financial crisis (the managers of the financial institutions and the Ministry of Finance—whose duty it was to supervise and guide those institutions) have not been called to account in the slightest degree.

The managers of the banks that received injections of public funds are hardly better than kidnappers looking for a ransom, and the

Ministry of Finance is the kidnappers' accomplice. The kidnappers (the bank managers) took a hostage (a financial panic) and neatly extorted a ransom (public funds). The police (the government) paid the ransom to rescue the hostage but then failed to arrest the criminals. Indeed, as far as the accomplice (the Ministry of Finance) was concerned, it ignored the crime altogether.

Public funds are taxes paid by the citizens. Therefore, those responsible for creating an excessive burden for the Japanese people ought to be severely punished. It seems that those in Japan's iron triangle of politicians, bureaucrats, and businessmen who are well connected with the authorities are rarely found guilty of a crime, no matter what kind of illegality they become involved in.

For example, Yamaichi Securities hid losses from failures in managing funds in a paper company overseas, and repeatedly dressed up its accounts. On December 21, 1999, Yamaichi Securities went on public trial for doctoring their accounts, but in its defense it claimed, "[The illegal conduct of concealing losses] was committed on the instructions of the then Ministry of Finance Securities Bureau Director General Matsuno" and "Why is no one from the government or the Bank of Japan sitting in the defendants' chairs?"

However, on March 28, 2000, the Tokyo District Court delivered a guilty verdict against former President Atsuo Miki and former Chairman Tsugio Yukihira of Yamaichi Securities for the filing of a false securities report and for making illegal distributions. The court gave the two a prison sentence and a suspended sentence respectively. The verdict stated that the concealment of losses was pernicious and the crimes of the defendants, which brought the company to bankruptcy, were grave. However, the person who had suggested the concealment of the losses was then Ministry of Finance Securities Bureau Director General Matsuno—who himself admitted this in testimony before the National Diet.

Amazingly, despite this confession, the Tokyo District Court did not utter a single word about this involvement by a ministry bureaucrat. The ordinary commonsense point of view would consider the involvement by a government official to be the most serious crime of all, but Japan's judiciary does not hold persons at the center of power accountable for such crimes. It is as though they are completely blind to crimes committed by anyone in the high-ranking government positions. Given that collusion between the administration and the judiciary still seems to be rampant, one can only be deeply worried about Japan's future and its implications for the U.S.

Moreover, requests to banks for the forgiveness of debts, centering on the construction industry, also pose a problem. One reason why banks are now carrying such a huge backlog of bad debts is that they extended excessive financing to general construction contractors investing in land during the bubble economy. Accordingly, the general construction contractors owe huge debts to the banks, and with the onset of the business crisis, the prices of many stocks are poised to fall below par value. As mentioned above, the construction industry in Japan is a hotbed of concessions from administrative and bureaucratic circles. If construction companies collapse, this will cause difficulties for politicians and civil servants. Therefore, the injection of public funds is directed not only toward saving the banks, but also toward bailing out the construction companies.

It isn't just the construction companies that are asking the banks to forgive their debts; manufacturing and trading concerns are doing so as well. For instance, the trading company Tomen is asking for the forgiveness of ¥200 billion in debts. Isn't it good business ethics— to say nothing of normal business practices—to repay debt out of future profits rather than to ask for the forgiveness of such extraordinary debts? If debts are so easily forgiven, what is the point, then, of taking out a loan? Simply open the vault doors and let everyone take what they want. Have the bank managers forgotten that loans are *supposed* to be paid back? An even more important question for the discussion at hand is will they be so forgiving with the loans that U.S. companies and government have taken out? Or will they look to the U.S. to pay back loans that Japanese companies are defaulting on?

The consequence of illegal conduct on the part of business and the Ministry of Finance is a heavy burden weighing down on the people of Japan. Of the ¥84.99 trillion budget for the year 2000, ¥32.61 trillion came from issuing national bonds. This amounted to some 38.4% of the budget. Subsequently, the total value of national bonds issued was expanded to ¥364 trillion. This represented money borrowed by the citizens of Japan and worked out to a loan of ¥3.03 million being borne by each citizen. For a family of four, the amount borrowed comes to more than ¥12 million or $85,714.

While ¥60 trillion in public funds has been prepared to bail out the financial institutions, the liability for the mammoth issuance of national bonds by the current government will be passed on to the next generation, which will be saddled with cleaning up the mess left behind from the illegalities perpetrated by the preceding generation. Right now in Japan, government officials have been declaring that a financial crisis has been averted and that recovery from the depths of the economic downturn is under way. But if the persons responsible for bringing Japan to the brink of disaster are never punished and the situation remains ambiguous at best, then it cannot be said that the future of Japan's economy is as rosy as the government would have its citizens—and the rest of the world—believe.

The American Response

When my son Robert testified in 1991 before a House subcommittee, no agency had yet conducted an impartial, official and, above all, comprehensive investigation of the structure and operation of Japan's securities and capital markets, and their implications for U.S. policy.

Robert was called in to testify on behalf of House Resolution 3283, the Foreign Capital and Securities Markets Study Act of 1991, which called upon the Treasury Department to conduct a one-year study of the structure, operation, and practices of Japan's capital and securities markets, and their implications for the United States.

In his 1992 speech to introduce the bill, Senator Daschle said:

Mr. President, the amendment directs the Treasury Department to conduct a one-year study of Japan's financial system. It is derived from S. 1861, legislation that I introduced last year and that is cosponsored by Senator Brown.

As witnesses have testified before the Finance Committee, United States policymakers need a better understanding of the Japanese financial system, its influence on the United States economy, and the competitive advantages the system confers on Japanese corporations.

Japan's financial structure has given Japanese firms access to cheap capital and other advantages. Financial ties among Japanese firms deter foreign investment in Japanese public corporations.

Japanese institutions have been heavily involved in financing the United States Government's budget deficit. Instability in Japanese financial markets could affect the ability of Japanese investors to finance our debt.

Because of the importance of the Japanese financial system to the competitiveness of American companies, and to the long-term stability of the United States economy, policymakers need a more thorough understanding of how the Japanese financial system works and how it affects our economy.

I am aware of no opposition to this amendment.

The bill was passed by both houses of Congress as part of the 1992 tax bill. Unfortunately, President Bush vetoed the tax bill. As a result, Robert was called to testify once more before the House Subcommittee on March 25, 1993, under the new Clinton administration. What follows is some of his testimony.

Thank you very much, Mr. Chairman. I am happy to be here. My name is Robert Wang, and I am from Los Angeles,

California. I am testifying today to urge the subcommittee to add the language of H.R. 420 to this year's Treasury Department to conduct a comprehensive year-long study of Japan's financial crisis and what that crisis may mean for the United States.

Nearly two years ago, I came to Washington to meet with government leaders. My purpose was to warn our government about a potential collapse of Japan's stock market. That prediction, sadly, proved accurate. I come to Washington today with another prediction. Within the next two years, one or more banks, major Japanese banks, will fail. And such a bank failure could ripple through the entire Japanese banking industry...

In 1991, I wrote a comprehensive white paper on Japan's financial crisis and among my conclusions are, one, that the Japanese stock market had collapsed and showed few signs of recovery...The sole criticism of the White Paper was from Deputy Vice Minister Takatoshi Kato of Japan's Ministry of Finance, who claimed that our family had failed to work for reform in Japan, while nothing can be further from the truth...

[With the massive bank scandals and lack of adequate loan loss reserves,] many smaller banks in Japan would have collapsed already if the Japanese government had not encouraged larger banks to merge with them. Because Japanese banks need to meet [international banking] capital standards by next Wednesday, the Japanese government has taken an utterly alien policy initiative.

It is aggressively intervening in the Tokyo stock market by investing billions of dollars of public funds and the government ministry is also pressuring the private sector to put billions more into the market. It would be as if the Treasury Department in the United States would use taxpayer dollars to invest directly in the New York Stock Exchange to prop up the Dow Jones index while the SEC would call around to pension funds and other financial institutions encouraging them to invest...

This massive market intervention is unlikely to prevent the bank failures that I predict. Not even a finance ministry can rewrite the laws of economics. But it does serve to illustrate how different the Japanese market is from our own and how little we understand about it. It is for this reason I am supporting H.R. 420.

The predictions that Robert gave in his testimony in 1991 and in 1993 proved to be very accurate. Japan's financial policy subsequently disintegrated, and numerous securities companies and banks went under.

Unfortunately, although this bill was passed, signed into law, and received widespread support, the study itself of Japan's policies received little attention. Although it is hard to speculate why this would be, perhaps the lack of attention was due to the overall ignorance of the Japanese problem. Perhaps the problems in Japan are viewed as far off or have little direct effect on America. Or perhaps the wounds from "losing" to the Japanese in the 1980s were still too raw and in some ways the problems in Japan were seen as "just desserts."

Whatever the reason, ignoring the problem with the Japanese system does not make it go away and certainly will not prevent the problems from reaching the shores of the United States.

Currently, Japan is suffering through one of its worst economic downturns. Despite this, even now, there seems to be little emphasis in the United States on understanding the Japanese problem, perhaps because the Japanese no longer seem to be the "threat" that they were during their bubble economy of the 1980s when it was feared they would "take over." And yet this same lackadaisical attitude could very well lead to a severe downturn in the United States' own economy, because if Japan was to suddenly sink into the black hole that it has created for itself, the U.S. could very well become entrapped. The time for action and to demand change from Japan is now, before it is too late. They need our help and direction and not a standoffish attitude.

Private Action by U.S. Investors

In 1996, James A. Baker, the former American Secretary of State and former Secretary of Treasury, sent the following letter to Securities Bureau Director General Atsushi Nagano of the Ministry of Finance in regard to the Oji Paper Company matter:

September 27, 1996
Mr. Atsushi Nagano
Director General, Securities Bureau
Ministry of Finance

Dear Mr. Nagano:

I represent in an advisory capacity Mr. T. H. Wang of Hong Kong, a prominent international financier and businessman whom I believe to be a man of principle, integrity, and tenacity. In that connection, I write to share with you my views on how the Securities Bureau (the "Bureau") of the Ministry of Finance (the "Ministry") can help resolve a longstanding dispute between Mr. Wang and the Japanese paper and pulp products company, Oji Paper and the four most substantial securities firms in Japan (i.e. Nomura, Nikko, Daiwa and Yamaichi or the "Big Four").

As U.S. Secretary of State and as Secretary of Treasury, I strongly supported and often espoused the critical importance of the close relationship between the United States and Japan. In doing so, I occasionally criticized (hopefully in a constructive and fair manner) what many in the West viewed as the reflexive insularity of the Japanese financial system. It seems to me that the Oji Paper matter has policy implications that exceed its commercial aspects, and therefore, I believe a mutually satisfactory resolution of the matter would demonstrate to the international financial community the substantial progress that Japan has made in opening its financial system. It would constitute a significant step in preserving and strengthening Japan's reputation as a nation of economic opportunity, and it would certainly strengthen the hand of those like myself who continue to speak out about the importance of a 'global partnership' between Japan and the United States. I am writing to you in this regard because the Bureau played a role in precipitating the dispute between Mr. Wang on the one hand and the Big Four and Oji Paper on the other, and I believe it can also play a critical role in resolving that dispute.

According to the findings of the Tokyo District Court, in September of 1977, the Bureau expressed concern to the Big Four over a pattern of acquisitions of Oji Paper stock by Mr. Wang and other Hong Kong investors. This concern was based on allegations on the part of Oji Paper, wholly unfounded, that Mr. Wang was seeking to "greenmail" Oji Paper. The Big Four indicated to Mr. Wang that the Bureau's expression of concern was intended as "guidance" reflecting the Ministry's objections to Mr. Wang's investments in Oji Paper stock, and as a result thereof, they instituted a "self-restraint program" under which they each agreed to refrain from executing further purchase orders on behalf of Mr. Wang and the Hong Kong investors. Prior to the Bureau's intervention, Mr. Wang and the Hong Kong investors had been acquiring Oji Paper stock in full compliance with Japanese law and upon the recommendation of several leading Japanese securities houses, notably including the Big Four.

The Bureau's response to the spurious charges made by Oji Paper thus set in motion a pattern of activity on the part of the Big Four that directly caused a number of adverse consequences for Mr. Wang. Specifically, those consequences included the following:

- As noted by the Tokyo District Court (the 'Court') in its judgment regarding this matter, Oji Paper and the Big Four arbitrarily, without notice or cause, stopped accepting purchase orders from Mr. Wang and the Hong Kong investors for Oji Paper stock.
- As further reflected in the Court's judgment, Mr. Wang was unfairly characterized as a "greenmailer," a personal insult for which there was no basis in fact.
- As revealed by a senior Nomura official's personal diary, which has just recently been authenticated by Nomura and accepted into evidence by the Tokyo High Court, the Big Four securities houses and Oji Paper colluded in setting the price for repurchase of the Oji Paper stock from Mr. Wang. (According to the Nomura official's diary, both the Ministry and the Tokyo Stock Exchange were made aware of this price-fixing activity, yet nothing was done to prevent it.)

Fundamentally, these consequences caused damage to Mr. Wang's reputation as an international investor and deprived his investor group of the economic opportunity of realizing a return on its investment.

The fallout of this dispute extends beyond the damage suffered by Mr. Wang, however. Oji Paper and the Big Four have suffered harm to their international reputations for their conduct in implementing and defending the Bureau's administrative guidance. Although the final outcome of Mr. Wang's litigation may well hold them accountable for their actions in a strict legal sense, it is my belief that they probably acted out of a perverse and ultimately counterproductive sense of duty to their government and country.

And therefore, this dispute will continue to be an embarrassment to Japan for as long as it goes on. The discriminatory treatment imposed on Mr. Wang by the Japanese financial establishment and legal system is known in international economic and financial circles. This dispute and particularly the Ministry's indifferent reaction to it merely serve to confirm serious concerns about the openness of Japanese capital markets to foreign investment on a fair and transparent basis.

Therefore, in the hope that this matter might be resolved in a mutually acceptable fashion, I would urge the Bureau to intervene once again, but this time in order to broker a resolution of this dispute and thereby eliminate what I would think would be a source of continuing embarrassment. Perhaps the Bureau could meet again with the Big Four and this time offer guidance to settle this matter. In this fashion, the Bureau and the Ministry could rectify, at least in part, the unfortunate consequences of its initial intervention nearly twenty years ago.

I look forward to hearing from you.

Sincerely,

James A. Baker, III

Despite the importance of the letter, Mr. Nagano failed to reply. Mr. Baker sent a subsequent note requesting a reply to his previous letter, but was once again ignored. If the Ministry of Finance had addressed the concerns expressed by Mr. Baker in his letter, perhaps more effective monetary and fiscal policies might have been implemented that would have minimized the subsequent financial collapse and recession.

A long-time friend of mine, Mr. Takujiro Hamada, was a states-
man who had served in the Ministry of Finance and who became the
Vice Minister for Foreign Affairs and Chairman of the Committee
on Judicial Affairs in the House of Representatives. He suggested I
write to Mr. Nagano as well, who was one year junior to him when
my friend was working in the Ministry of Finance. I took his suggestion and wrote to him in September 1996 after he personally visited Mr. Nagano on August 27th to drop off some of my documents
and discuss them with him.

Here is part of my letter to him:

> Mr. Hamada told me later that during the meeting, you
> had ardently talked about the necessity to revitalize the
> Japanese securities market and to promote the participation
> of individual investors in stock investment. I hold a view,
> however, that regaining the individual investors' confidence
> in the Tokyo securities market is a prerequisite.
>
> When the Nikkei average rose over ¥40,000, companies
> seized the opportunity and issued tens of trillion yen shares
> at market price to raise funds from individual investors. The
> bursting of the bubble economy triggered a steep decline in
> share prices, as a result of which such individual investors
> suffered a great loss. However, the Ministry of Finance
> turned a blind eye to all this. Unless the normalization of the
> Tokyo securities market is implemented, individual investors
> will not be easily enticed after the bitter lesson they have
> learned.
>
> Under the present economic system in Japan, numerous
> unjust, unlawful acts are allowed to happen. Manipulation of
> share prices is a semi-open secret, and collusion between
> issuing companies and securities companies is as common as
> a cold. The supervising authorities of the Ministry of
> Finance and the Tokyo Stock Exchange turn a blind eye to
> such malpractices, breaching their due diligence and commit-

ting unlawful acts in collusion with them. It would be very difficult to revitalize the securities market without addressing the issues of the Japanese system that allows a back-scratching alliance of government and big business with their collusive hush-ups.

The evidence and documents I have shown you in relation to the "Oji Paper Company Ltd. Incident" will clearly indicate the seriousness of the collusive nature of the relationship between politics and business in Japan.

As he did with Mr. Baker's letter, Mr. Nagano also ignored my letter.

In 1998, it was discovered that Nagano, this same Securities Bureau Director General, had accepted a large amount of entertainment from the financial establishment and was forced to resign. This was regrettable for him personally, but perhaps his lack of integrity demonstrates why he took no action in regard to either Mr. Baker's letter or my own.

Further Efforts

I have undertaken many other efforts to try to bring about change in Japan, not least of which is the writing of this book and publishing it in America. It is my firm belief and great hope that those U.S. citizens who read this book will feel inspired to act as well. There is no such thing as a "Japanese Problem." It's a world problem, just as one cannot drop a stone in a pool without the ripples reaching the other shores. The citizens of Japan need our help and it is very apparent that the Japanese government seems frozen, incapable of making change on its own.

Yosahiko Sakurai, writing in the August 17, 1994, issue of the *Nikkei Financial Daily*, commented on a letter my son Robert had received from Robert Colby, Deputy Director of the Division of Market Regulation of the SEC.

Mr. Colby had indicated the SEC's willingness to take up the issues brought up by Mr. Wang by saying in his reply letter that "We at the SEC routinely meet with our counterparts from Japan's Ministry of Finance...We also use these meetings to address matters of concern to U.S. persons participating in the Japanese securities markets."

Is Japan, the undersigned wonders, really unable to change its system unless it is forced to do so by "*gaiatsu*" [(foreign pressure)] from the United States?

Individual American investors in Japanese securities can indeed act in a number of ways to encourage reform in Japan. These steps can be both passive and active.

U.S. investors simply can "vote with their feet" on the acceptability of the structure and operation of Japan's securities markets, for example. By taking their money out of Japan's markets and refusing to invest in the future until meaningful reforms are effectuated, American investors can shine critical illumination on the problems.

American shareholders can take more active approaches with companies in which they already own shares. They can refuse to invest in a stock of a company that failed to adhere to free-market principles and make it known to them why they chose not to invest. If they already hold shares in a company, they could ask that these corporations denounce the use of *sokaiya* to intimidate shareholders. American shareholders could ask for the creation of a board committee to supervise and report to shareholders on the management of the company's stock portfolio and also ask the company for commitments to pay dividends commensurate with the company's profitability.

This more active approach was demonstrated during the summer of 1991. Two U.S. pension funds—California Public Employees' Retirement System (CalPERS) and College Retirement Equities Fund (CREF)—both objected to loss guarantee payments by the Big Four. CalPERS placed Nomura Capital Management, which handles $380 million in CalPERS assets, on "probation" for its activities. Both pension funds questioned the volume of future trading in which they would engage with Japanese securities firms.

In the summer of 1991, American investors registered their displeasure with barriers to participation in corporate governance of such major Japanese corporations as Sony and Sumitomo Bank by casting proxy votes against management policies. In the words of CalPERS director Dale Hanson, the U.S. investors were "just trying to import some Yankee activism over to Japan."

These examples of "Yankee activism" illustrate how private American investors can apply "*gaiatsu*"—or foreign pressure—to encourage reform in Japan.

American pressure could go beyond such immediate corporate concerns, however, to insist that the Japanese company itself work for reforms such as: the tighter de-listing standards to discourage stable shareholding and encourage greater market liquidity; the immediate deregulation of brokerage commissions; and creation of an independent stock market regulatory agency. Disclosure of *keiretsu* and similar relationships could and should also be demanded.

In this manner, Japanese corporations, stimulated by American investors, could be transformed into agents for change in Japan—changes that would benefit Japan as well as its trading partners.

While it is understandable for readers to feel that they are only one small voice and may be hesitant to approach Japanese corporate managers, I would hope that American readers would put such fears behind them. After all, this is the same attitude of the Japanese people that has allowed the Japanese corporate and financial structure to deteriorate into what it is today: a mess. The Japanese people need the assistance of the American people and by adding our voices to those brave souls in Japan who are asking for reform, it may be that we can truly bring about change.

One further idea is for American readers to approach their representatives and senators and encourage them to investigate the

Japanese financial structure and also encourage them do something about it rather than merely investigate it.

I have been contacting congressmen and have also approached the SEC. On December 22, 2000, I wrote to the SEC because I was concerned when I found out that securities companies in Japan were seeking public listing in the United States. I wanted to be sure that the securities companies would have to make a full disclosure of their unethical business practices to the SEC and I enclosed a briefing on some of my experiences in dealing with the Japanese to put the SEC on alert that many of the Japanese securities companies' practices would violate U.S. law. I was encouraged when I received a reply on February 1, 2001, not only welcoming my letter but also reassuring me that "should Nomura Securities seek a listing in the United States, it will be required to disclose information regarding litigation or potential litigation in the United States or elsewhere that is material to an investment decision." Also encouraging was that they said, "We appreciate your interest in writing...Please communicate with us in the future regarding any matters you believe we should consider regarding United States securities laws."

What a difference from their Japanese counterparts!

Needless to say, I was only too happy to provide them with additional material.

I truly believe that the U.S. can and should bring pressure to bear on Japan to change its ways. We in America rightfully demand and expect fair play. If the Japanese corporations and investors expect to have free access to our markets here in the U.S., then it is only right that we have equal access to the Japanese markets. The rules that apply here which guarantee free access to the markets should apply equally in Japan.

Finally, by raising our voices together, we will be able to help free the Japanese investors from the tyranny of the Japanese bureaucracy. If Japan's politicians, bureaucrats, and businessmen fail to listen to our advice, Japan will be left trailing in the wake of the global society. But unfortunately, that may have dire consequences for the U.S. as well. We need to bring pressure on them to change before it is too late.

I sincerely hope that you will add your voice to mine and perhaps together we can help change Japan's corrupt system, averting a worldwide financial crisis.

Chapter Nine

The End of the Katakura Affair

In one's youth, it's easy to believe in the sanctity of mankind's institutions. The courts and elected officials are held in a certain esteem or reverence, and one looks up to them as protectors of justice and upholders of the law. However, as one grows older, one becomes wiser. Wisdom is not always an easy thing to come by and it is sometimes very costly in many ways.

It had been difficult during the Oji Paper affair to believe that so many people would conspire against us Hong Kong investors. When first confronted with such a conspiracy, it defies logic, as though your brain refuses to accept what is happening. Not only was it difficult to believe, it was even harder to accept what had happened.

Now, here again in the Katakura affair, there were people who conspired against us. This time, though, the attack seemed almost more blatant and even more savage. First, we had been intentionally set up by the securities companies, which had prepared a false report in order to convince us to buy shares of Katakura Industries. When we tried to protect our investment by making suggestions to Katakura, we were told to leave them alone and leave them to their own devices; methods we surely knew would not benefit the shareholders of Katakura Industries, but only those on the inside who had their own interests at heart.

Then, when the government tried to open up the doors to foreign investment—a move that would have allowed us to gain greater control of Katakura Industries—the management of Katakura appealed to the government to protect them. Astonishingly, the government agreed to assist them—much to our dismay and to the embarrassment of Japanese citizens. When we filed complaints against those in power who were responsible for such an action, the government suddenly dropped their designation.

It was the lies and the direct actions against me and my friends that astounded me. Collusion was one thing, but a lie is something that is designed to hurt an individual and protect oneself. Why should the effort of simply trying to invest in companies that I believed in and in which I thought could give me a good return on my money be such a struggle? All I wanted was a simple investment. This should not be a difficult matter and yet it seemed every time I tried to have a simple investment, it turned against me.

The Shareholders' Representative Suit

Although the request for an auditor to look into Katakura's affair had been denied, I lodged a shareholders' representative suit in the Tokyo District Court, with all the directors of Katakura Industries as the defendants, seeking that they pay compensation to the company's shareholders for losses in the amount of ¥730 million due to their illegal activities.

During the course of this trial, the methods that the defendants used to slander and defame me were exactly the same as those employed in the Oji Paper case. They claimed that we had collected various stocks (Kao Soap, Ajinomoto, Meiji Milk, and Oji Paper) and then sold them through securities companies via cross-trading, requesting that the issuing companies either buy the shares themselves or make arrangements for someone else to buy the shares.

Of course all of this was groundless. However, in judging this case, the judge presumed a factual pattern as follows.

The plaintiffs, the Hong Kong investors group, collected from 10 million to 37 million shares in various companies, i.e., Kao Soap Corp. in 1975; Ajinomoto Co., Inc. and Meiji Milk Products Co., Ltd. in 1976; and Oji Paper Co., Ltd. in 1977, and within the space of around a year and a half after the respective acquisitions, sold all or most of the shares in the respective companies through Daiwa Securities and other securities firms by means of so-called cross-trading (trading in which a transaction is established by having the same securities company become a seller and a buyer at the same time), and [the Hong Kong investors] earned a considerable profit on transactions in the stocks of the first three companies.

In cases where it is desired to sell a large volume of shares by cross-trading, it normally happens that seeking a buyer is not possible without substantial involvement by the issuing company, and it can be surmised that the various companies above were also involved in the cross-trading of their respective shares (however, there is no evidence sufficient to conclude that the plaintiff's side requested the respective issuing companies to purchase the shares or to arrange for buyers).

Even in this written judgment, the judge used expressions filled with animosity. He stated that I engaged in greenmail demands, even while saying that there was no proof.

This is totally incoherent logic. It isn't the judge's job to speculate on what the lack of evidence implies. It would be like concluding a person should be branded a murderer even though there was no evidence to support it.

The judge also said that it is normally not possible to find a buyer for such large volume of shares without the substantial involvement of the issuing company. This is a reference to the normal business practice of involving the issuing company in large share transactions and, in particular, refers to the practice of shares purchased by the issuing company being placed with stable shareholders with whom the issuing company has cross-holdings.

But I have never—not even once—asked for the involvement of an issuing company in selling a large volume of its shares. To the contrary, I have been embroiled in outrageous difficulties because of them, and not because of anything that I have done or any laws that I have broken.

In short, all this judge did was give approval to the illegal Japanese-style securities transactions that are not accepted in international society and which would in fact be illegal in other countries. Such business practices must come to a halt if Japan wants to truly join the rest of the global economy.

Have the Japanese Lost Their Integrity?

I had long held the Japanese people in high regard for being devoted to justice and for being loyal to the truth. But during the above proceedings, Daiwa Managing Director Hosoi stood to testify in court, and under oath declared, "I only met Mr. T. H. Wang once." He also made a statement that I had wanted to settle. Unless you yourself have been coldly betrayed by someone you trusted, you cannot imagine the shock and deep pain of it. To have someone lie about you when you had thought they might support you, chills one to the bone.

You may recall from Chapter Two that when Vice President Chino of Daiwa Securities and President Yamanaka of Daiwa Hong Kong came to visit me, it was in gratitude for the sale of the Kao Soap shares. The reason that the top people at Daiwa Securities came one after another to show their gratitude was because the buyback of the Kao Soap shares from me had been very much appreciated by the Japanese side.

I also received a visit from Managing Director Hosoi of Daiwa, who said that he would like to be introduced to Hong Kong clients. I also introduced him to the consul-general of the Republic of

Nauru, an island country in the Pacific Ocean that is rich in phosphate ore. At the time, the consulate-general of this republic was leasing office space in a building that I owned, and I was also on close terms with the president. Through that connection, I introduced Managing Director Hosoi to the consul-general. From a subsequent newspaper report, I learned that an investment consultancy company from the Daiwa Securities *keiretsu* had been entrusted with the management of a large volume of funds from the Republic of Nauru.

Later, Managing Director Hosoi came to visit me in Hong Kong once again. At that time, he asked me to introduce him to various Hong Kong business figures. I introduced him to three of my friends, who were not only some of the richest men in Hong Kong, but also in the world. I went out of my way to manage these connections for him by juggling not only Managing Director Hosoi's tight schedule but those of the people I was trying to introduce him to, and it was only by being unreasonably pushy that I was able to arrange for him to meet all three persons on the same day.

Despite what I had done for him, Managing Director Hosoi of Daiwa Securities gave testimony in court in which he lied about me and was unfavorable to me. I still feel sick about it to this day, thinking what a betrayal it was. Even though I don't particularly want thanks, I remember very clearly that he had thanked me at the time I had made the connection on his behalf. But I have absolutely no memory of having done anything to deserve being stabbed in the back like this.

All I was doing by this lawsuit was saying that I would not tolerate illegal conduct on the part of the companies that I invested in, but perhaps he thought I had other motives and that was why he decided to betray me. In this action, I was simply requesting the defendants repay the losses that they had caused the shareholders of Katakura. Even if I won the suit, I wouldn't earn a single penny. Quite to the contrary, all it did was cost me considerable time, effort, and expense. I simply wanted to recover my good name.

Share Price Manipulation

Katakura worked very hard to keep control of their own shares, despite the fact that they were a publicly listed corporation. It was as though they wanted people to simply give them their money but did not want to have any of the responsibility or accountability that would go along with that.

As you'll recall from the earlier chapter on Katakura, I didn't trust the Bank of Japan's answer to our inquiries about the availability of shares to foreigners and therefore had one of my son's American friends buy some shares, which he managed to do. However, they soon cut him off as well, saying in their defense that the shares weren't suitable for American investors due to their "wildly speculative nature." During August 1981, when he had managed to purchase 10,000 shares, Katakura Industries shares ranged from an average high of ¥400 to an average low of ¥395—a range of just five yen—and the turnover was no more than 250,000 shares per month. This was wildly speculative?

This amazing stability and absolute lack of volatility continued. For approximately three years, starting from when Katakura Industries became a designated company in 1980, the price hovered around ¥400 per share.

But it was not only foreign investors who were being pressured by Katakura. There are also some examples of coercion being put on Japanese investors. In 1982, when it was still impossible for me to go on buying any more shares in Katakura Industries (the government restriction was not lifted until May 1984), I recommended the company to a Japanese friend who was my golfing partner in Hong Kong. Even though I couldn't personally buy shares, I still thought Katakura was a good investment because of their latent assets, despite the false entries I'd discovered.

But when he invested, he was pressured by the following report from the securities companies.

On November 1, 1982, an order was received at the request of the client [name withheld] for the purchase of 50,000 shares in Katakura Industries (Co. Ltd.). However, since there is currently an ongoing dispute with a Hong Kong shareholder, we have made the following purchase this day on the condition that it is confirmed that the person in question is the true investor and that the shares will definitely be kept by the company after they have been transferred to the name of the person in question. (Remainder omitted).

Using this report as a means of intimidation, he was then forced to sign the following memorandum for the securities company:

Memorandum

1. Shares in Katakura Industries Co., Ltd.—32,000 shares.

The above are shares that I have purchased finally and solely with my own assets, and I hereby pledge that in the future I will not cause any trouble for your company.

Signed (Name omitted)
November 12, 1982

On being subjected to this kind of blatant pressure, neither Japanese investors nor foreigners could buy Katakura Industries shares with any sort of freedom. It's no wonder, then, that the share price of Katakura Industries remained stagnant.

The Sale of Katakura

As you'll recall, in March 1983, we decided to try to sell off the Katakura shares, but even this proved to be difficult. At first they had successfully blocked us from buying any more shares. Now, it seemed that they wanted to hold on to our money.

When I sent letters to eleven Japanese securities companies in Hong Kong asking them to sell, each of the leading securities firms (the "Big Four" and New Japan, Kankaku, Wako, Okasan, Yamatane, Sanyo, and Kokusai) ignored the letters. I sent letter after letter asking to sell, and in the end I received answers from only four companies, namely, Nomura, Yamatane, Wako and Kokusai. However, the answers from all four companies were to the effect that: "There is no interest in Katakura shares" or "We cannot find any buyers."

It is simply impossible that eleven securities houses, one and all, would ignore a sale order for shares or be unable to find buyers. It is unbelievable for securities companies to say that there is no interest in a client's order, even though they earn large commissions on orders for large volume sales. This was the same kind of set-up as the unanimous self-restraint program by the eight securities companies in the Oji Paper Company case. One can only imagine that Katakura Industries may have even appealed to the Ministry of Finance to prevail on the securities companies to act in unison. Besides, the securities companies' statement to us that there was no interest in Katakura shares was a ridiculous and false statement, one that we knew not to be true since we could plainly see from the newspaper reports of the TSE transactions that shares in Katakura were indeed being traded. If no one was interested in them, then the volume of shares traded would be zero.

After much struggle, we did finally manage to sell small amounts of shares in October 1983. However, under the circumstances, taking this to be a repetition of the Oji Paper Company matter and considering that the share price would absolutely not rise, I decided to change tactics. I decided to place market orders with all the securities companies of around 5,000 shares each time at any price, not caring even if it went down to ¥1 per share. This was because with market orders, the price would go down, but the securities companies could not refuse my buy order because by now, the restrictions had been lifted.

At this time, I had brought a suit in Hong Kong claiming compensation for losses against Nikko, Yamaichi, and Kankaku, the three securities companies that had encouraged our investment based on documents with false information on the latent assets of Katakura Industries. From around February 1984, when it became clear that the Japanese side would lose in the Hong Kong case, the share price of Katakura Industries suddenly began to go up, reaching a high of ¥730. At this point, my lawyer came to me and told me that if I made a profit on the sale owing to the rising price then my case for compensation for losses wouldn't stand because I couldn't show that I'd suffered a loss.

It's my own personal belief that there were "black hands" behind the scenes here at work to prop up the share prices and stifle my case. Unfortunately, I have no way to prove such a thing but that is still my educated belief.

So I took my lawyer's advice and I sold everything, keeping only the 1,000 shares required to maintain my case.

By December 1989, having sold all the shares I owned in Katakura Industries, the price reached a high of ¥7,400; and again in February 1990, it surged as high as ¥7,750. The shares that had been in the deep freeze at a low price of around ¥400 for eight years after Katakura Industries had been designated a strategic company, sky-rocketed after I finished selling them all off, ultimately reaching about twenty times the initial price. After having such things happen to me after sales of other stocks, it did not surprise me at all.

The First Victory

The judgment of the Tokyo District Court was pronounced on April 18, 1991, on my suit against the board of directors for their causing a loss to the company.

I actually won.

However, the Tokyo District Court reduced the compensation from ¥730 million to just over ¥151 million. This was because the court calculated the amount by which the value of shares of the subsidiary owned by Katakura Industries had been reduced owing to the losses incurred by the subsidiary, and took this reduced figure as the amount of the loss to Katakura Industries. To my amateur eyes, it seemed that the court's calculation was too technical and contrary to the common practice of ordinary companies.

Although it was a partial victory, it seems the judges couldn't resist the temptation to intersperse the text of the judgment at various points with groundless hearsay about me that had been spread about in the Oji Paper case. Even so, the judge had no choice but to admit the losses had in fact occurred due to the blatant self-dealing.

Katakura Industries and I were both displeased with this judgment, and appealed to the Tokyo High Court so that my friends and I might be fully vindicated. The judgment of the Tokyo High Court was pronounced on August 29, 1994. The judgment dismissed the appeals and upheld the partial claim.

As for the amount of compensation due, however, my claim was recognized as correct for the first time in this trial before the Tokyo High Court. Without any malice or prejudice toward me, without being led astray by slander and defamation, the contention of the defendants' side about the abuse of minority shareholders' rights was rejected. For me, it was the first honest judgment and I finally felt as though there was at least the semblance of justice in this system.

Upon consultation with my lawyer, I decided to appeal to the Supreme Court and the defendants' side also made an appeal.

During the original trial before the District Court, I had succeeded in freezing all of the board of directors' assets. However, during the course of the trial, I had petitioned the court to release the frozen assets of the directors except for the managing director and the chairman. The prevailing norm at Japanese companies is that it is rare for ordinary directors to be permitted even to speak at board meetings; they just silently affix their seals to whatever the company leaders have decided. Considering that it would be too much of a pity for such people to shoulder amounts of compensation that would bankrupt them, I decided to exclude them from the defendants.

Moreover, since the trial began, the former president Mr. Shinichi Funatsu had died and his widow and heirs succeeded to the case. Therefore, at this point in time, the defendants from whom I was claiming compensation for the company were six persons: the five heirs of former President Funatsu and former Managing Director Mr. Haruo Yanagisawa. In order to ensure the compensation, I submitted a guarantee and placed a provisional attachment on the Funatsu residence in Suginami and the Yanagisawa residence in Nerima. To secure this provisional attachment, I placed ¥177.5 million ($1.5 million) of my own money with the court as a deposit. I had also made provisional attachments on the assets of the ordinary directors, which were released as soon as they were excluded from the defendants.

Withdrawal of the Suit

Before the Supreme Court could pass judgment on my appeal, there was the announcement of a complete victory by the shareholders' side in a shareholders' representative suit regarding the self-dealing in Mitsui Mining shares. This was a case brought against Mitsui Mining that was very similar to my own against Katakura Industries. The Supreme Court found the parent company, Mitsui Mining, to have suffered losses equal to those incurred by its wholly owned subsidiary, Miike Development.

Taking hope at the decision of the Supreme Court in the Mitsui Mining case, the partial judgment of the Tokyo District Court was incorrect and it was very likely that I would win a complete victory as well.

However, I was torn. If the Supreme Court delivered a judgment in favor of our side, the bereaved family of the former president and the former managing director would be liable for a claim of roughly ¥1.55 billion (US $12.3 million) since the legally prescribed interest would be added in at the rate of five percent per annum. In order to repay compensation to Katakura, the defendants—the bereaved fam-

ily and the former managing director—would have to sell their houses, land, and other possessions. I felt that no matter what had happened, such a thing would be too cruel.

Before the issuing of the judgment of the Supreme Court, I
decided to withdraw the suit.

Following my withdrawal, an article appeared in the Japanese
media on August 12, 1996:

Letter of Withdrawal of Suit

Newpis Hong Kong Limited, will completely withdraw
the lawsuit in the matter of the claim for compensation in the
case against the aforesaid respondents, Shige Funatsu, and
five others…

The aims for which the aforesaid appellant has instituted
and pursued this suit have been to prosecute abuses that have
long been entrenched in Japan's corporate culture (tendencies
of Japanese companies that are not tolerated internationally)
and seek their improvement.

It is possible to judge that the above aims have, to some
degree, been achieved through the judgments of the Court of
First Instance and the Court of Appeals, which partially
acknowledged the claims of the appellant.

On the other hand, if the Supreme Court judgment were
to come down as things stand, with the appellant winning the
suit and the respondents losing, an auction of the individual
assets of the respondents would become inevitable.

However, the late Mr. Shinichi Funatsu and the respon-
dent Mr. Haruo Yanagisawa did not gain personal advantages
from the acquisition of the company's own shares in this
case. Depending on one's viewpoint, it might not be too
much to say that the two gentlemen above were victims
themselves of the aforesaid abuses, by which they were
forced into the illegal acquisition of the company's own
shares.

It is difficult for the appellant to forgive the testimony given in this case by the two gentlemen above, especially that of Mr. Haruo Yanagisawa, which denounced and slandered the appellant's representative; nevertheless, it would really be a pity if even the latter gentleman, but especially the bereaved family of the late Mr. Funatsu, were forced to make compensation for the loss using their individual assets, and one cannot help but sympathize. From the outset, such a situation has never been the purpose of the appellant in instituting and pursuing this suit.

Accordingly, in the present situation the representative of the appellant has decided to withdraw the lawsuit against the respondents unconditionally.

It goes without saying that this case is a shareholders' representative suit, and has never been a vehicle for pursuing the appellant's individual benefit.

Since the good name of the appellant and its representative has been involved, the withdrawal of the suit on this occasion, if we may dare make it clear here, is based on the individual discretion of the appellant. One time, several months after the judgment of the Court of Appeals was pronounced, there were circumstances in which the lawyer for the respondents indicated certain reasonable conditions for an out-of-court settlement, and the appellant refused them. However, the present withdrawal of the suit, as opposed to the above, is completely unconditional. Therefore, the costs for the appellant's lodging and pursuit of the lawsuit, lawyers' fees and the like shall all, it goes without saying, be borne by the appellant, and there is no intention of passing them on to the company or to the respondents.

On withdrawing the aforesaid lawsuit, the appellant and its representative continue to hope that the spirit of the judgments of the Court of First Instance and of the Court of

Appeals will fully permeate Japan's corporate culture and that
the long-entrenched abuses…that the appellant has repeatedly emphasized in this suit will be improved, even marginal-
ly.

On the day after I submitted the Letter of Withdrawal to the
Supreme Court, the August 13, 1996 *Asahi Shimbun* had an extensive
report in the general news pages with the gigantic headline,
"Regrettable High Compensation for White-Collar Directors."

Regarding the self-dealing in shares of the textile manufacturer 'Katakura Industries' (head office: Tokyo), the Hong
Kong shareholder who lodged the shareholders' representative lawsuit against two officers at the time and won in the
Court of First Instance and the Court of Appeals took steps
on the 12th to withdraw the suit at the third stage with the
Petty Bench of the Supreme Court for the hearing of the
final appeal.

The reasons given: "In the trials up to now, the goal of
prosecuting the abuses of closed Japanese corporations has
been achieved," and "It would really be regrettable to seek a
compensation payment from white-collar officers." The consent of the defendants' side was necessary, but the former
officers, who had been ordered in the judgment to pay
approximately ¥150 million, welcomed it, saying that they
were "relieved."

The defendants in the shareholders' representative lawsuit
were held liable as the management, and compensation to the
company was sought. In the event that they lost the suit, the
amount of compensation would have had to be borne individually, and they might be called on to shoulder a burden
that they could not possibly pay with their personal assets.

…Regarding the withdrawal of the suit, the bereaved family of former President Funatsu, who succeeded to the suit,

rejoiced: "It's tremendous. We're very grateful for this," while Chairman Yanagisawa said, "I've been suffering for a long time, but in these circumstances it has ended without my having to sell my house. I'm going to give a report at the graveside of former President Funatsu, who passed away during the trial."

The party that withdrew the suit was the Hong Kong investment company "Newpis Hong Kong Limited" (President T. H. Wang). Mr. Wang was born in Taipei and has British nationality; he deals in property, shares, gold, and silver from bases in Hong Kong and the United States. Reputed to be one of Hong Kong's many men of property, he is also the author of the book *Confronting Japan, Inc.* (Tokuma Shoten).

In the Letter of Withdrawal, Mr. Wang explained: "The aim of continuing the lawsuit was to prosecute the exclusivist predisposition of Japanese companies, which is not tolerated internationally. With the victories in the Court of First Instance and the Court of Appeal, the aim was met to a certain extent." In addition, he stated: "If we won in the Supreme Court as well, the bereaved family of the former president and the former managing director would not be able to pay the compensation without auctioning their personal assets, which would really be a pity, and one cannot help but sympathize."

On reading this newspaper article, I felt to some extent that I had been vindicated. I learned that the bereaved family of former President Funatsu and even former Managing Director Yanagisawa, who had done nothing but call me a miserable villain in the trial, were happy. Of course, I had decided to bear all the expenses incurred in the trials, and was not asking the defendants for a single penny. My withdrawal of the lawsuit before the Supreme Court came down with the decision earned me a good reputation with Japan's media.

However, in Japan's mass media there were still those who suspected that I had obtained a tidy sum through a transaction behind the scenes. (While it was true that I had been offered a settlement of ¥100 million, I had declined and told them I was not in the lawsuit to make money.) There is absolutely no way to describe this except as vulgar suspicion. They are a mean-natured lot and would not have believed anything kind about me no matter what was written.

Despite the stubbornness of some Japanese who refused to believe that I had only good intentions at heart, even years after this incident, I continued to receive notes of encouragement from Japanese individuals who felt badly about the whole incident. In January 1997, I received a note from the former Chief Justice of the Supreme Court of Japan, Ekizo Fujibaysahi, who was still very moved by my action and voiced his support for me. He had visited me in Hong Kong in 1983 after I'd personally invited him. In his note, he said, "I was sorting out the news scraps of last year and read the news story (article) once again about you dropping the case in Tokyo against the Katakura Industries Co. Ltd. and felt the deep emotion about it." If only more of Japan's judges were of his mind, maybe there would be less injustice in Japan's judicial system.

One final note to make here is that Yamaichi Securities, which had been the one to set us up to begin with, was pushed to voluntary closure when off-book debts of approximately ¥260 billion were discovered in November 1997. Upon subsequent investigation, the old management of Yamaichi Securities was arrested on March 4, 1998, on suspicion of having hidden mammoth losses by means of "*tobashi* transactions" (transactions where losses are "parked" elsewhere) and of having submitted false securities reports over a period of six years.

While I do not wish harm on anyone, in some sense, perhaps this was justice at work.

Chapter Ten

Troubles Continue: The Saibo Case

In the late 1980s, I decided to swear off investing in Japanese securities. I was tired of dealing with such treacherous people and a system that seemed set up only to reward those inside the system while punishing those who only had innocent and decent intentions. Where else in the world, I felt, were investors dealt with so badly? Where else could a simple, ordinary investment decision go so horribly wrong?

I felt badly for the Japanese people and for the everyday investor, who are really at the whim of the securities companies, Ministry of Finance, and Tokyo Stock Exchange. To stop investing in a country that I saw as my second homeland was a hard decision to make. I still had many friends and family in Japan, but I just couldn't deal with such a system anymore. My court cases against Katakura were underway at this time, too, so the easiest thing to do was to pull up stakes and invest somewhere else. I wanted to find companies where my investments would be treated honorably, where they would be welcomed, and where I wouldn't fall under suspicion and contempt simply for investing in a company.

During the late 1980s, the way that I'd been treated by the Japanese financial system drew some attention in Japan's national media. Also, as the court cases progressed and as Japan struggled with the idea of internationalization, the media again focused on my struggles as a prominent foreign investor.

In November 1988, I granted an interview with Soichiro Tawara of the *Shukan Post*. In this article, I stated that the Tokyo Stock Market was a "manipulated share priced market" and that I wouldn't buy any more Japanese shares.

Hong Kong Dollars Angered at the Tokyo Stock Market.

With the Recruit Cosmos affair, the Meiden Construction affair, and the suspected insider trading connected with the Shin Nittetsu/Sankyo Seiki joint operation, there has been a succession of scandals involved with trading in shares, leading to repeated questioning as to the ways in which share trading is carried out in Japan and the operating of the stock markets. And on top of everything, a scalding criticism, in fact a bomb stating "the Tokyo Stock Market is unhealthy in the extreme and rampant with irregular trading practices" has been cast from abroad.

The individual who has cast this bomb is Mr. Tseng Hsiang Wang, a Hong Kong investor...That this individual who in practice has the power and ability to partition off Hong Kong dollars said to be amounting to funds of several thousands of millions of dollars [through his sphere of influence] has chosen to cast a bomb in the form of naming a top enterprise Nomura Securities in legal actions, alleging that "the Japanese stock market is controlled and manipulated by the securities companies and the government" is a topic that one just cannot fail to be deeply involved in.

At the very start of my telephone interview, Mr. Wang suddenly flung a shower of bitter words in Japanese at me. It was a sort of rough pitch that we rarely hear in Tokyo today.

Wang: Frankly speaking, the stock market of Japan is extremely unhealthy. Share prices change as a result of collusion. All the investors in Hong Kong are incensed at this… This kind of operation is totally unwarranted in today's world. If the stock market still continues to carry on in this manner, no foreigner will want to buy shares anymore.

— Mr. Wang, I understand that you trade in stock markets all over the world, but is the Tokyo Stock Market so unhealthy in comparison with, say, New York or London? I would like to hear more specifically about how you think.

Wang: I was swindled in connection with Katakura Industries shares and sued the company…Katakura remained unchanged at ¥400 for around eight years. As soon as I sold them, it rose rapidly and at present it's ¥2,000. Before that there was Japan Line. About fifteen years ago [in 1973], I held about 11 million shares. I bought them at about ¥60 per share but Nikko Securities of Hong Kong convinced me to sell to Mr. Toshio Kawamoto of Sanko Kisen. Thus, I sold a big percentage to Sanko Kisen and the rest to various securities companies. The average sale price was roughly around ¥70 a share. Six months after that, the price rose to ¥960 so I failed to gain a profit of about ¥10,000 million.

— Surely you just can't take it for granted that the Tokyo Stock Market is controlled and manipulated by the leading securities companies and the government on these grounds alone?

Wang: That's why I've specifically sued Nomura. Let me speak more frankly and specifically. Ishikawajima Harima Heavy Industries. Isn't this a company paying no dividend? And then the shares of this company paying no dividend suddenly start to rise from the summer of 1986. At the beginning it was around ¥200 or so, and then by April or

May 1987 it had jumped to over ¥700, and by the summer of 1988 it reached the ¥1,200 mark. It's not normal. Anybody would think it strange, wouldn't they?

— Yes, but why did this lead to your lodging a complaint against Nomura?

Wang: During the period that this strange movement persisted (from August 1986 – July 1988), Nomura had purchased 42.7% and sold 38.9% of the total volume of Ishikawajima Harima shares traded during that time. Can you understand the horrendousness of this?

— In other words, Nomura Securities was over-monopolizing the market. Therefore they were disgraceful, is that what you mean?

Wang: Monopolizing...no, that would be dangerous. But even so, I wouldn't have sued them if they had been doing proper business. No, Nomura drew up false data and stimulated the market. This is a sort of confidence trick.

— False data? Confidence trick? Those are certainly unusual words. What was false and what was the confidence trick?

Wang: In an inter-company report entitled 'Portfolio Weekly' they carried articles on Ishikawajima Harima for a consecutive thirty-six weeks and thus stimulated public interest in their shares. The alleged reason was the Tokyo Waterfront Project, which is a topic of discussion now; Ishikawajima Harima has a factory site of 380,000 square meters in Toyosu... This will become a financial center in the future. So even if only half of the area were to be developed, it would result in an annual increase in ordinary profit of ¥40 billion—so they emphasized.

In other words, they maintained that this non-dividend paying company Ishikawajima Harima held vast latent assets that could be utilized in the full under the Waterfront

Project, so therefore investing in Ishikawajima Harima would be a 'clever' move.

The problem was that this report turned out to be false. Nomura told lies and stimulated interest in Ishikawajima Harima in the market and as a result of this, the share price rose rapidly."

— What do you mean by 'lies'?

Wang: The Tokyo Metropolitan Government announced the Waterfront Project plans this March, but the Ishikawajima Harima site isn't included in the plans for the financial center. The plans have already been made public, so anybody can check if they wish. In other words, the Nomura report was false.

As part of the article, the reporter contacted Nomura to check their side of the story and they offered an explanation that did not deny their including Ishikawajima Harima in their Portfolio Weekly but did deny that they intended to say that the Ishikawajima Harima site would definitely be developed. "We only stated," the Nomura representative said, "that once this project is launched and matters progress, attention will be focused on this site… This is neither false nor a lie."

In response, the reporter said, "As Japanese, we can understand and accept Nomura's explanation as it is, but this does not appear to be so in the case of Mr. Wang. He maintains that it is a 'typical Japanese collusion, a reason of the artful dodge type'."

I went on to explain in the article about the Oji Paper affair and the difficulties involved in it. The reporter asked me why then, if I suffered so badly in Oji Paper, did I invest in Katakura. I replied that's exactly my point: that I was promised that the problems I'd experienced with Oji Paper would not be repeated. I explained in detail the deep collusion between not only the securities companies but also the government.

Wang: ...Now why did Katakura, a producer of shirts and pants, even get to be included on this [list of protected industries]? Can this be said to be the normal picture of the stock market that forms the basis for economic liberalism?

— I would like to confirm this again. In what way does the Japanese Stock Market differ from those in New York or London?

Wang: In Japan there is collusion and ambiguity... Even if illegal trading or irregular actions are committed, the parties are not arrested. In the case of America, there is the Securities and Exchange Commission that has no mercy on offenders. The rules are clear as to what can be done and what should not be done.

However, in the Japanese stock market, there are not true rules. Even if there may be so-called rules, they are not true rules, they allow a typical Japanese type of collusion and are incomprehensible to a foreigner. It makes me so mad...

The reporter closed with:

Although some of Mr. Wang's reasoning may be open to doubt, the fact remains that the stock market of Japan is viewed by many foreigners with a feeling of malaise and displeasure. It is obvious that the time has come when all traces of the typical Japanese ambiguity and collusion must be wiped out completely and reforms introduced to re-create an open market operating under clearly defined rules.

Saibo

In 1989, President Fukumaru of Ichiyoshi Securities Hong Kong visited me while I was in Hong Kong. "There's a textile company on the Tokyo second market called Saibo that has huge latent assets in the form of land," he said enthusiastically. "You really ought to invest in it. Why don't you give them some consideration?"

Saibo was primarily a textile company that had a broad line of products including cotton goods, synthetic textile products, apparel, lace, and bedroom textiles. Saibo also had an import-export operation for textile products and materials as well as other activities, including the sales, leasing, and management of real estate and the production of painted metal plates for automobiles. The trading division was the largest division, accounting for roughly 40% of Saibo's revenues, though the textile division was its main business.

President Fukumaru showed me a survey report on the latent assets. According to that survey report, the land held by Saibo in Kawaguchi City, Saitama Prefecture covered 240,000 square meters, and this land's latent profit alone was said to be ¥132.2 billion, which amounted to ¥11,016 per share. Needless to say, this was extremely impressive.

While latent assets are always impressive, what is important if that the company can actually capitalize on those assets. As I had painfully learned with Katakura—which had a great deal of latent assents—just because a company has latent assets, it does not necessarily mean the company will utilize them profitably. In the case of Katakura, as you'll remember, they had refused to sell off their landed assets to pay down debt and further gave a below-market lease to Ito-Yokado.

But Saibo looked especially promising because Kawaguchi City had been an industrial area that had centered on the casting industry since before World War II. The area had lagged in transforming its surroundings into housing, but had recently embarked on urbanization, so that the city was improving itself. It was observed that if major developers or prominent local enterprises began to promote redevelopment in earnest, the land prices would rise to a maximum of anywhere from ¥1.5 million to ¥2.5 million per 3.3 square meters.

Among the latent assets in the report were the head office, the main factory, two other factories, an auto school, and a golf course.

Altogether, they had 231,523 square meters of very valuable land with a latent worth of ¥132.2 billion. This meant that the 12 million shares were worth ¥11,016 based solely on the land itself, to say nothing of the actual operation of the company.

Owing to my previous experience of handling property development around Kai Tak Airport in Hong Kong, this report truly caught my attention. I was absolutely sure that if Saibo embarked on the development of land in Kawaguchi City, which was a mere twenty-minute train ride from Tokyo, not only would it reap enormous profits, but it would also contribute to the local development of Kawaguchi City. This was 1989; Japan was at the height of its bubble economy and land prices were shooting up. Therefore, Saibo's latent assets in land were rising, not falling. Naturally, the latent profit of the shares would rise in tandem.

In addition to the land, Saibo possessed around ¥7.6 billion in securities and had a reputation, moreover, as a company without debts. Saibo was essentially a family-run business, with the majority of the directors being from the Iizuka family; in fact, the chairman, Mr. Naoji Iizuka, and the president, Mr. Hirobumi Iizuka, were father and son.

I thought Saibo to be a good target for investment, just as President Fukumaru had said. Therefore, I decided to invest in Saibo, bringing in one of my prominent friends from Hong Kong. Together we began to slowly acquire some 600,000 shares over the course of a couple of years.

It was when we acquired some five percent of the outstanding shares that the trouble began.

When the management of Saibo learned that my friends and I had acquired so many shares, they panicked, fearing that the company would be taken over by foreign shareholders and moved to prevent any such thing.

To dilute our percentage, on March 7, 1991, they decided to issue 2 million new shares, raising the total of issued shares to roughly 14 million. That alone would not be such a bad thing, because issuing the shares and placing them on the open market would have allowed us to buy at least some additional shares in order to keep our position of five percent. Instead, Saibo allotted all 2 million of them to two of their daughter companies—Saiei Fudosan Company and Saitama Kogyo Company—one million to each company. On the surface it was an increase of capital allotted to third parties, but since it was in fact merely placing the newly issued shares in companies controlled by the managers themselves, this amounted to self-dealing and was completely outrageous and devious on the part of the management. By issuing their own shares and then "selling" them to their daughter companies, the Iizuka management essentially printed their own money and strengthened their position while simultaneously weakening the position of all the other shareholders.

When new shares are issued, it is common practice and trite company law that all newly issue shares should be allotted proportionally to all the company's existing shareholders. It is only when some shareholders decline in subscribing for their new shares that they are then offered to other interested shareholders or outside parties. Although Saibo had stable shareholders, such as Saitama Bank (now Asahi Bank), Nissan Fire and Marine Insurance, Toyoda Automatic Loom Works, and Toyo Menka Kaisha (Tomen), Saibo's management apparently either did not ask them to undertake the new shares or the stable shareholders declined to take the new shares for whatever reason. (Saibo, in fact, did later claim just that—that they had offered and that these companies had declined.) In any event, they certainly did not ask my friend and me nor, for that matter, did they ask any of the smaller shareholders if they wanted to purchase additional shares, nor did they even put them on the market.

As if the issuance of new shares was not enough, there was a problem with the price of the newly issued shares. According to a survey of the prices of all the land owned by Saibo, done at my request by a property appraiser, the current value (not the latent value) of the approximately 240,000 square meters of land owned by Saibo was ¥62.8 billion. In addition, because the value of the stock and securities that Saibo owned was approximately ¥7.6 billion, and was, moreover, a company without debts, their total assets amounted to approximately ¥70.4 billion. Since Saibo had 12 million shares, if one divided ¥70.4 billion by the 12 million issued shares, this clearly meant that one share of Saibo would be worth more than ¥5,000. However, the management of Saibo issued the new shares at a price of only ¥801 per share.

This was an outrage. Not only was it self-serving, but every single shareholder of Saibo suffered as a result. How many shareholders would have jumped for joy at the chance to buy shares with a value of more then ¥5,000 (and a latent value of up to ¥11,000) for a mere ¥801 per share? It was a slap in the face to every shareholder, since they could have claimed additional shares at a discounted rate, but were not even given the opportunity to do so. Apparently, the management didn't view the company's own "lesser shareholders" as worthy of even having a right of first refusal.

As a result of issuing and holding the new shares, the proportion held by the managers was lifted from 16.4% to 28.4%, and, conversely, the proportion of shares that we held was reduced from 5% to just over 4%. By this taking this move, the management was obviously only thinking of their own best interest and not caring a whit about the company's true owners, the shareholders.

Although I was outraged at this move by Saibo, I was not surprised by it either. It was just another example of how poorly the Japanese system works to protect individual shareholders and how easily those in power could quickly move to protect their position. I wish, though, that the Japanese people could understand what was really happening, and that this was not a case of the owners of a company protecting their company. Not at all. This was the management protecting themselves regardless of the wishes of the owners. It is as if the Japanese people cannot see that as shareholders, *they* are the owners of the company—*not* the management. This concept seems utterly lost on them.

If a Japanese person owned a small shop and an employee was stealing cash and items from the shelves, would they simply look the other way and ignore it? Or would they fire the employee and report him to the police? If the employee performed badly and did not do his job and cost the small shop money because of his bad decisions, would the owner simply shrug and do nothing?

Yet somehow, as shareholders, the Japanese seem to think nothing of an "employee" of theirs that misuses company funds. Time and time again this situation has repeated itself.

This is also evident by the fact that none of the other shareholders saw fit to complain to the Iizuka management. One and all, they acquiesced like mild sheep and saw nothing at all wrong with the fact that Saibo saw fit to weaken their position—or, if they did, they did nothing about it.

What was more reprehensible is that some of the major shareholders were also publicly held corporations, such as Asahi Bank and Toyoda Loom Works. These Japanese corporations that held stock in Saibo had duties and responsibilities to their own shareholders to protect their assets, which included the Saibo shares that these corporations held. By allowing Saibo to dilute the shares, these corporations in turn weakened their own holdings and therefore failed in their duties to their own shareholders because they should have been protecting the assets of their own company. A responsible corporate shareholder should have fought to protect their assets rather than allow this to happen.

Though Saibo's move was not surprising, it was still disappointing to see this type of thing happening once again.

After a couple of years, the shares of Saibo did not show the growth that my friend and I had anticipated. One of Saibo's greatest weaknesses was that its textile business was sorely lagging and creating a real drain on the company. This was unfortunate because Saibo had no debt and yet its textile department had been running at a substantial loss since 1984 that was equivalent to almost six times that of the company's capital and showed no signs of improving any time soon.

As a shareholder, I began to make repeated recommendations to Saibo that they liquidate this poorly performing company, but my suggestions fell on deaf ears each time.

All of this was happening during the early 1990s when there were a great many other things that were going on in my life. In 1989, I'd become incensed at the interview by president of Oji Paper and this fight would drag on for years through the early 1990s; also, the Katakura court fights and their subsequent appeals were in full swing and would not end until 1997.

In spite of everything else that was already happening, I felt compelled to do something and to try to change the system for the betterment of all shareholders who could not speak up for themselves due to the expense of court proceedings. Perhaps it was Fate once again acting in my life, urging me to fight the good fight for the people of Japan. So I decided to once again seek court action against a Japanese company and began to put the wheels into motion for the court battle.

Saibo Court Case

I started by writing letters to the other major shareholders, such as Asahi Bank and Toyoda Automatic Loom Works, but they showed no interest in pursuing any legal means against Saibo, even though the self-dealing to their daughter companies represented a great loss to Saibo in the area of ¥8.4 billion (the difference between ¥5,000 and ¥801 multiplied by 2 million shares), and thereby represented a substantial loss to all of the shareholders of Saibo. I pointed out to them that they had fiduciary responsibilities to their own shareholders to protect the assets of their own companies, and by allowing Saibo to issue the new shares, it had weakened their own position.

Despite my efforts, none of them replied or joined in the fight. This was very disappointing, since such respected Japanese companies could have bravely taken a stand against the management of Saibo and such corrupt practices.

By February 15, 1995, I was ready to go to court and filed a derivative action by my company, Newpis, against members of the Iizuka family and others who made up the board members of Saibo. In this lawsuit, I claimed on behalf of the shareholders that the Iizukas and their related companies, Saiei Fudosan and Saitama, should compensate the Saibo shareholders in this unlawful transaction, and therefore sought to collect the difference between the fair market price of 2 million shares and the unfair price used when they were issued to the daughter companies of Saibo. This suit was filed not only on my own behalf, but also on behalf of all the shareholders of Saibo.

As a spoiling move, however, the management of Saibo petitioned the District Court of Urawa (where Saibo is located) for me to put down a deposit of a ¥282 million guarantee before I could continue the lawsuit in order to secure Saibo against losses on the grounds that my suit had been lodged in bad faith. This was a deposit designed to discourage frivolous lawsuits and Saibo was alleging that my lawsuit was an abuse of my right to sue and that I was a troublemaker.

To defend against this request for a petition, I hired a land evaluator who assessed the land owned by Saibo. He assessed the fair value of each Saibo share according to the latent assets of the company by taking into account the market value of the lands, the stocks and securities that Saibo held, and Saibo's other assets. Using this valuation, he arrived at a value of about ¥5,000 per share.

In response to this petition, the District Court of Urawa agreed with my appraisal report that supported a higher value for the stock price and which showed the shares were worth more than ¥5,000. The Urawa District Court therefore ruled that the lawsuit was not frivolous and denied Saibo's petition for me to put up a bond, saying,

"From the very fact that the trading volume of Saibo shares on the Tokyo Stock Exchange had been moving along on a low base means that when an issue price has been determined solely on the basis of the aforesaid share price, a more careful examination will be required into whether it can be said right off that such issue price was fair. Furthermore, taking into consideration the fact that the claim is being advanced on the basis of the results of a survey on fair pricing carried out by the plaintiff through a property appraisal agency stating that the value of one share was at least ¥5,000, it cannot be accepted *prima facie* that this suit lacks a rationale."

The court also took note of the fact that Saibo used the calculation of ¥870 per share in their petition because that was the average share price in the month preceding the sale to their daughter companies. Perhaps the court was indicating to Saibo that the sale price by its own standard was rather dubious. I felt this was encouraging because that alone showed that sale price of ¥801 per share was rather dubious. The difference would represent a loss of ¥138 million to the shareholders of Saibo.

Saibo decided to appeal the decision to the Tokyo High Court. However, the Tokyo High Court upheld the lower court ruling. In making their ruling, they agreed with the Urawa District Court and further stated that "The number of shares bought and sold both before and after the issuance of the new shares has been small, and it cannot be deemed that no doubt exists about the conclusion that as many as 2 million shares out of the total of 12 million Saibo shares issued could have been purchased in the market at ¥801 per share."

With these rulings out of the way, my court case could proceed. Even though it had been a bit of a pain to defend this request for a deposit, all of this was extremely encouraging. Not one but two courts had agreed that the case was not frivolous and had used the evaluation I'd prepared as the basis for their decisions. If the court agreed just with the evaluation of ¥5,000—to say nothing of the latent assets that could push the share price up to ¥11,000 per share—then the potential boon to the shareholders would mean a judgment of ¥8.4 billion.

The Trial

During the trial, President Iizuka contended that the standard they used for determining the price of the 2 million new shares was the market price, but this wasn't quite proper since Saibo had an extremely small turnover rate, which is one reason why Saibo was listed on the Second Market. In fact, the month before the new issuance, the trading volume was only 14,000. As such, it wasn't proper to price a large disbursement on such a small trading volume. Moreover, using Saibo's own valuations for their assets and dividing it by the outstanding 12 million shares, yielded a figure of ¥4,029 per share. Certainly, all of the directors must have known what the true value of their shares were, which corroborated my contention that the price of ¥801 determined by Saibo's board of directors was a fabricated price and without foundation.

Another fact that came out was that Saibo had made no record of certain land they owned in their securities report—land that was valued at more than ¥7.6 billion. Obviously, the failure to report such an asset is illegal. However, no action was taken against Saibo for their failure to report it.

Like Katakura, whose main industry of silk manufacturing was in the doldrums, Saibo had been showing little profit over the years, despite the vast amount of landed assets they owned. In fact, the cumulative losses in Saibo's textile sectors reached ¥7.0 billion over a seventeen-year period. Managers from any normal company would have long ago withdrawn from such an unprofitable sector. Even today Saibo continues to register massive annual losses in their textile division. This means that the majority of shareholders has been suffering losses and continues to do so. Why is this? The only possible explanation is that the managers have ulterior motives in mind.

Faced with such obvious mismanagement of Saibo's assets and profits, Saibo's own president said that the formation of the share price was beyond his control. If there are such huge and ongoing losses affecting the share price, shouldn't a manager pull out of unprofitable endeavors? That's the only way to shake free of a depressed share price.

Even though prestigious family enterprises and large-scale corporations are abandoning and withdrawing from losing sectors, Saibo has continued to wallow in an interminable river of red ink. If Saibo were a private corporation, no one would raise a peep even if they churned out losses for one hundred years in a row. However, Saibo is not a private company, they are a publicly listed company, which makes them responsible to their shareholders, much in the same way that a democratically elected government is responsible to those that elected it.

Additionally, the Iizuka family bought 100,000 shares through Yamaichi at ¥1,300, which clearly indicates that the Iizuka family acknowledged that the stock was worth at least ¥1,300. When President Iizuka was asked in court whether he was involved personally in this purchase, he carefully answered, "I don't know" rather than a simple "no," perhaps in an effort to avoid committing perjury.

When my lawyer questioned President Iizuka about the need for issuing the new shares, he gave some interesting responses. Saibo was a company without any debt at the time they issued the new shares, so the normal method would have been to borrow from the banks— which would have been only too happy to loan them money. They could have raised capital by selling off some of the ¥7.6 billion in securities that they owned. Also, in issuing the new shares, the shares were undervalued at ¥801 per share when we were not even able to buy them at ¥1,300 per share. So if Saibo truly needed more capital, they should have issued them at a higher price. I know I would certainly have jumped at the chance to buy them at that price. But, as President Iizuka was forced to admit under oath, I was not even asked, despite the fact that I owned nearly 5% of the company. It became obvious that the issuance of the new shares was not to raise additional capital, as President Iizuka claimed, but rather to place the additional 2 million shares in the hands of affiliates under the Iizuka family control.

If you would like to read some of the actual court testimony along with additional comments on these and other points, please see Appendix D.

The Outcome of the Trial

Given the rulings of the Urawa District Court and the Tokyo High Court, both of which denied Saibo's petition for a bond, most people believed that I would prevail in this court action.

But to everyone's surprise, I lost the case and the judge of the Urawa District Court dismissed my complaint in its entirety on October 8, 1997. This was no doubt due in large part to the fact that the judge refused to allow me to call the real estate evaluator as a witness in this case, even though the Urawa District Court and the Tokyo High Court had both admitted his testimony during the trial for Saibo's petition for a bond. It was inexplicable, especially since the judge in charge was the very same judge who had dismissed the bonding petition.

Naturally, I appealed the case to the Tokyo High Court, hoping that this court—which had also heard and upheld the lower court's decision on the bonding petition—would find in my favor.

Again, despite the fact that they had allowed the evidence by the real estate evaluator in the previous case, they upheld the lower court's decision and dismissed my shareholders' suit.

Commonsense would dictate that to maintain judicial consistency, the Urawa District Court and the Tokyo High Court should have both permitted me to call the real estate evaluator as a witness. After all, they had previously dismissed Saibo's bonding petition by supporting the conclusions of the real estate evaluation. If they had done so, then they might have found in the shareholders' favor.

Perhaps, though, this loss in the Tokyo High Court should not have surprised me after all. Two of the three judges presiding at the Tokyo High Court—the chief judge and one of his associates—were the same ones who had rejected my appeal in the Oji Paper case, which I had been absolutely confident of winning. The normal procedure is to have a rotation system for the judges hearing cases. Could it have been mere coincidence that from among the plethora of judges, the two judges mentioned above were assigned to my case? Hardly. The Tokyo High Court must have deliberately assigned these two persons to the Saibo case.

A Change in Tactics

After the denial from the High Court, I decided not to take the Saibo case to the Supreme Court because the whole process was obviously rigged from the beginning. Therefore, it seemed pointless to me to appeal. However, I changed my strategy, which became to write books such as this one to inform the general public of these unfair practices.

If Japanese courts acquiesce in improper third party allocations of capital increases as in the Saibo case, it will become absolutely impossible for foreign investors to buy a majority of the shares in a Japanese company through the stock market. Any time a company feels "threatened," all they need to do is immediately issue a third party allocation of shares, as it was in my case, and the new shares from the capital increase can all be assigned to the management family. No matter how many shares an outsider tries to buy, anytime he gets close, the company can simply print their own money by continuously adding to their own shares. Therefore, this closes out the possibility of takeovers of Japanese companies, which seriously damages the reputation and international standing of the Japanese financial system.

From my experiences with Saibo, Katakura Industries, and Oji Paper Company, it is easy to see that even the judiciary in Japan works to preserve the establishment. I have gathered the opinions of Japanese and American legal experts about the evils of an establishment society such as Japan's and one and all, they have agreed with me.

These individuals are: Professor of Law Tatsuo Kamimura of Waseda University, Professor of Law William L. Reynolds of Maryland University, Professor of Law Howell E. Jackson of Harvard University, and Professor Howard V. Perlmutter of the Wharton Business School of the University of Pennsylvania on the Oji Paper case; Professor of Law Katsuro Kanzaki of Kobe University on the Katakura Industries case; and Professor of Law Mark A. Sargent of Maryland University on the Saibo case. And although they do not appear in this work, I have also benefited from the opinions of economics commentator Mr. Atsuo Mihara on the Oji Paper case, and of Professor of Law Kazuo Yamauchi of Gakushuin University and Assistant Professor of Law Masafumy Kaneko of Dokkyo University suit against the four Ministers of Japan, including the Ministry of Finance, for listing Katakura Industries as one of the eleven protected companies for national security.

With so many top legal minds in agreement, it is sad to see Japan stand alone in the world and refuse to change its system. It is unfortunate, because the rest of the world will not stand still to wait for Japan to catch up. Given its current financial problems, Japan must make some hard choices about its ingrained collusion, or it is in danger of being shunned by the global community, and that will be unfortunate not only for Japan but for the Japanese people themselves.

Professor Kamimura especially understands the importance of changing the Japanese mindset. I have consulted with him in the past for some of my other books, and he wrote me a note after I sent him a copy of one of them. I give his letter in its entirety to demonstrate that not all Japanese believe in the status quo. (Unfortunately, those who don't are sorely in the minority and are also keenly aware of the fact that they hold a minority view.)

Dear Mr. Tseng-Hsiang Wang:

I am sure that you are spending very busy days during this hot weather. I am writing to you for the first time. I am writing this letter in Japanese, because I understand that you are very fluent in the Japanese language.

I thank you very much for your sending me the book *The Eve of the Financial and Securities Collapse* authored by you. I was a little surprised to find that my appraisal was mentioned as it was, but I am satisfied with that because this will give an opportunity for it to be seen by many people. After I read your much-too-high evaluation for my appraisal in your previous book *Evil Deeds*, I did not thank you and I hope you do take my apology for that. In any case, I do think all your concern over the securities market in Japan is totally right. I do also agree that the court itself has become a "salary-man-like" institution and is not fulfilling its mission. Since Mr. Kawai, a Judge of the Supreme Court, has defended securities groups together with Professor Ichiro Kawamoto [Komoto], I think he should not even be involved in the Oji Paper court case. But, I heard that there was much heated debate in the Council of the Supreme Court about the judicial decision.

In Japan, we have dealt too loosely with legal, economic, and accounting matters without the true understanding of the meaning. There is no respect for academic learning. I think there is no visible sign of the true meaning of regret or any intention of reform, even at this point. There seems to be no determination of pushing through a reform accompanied by pain. It is not only the matter of dealing with bad debt and economic recovery, but they don't try to find out what is the cause of those problems. I think we have to make a commitment to overcome the big hurdle that Japan is notoriously weakest in dealing with. This final big wall is namely "The Wealth and Legal Power of the Nation," which was preceded by "The Wealth and Military Power of the Nation" (in the Meiji Era), that was followed by the "Wealth and Strong Economy of the Nation" after the war. Japan needs to find a determined commitment to become the first non-Western country in truly challenging this big wall.

In any case, there are many people who understand your passionate opinion in their hearts. I hope that you continue ringing the timely warning about the situation. I have also read your book, *The Challenge of Hong Kong*, and always thought of you as one who would speak the right opinion.

With heartfelt thanks…

Sincerely yours,

Tatsuo Kamimura,
Professor of Waseda University

Further Problems with Saibo

On February 20, 1997, just a few months before President Hirobumi Iizuka would testify before the Urawa District Court, I received a telephone call from Kankaku Asia, the local Hong Kong subsidiary of Kankaku Securities. By this time, my friend and I had acquired about thirteen percent of Saibo's shares.

"In the future," the staff person said, "we would like you to refrain from placing purchase orders for Saibo shares at the bid price of ¥1,300."

"Why is that?"

"We had a telephone call from Japan's Ministry of Finance."

I demanded to know who it was at the Ministry of Finance who had given such a direction, but they would not tell me.

The following day, another person from Kankaku Asia called me and said that the instruction was not from the Ministry of Finance after all but from the Kankaku's Tokyo head office. By so quickly changing their story, and after all that had happened to me in trying to make simple investments in Japan, it was obviously suspicious and did not bode well for the future. My stomach sank, which is what happens when one is under a constant barrage of abuse. I was sickened at the thought of what was going to happen next.

But what was especially troubling about this call from Kankaku was that I was one of the founders of Kankaku Asia, as well as being a major shareholder and a director. Obviously, the situation must have been quite serious for them to refuse purchase orders from one of their own shareholders and directors.

Accordingly, I tried to inquire of the head office of Kankaku in Tokyo through a lawyer. The written reply that came back read as follows:

> First of all, it is not a fact that our company failed to execute your purchase orders for Saibo shares. Therefore, there was actually no case of "refusing an order" ... However, prior to the execution of your order, we sounded out your intention by asking whether you would like to refrain from ordering Saibo shares... It was not a fact that "We had a telephone call from Japan's Ministry of Finance." However, it is the case that we received a request from the authorities to submit information regarding transactions in Saibo shares.

When a securities company refers to "the authorities," it definitely means either the Ministry of Finance or the TSE. And, if they were ordered by the authorities to submit information about an individual transaction, for a securities company that would be the same as being advised to refrain from involvement in that transaction. Kankaku Securities took the intention of the authorities to heart and asked my Hong Kong friend and I to refrain from orders for Saibo shares.

We have never made illegal investments, so why would the authorities put pressure on Kankaku Securities to prevent us from buying Saibo shares? There is no doubt that someone who did not want us to buy Saibo shares had influenced the authorities. I am certain that the culprit was the Saibo management urging them to make it impossible for us to buy additional shares at ¥1,300 apiece even though we had continued to place purchase orders all along at that level.

Such events having occurred, we could not buy even though we placed orders at ¥1,300 per share. However, as soon as we left Saibo shares alone, the price dropped steadily, and as of January 2000 it had reached ¥455 per share.

The turnover is also exceedingly small; so much so that there is doubt as to whether the Saibo stock continues to fulfill the TSE listing standards for publicly listed corporations. The turnover for the entire month of January 2000 was no more than a paltry 1,000 shares and, as I have stated, in 1999, there was even a month when no shares were traded at all. I feel that there is something unnatural about the price trend for Saibo shares. Since I had bought them with my own funds and because Saibo is not a significant investment for me and I consider it be a low risk, I wasn't too troubled. But if there were people who borrowed money from the bank to buy Saibo shares, they would have certainly gone bankrupt by this type of share price suppression.

Chao Hui Trading Company

In 1999, I attempted to exercise my rights as a Saibo shareholder. As specified by law, any shareholder who held at least 3% of the shares of a listed company could submit proposals. I therefore submitted an Instrument for the Exercise of the Right of Proposal calling for the dismissal of two directors, two inspectors, and the auditor.

I am sure you will not find it difficult to guess how far this proposal got. Needless to say, Saibo completely ignored my exercising my rights as shareholder and simply ignored my proposal. But let me tell the story in a bit more detail.

At the end of 1998, on examining Saibo's securities report and discovering the name of a company called "Jaffe Trading" in the investment securities column, I had the feeling that something was not quite right. Jaffe Trading was a company I had never heard of, but evidently, Saibo owned shares of this company and listed it in their securities report.

When the new year came around, I sent a letter of inquiry to Saibo to ask them about this company. They wrote back and said that the formal transcription for Jaffe Trading was "Chao Hui Trading," and that they were a textile-related trading company located in the City of Taipei in Taiwan. The purpose of Saibo's investment in them was to strengthen the relationship with Jaffe Trading, which was a customer for Saibo's knitted material.

After receiving this reply, I sent another letter, asking why Jaffe Trading's official designation in Chinese had not been used in the securities report, as well as to inquire how high the transaction volume with Jaffe Trading was.

Saibo wrote back, saying, "Since there is no official designation for Jaffe Trading in Japanese, the name of Jaffe Trading, by which it is ordinarily known, was entered in the securities report." However, this did not seem plausible, since the Chinese designation for Jaffe Trading, i.e., "Chao Hui Trading," consists of Chinese characters that are found on Japanese language word processors. The deliberate failure to use the officially designated company name constituted a false entry in a securities report but I believed there was something else behind this as well.

I also found out from Saibo that in its peak year, Chao Hui Trading had a huge transaction volume with Saibo totaling more than ¥1.36 billion. Thereupon, I immediately commissioned an investigation company in Taiwan to run a check on Chao Hui Trading.

From the investigation report I learned that Chao Hui Trading was a small six-person enterprise whose representative was Mr. Lin Ying-chieh, a former bank clerk, that the personal name of Saibo President Hirobumi Iizuka was entered in the register of shareholders, and that the Taipei branch of Saibo was located in the same building on the same floor and in the same office as Chao Hui Trading. On reading this investigation report, my suspicions grew even larger.

First of all, although Saibo had invested in Chao Hui Trading as a corporation, why was it that the personal name of Mr. Hirobumi Iizuka, the president of Saibo, was listed among the shareholders instead of Saibo? Under the circumstances, it amounted to the president making a personal investment with the company's money. Isn't it embezzlement to use the company's money as one's own? Furthermore, given that it was actually the president who personally became the shareholder, Saibo's statement in the securities report that they had invested in Chao Hui Trading as a company would constitute making a false entry in a securities report.

Secondly, from the fact that Saibo's Taipei branch shared an office with Chao Hui Trading, there is no doubt that their close relationship of interests went far beyond that of simple business acquaintances. Saibo contended that there was only one locally recruited part-time employee serving in its Taipei branch, but there was a sign written in Japanese posted on the door of this office saying "Watch your step!" which indicated that the office was being operated by Japanese.

Thus, numerous doubts existed about the relationship between Saibo and Chao Hui Trading. Accordingly, I sent letters to Saibo on several occasions asking them to clarify the actual situation. Saibo sent letters of reply, but when it came to vital matters regarding Chao Hui Trading, they simply refused to answer, saying, "It is merely a customer and is an absolutely different company, so no information can be disclosed."

Nevertheless, I was able to learn more details of what was really happening.

I requested the disclosure of the accounts of Chao Hui Trading, but Saibo consistently rejected my requests. Undoubtedly, if they disclosed the accounts, their evil deeds would come to light. Nevertheless, I received an answer saying that the accounts and the dividends had been sent to Saibo. However, the accounts and the dividends are sent to the shareholders themselves. Since the name and the residential address of Mr. Hirobumi Iizuka, the president of Saibo, were entered in the register of shareholders, they would be sent to him as a matter of course rather than to Saibo. The fact that the accounts were actually sent to Saibo was because someone had given instructions for that to be done. In other words, such a thing could not have been done unless there was a three-part conspiracy by Saibo, President Hirobumi Iizuka, and Chao Hui Trading.

In addition, Saibo failed to fully answer the questions in my letter querying the circumstances under which the name of Mr. Hirobumi Iizuka came to be entered into the register of shareholders. They merely excused it as a simple error, but it seems unlikely if not impossible that this error would not have been noticed for a period of nine years from the initial investment. The fact that the correction took four months from the time that I pointed the matter out—even though a correction of a register of shareholders can be accomplished in two to three days—makes it a certainty that operations to cover up their crimes were carried out during that period.

There is something even more mysterious. In 1996, Chao Hui Trading distributed a huge dividend, amounting to as much as three times the value of the capital fund. Moreover, in the nine years since Saibo's first investment, this was the first and only occasion on which they had ever paid a dividend. Under even the most ordinary of circumstances, such a huge dividend would be unimaginably abnormal. Since Taiwan's textile export industry is fiercely competitive, and it is a depressed business sector, the situation could not be such that it would permit such an enormous dividend. I felt that there had to be some sort of trickery behind this abnormally large dividend.

On getting hold of so much evidence, I wanted to lodge a suit in the Japanese courts. However, after all of my experience in the court system, I had completely lost faith in the courts to pursue justice or to actually punish criminals. I had given up on the Japanese system of "justice" and I knew that even if I brought the case to court, it was abundantly clear to me that the Japanese courts wouldn't believe it and I knew I would lose.

Perhaps the Japanese people might read this book and they might judge for themselves the rights and wrongs of the matter. My purpose in writing this book is not simply to expose the improper conduct of Saibo or Oji Paper or Katakura or any of the other companies in Japan. There are widespread examples in the Japanese media of the wrongdoings of such corporations. Instead, I have written this book because I do not believe that the rebirth of my beloved Japan can take place unless the dishonesty prevalent in the country's corporate culture is rectified. It is time for the Japanese people to take up the fight as well.

The Newest Trick

The intervention by the powers that be didn't stop with trying to prevent me from purchasing additional shares of Saibo. The conspiracy and abuse would not have been complete if I had been able to simply sell my shares and get my investment back. Instead, it would seem that the same forces that ruthlessly attacked me during the Oji Paper and Katakura affairs seemed to be hard at work once again.

At around 10:00 a.m. on May 11, 1999, I suddenly received a telephone call while in Los Angeles from President Toyama of Ichiyoshi Securities Hong Kong. It was a unilateral request to quit as the permanent representative for the Saibo share certificates that were deposited with his company.

It was incomprehensible for such a proposal to come from Ichiyoshi Securities, for whom our company's deposit of Saibo shares should have been a great advantage.

Just before this request from President Toyama of Ichiyoshi Securities Hong Kong, I had filed my shareholder's Instrument for the Exercise of Right of Proposal but when it was ignored, I followed it up with a letter to Saibo and requested an answer regarding my suspicions of dishonest conduct on the part of the Saibo management. In my letter, I asked for a reply by May 12. And then the day before the appointed date, I received this phone call from President Toyama in which he arbitrarily decided to stop acting as the custody agent for the physical certificates.

To the average reader, this refusal may appear to be rather unimportant, but it is actually extremely serious. By refusing to act as the custody agent, this is tantamount to a complete blocking of any sale of Japanese securities by a foreign investor. This is because the Tokyo Stock Exchange requires the clearing of all sold shares to be completed within four days. In order for the clearance to be achieved within four days, all Japanese shares are left in the custody of the securities companies from whom the customers bought them. Doing so works to the mutual benefit of the securities companies and to the customers; the former would have future business guaranteed when the customers wanted to sell their shares, and the latter would be able to obtain a credit margin on the shares.

However, if the customer keeps the shares rather than keeping them in the custody of securities companies, the authenticity of the shares would have to be verified by the issuing company. This process takes a minimum of seven days because the shares need to clear customs. As a result, we would never be able to sell our Saibo shares in the market unless we had a Japanese securities company to act as their custody agent.

They had found a new and clever way to stop sell orders. And once again we see the collusion between securities houses, issuing companies, the Tokyo Stock Exchange, and government bureaucrats.

On May 18, 1999, I therefore sent a letter to President Toyama of Ichiyoshi Securities Hong Kong.

Dear Sir:

I am glad to hear that you are well and prospering.

In regard to your telephone call to me the other day while I was staying in Los Angeles, I must express regret at your unilateral declaration that your company wishes to resign as the permanent representative for Saibo (thereby making it necessary to transfer the Saibo share certificates).

Our company has deposited approximately 5% of the shares issued in Saibo with your company, and I believe that you are aware that it is a great advantage to be the permanent representative of Saibo. For a securities house to have a large volume of shares on deposit is the same as a bank having a large quantity of funds on deposit. The transfer of share certificates is equivalent to having a depositor withdraw his money and ask another bank to take care of it. It is totally incomprehensible why, despite that fact, you wish to resign as the permanent representative and to have the share certificates transferred.

Therefore, what comes to mind is that the reason for the resignation as the permanent representative is not based on your company's circumstances, but more likely on the fact that Saibo has influenced the authorities concerned to put pressure on you. As you are aware, in the past matters of Oji Paper and Katakura Industries, there have been cases in which our company has suffered losses when the Ministry of Finance, the TSE, the "Big Four," and the issuing company have colluded to exert unjust pressure. Taking those matters into consideration, one may surmise that some sort of pressure has certainly been involved in this resignation as permanent representative as well. This matter, which so closely mirrors what happened some twenty years ago when politicians, bureaucrats, and business conspired to exclude us Hong Kong investors, means that things are still being done the

same way now, without any improvement. This is an extremely regrettable matter.

(Remainder omitted)

President Toyama of Ichiyoshi Securities responded to my letter
by saying, "The reason for resigning as the permanent representative
for Saibo is that Ichiyoshi Hong Kong is going to close."

While on the surface, this might sound reasonable, if Ichiyoshi
Hong Kong was actually going to close, it would have been perfectly in order for their head office in Tokyo to take over as the permanent representative. I had chosen Ichiyoshi Securities Hong Kong to
begin because Mr. Kurihara had become their special advisor. Mr.
Kurihara was the former managing director of Nomura Securities
who provided me with the "Kurihara diary" that became key evidence in the Oji Paper case. What is more, three persons—Mr.
Kurihara, former President Sasaki, and his successor, President
Fukumaru—worked at Ichiyoshi who understood me well and were
persons filled with a sense of justice. I had also traded approximately 30 million shares in Nippon Steel through Ichiyoshi Hong Kong.
Ichiyoshi must have earned several tens of millions of yen in commissions alone. The fact that they changed so suddenly and adopted
such behavior is an utterly callous way of doing business.

On December 17, 1999, some seven months after this all began,
President Suehiro of Kokusai Securities Hong Kong came to visit
me at my office.

"Japan's securities houses have changed their way of thinking," he
said, "and we would again like to request you to do business."

Since he had taken the trouble to pay a visit, I said, "Let's transfer
the 699,000 Saibo shares from Ichiyoshi Securities Hong Kong to
Kokusai Securities Hong Kong."

President Suehiro left a very happy man. Four days later, on
December 21, Mr. Motoki of Kokusai Securities Hong Kong came
to visit me, indicating that President Suehiro had sent him. He had

brought along the documents for opening an account, so I signed and returned them.

However, the next day there was a telephone call from Kokusai Securities Hong Kong.

"It is not possible to open a corporate account," they said.

Their contention was that they couldn't accept the deposit of the Saibo shares in the name of my company. Upon further questioning, they would not give me an explanation and merely said they couldn't open the account after all.

Six days later, on December 28, President Suehiro and Mr. Motoki both arrived at my office to explain.

"I'd like an answer in writing," I said, "on why it isn't possible to open an account in a corporate name."

"We can't answer in writing, which is why we came here to explain."

I listened to all the words pouring out as they tearfully apologized. "We got a severe dressing down from the officials from the head office. We are very, very sorry."

I felt badly for these two men who were at the mercy of their head office and who were simply trying to conduct honest business.

Just to make sure that this was a true conspiracy, I also requested Okasan Securities Hong Kong to take deposit of the Saibo shares. I'd had quite a few transactions with Okasan Securities, including purchasing 500,000 shares of Nissan Diesel as a favor to them—a favor that ended up costing me ¥10 million in loss.

Despite my past relationship with them, Okasan Securities Hong Kong also refused to take deposit of the Saibo shares.

This left no doubt in my mind that the power of the authorities and politicians was at work in the background. Under these circumstances, this was the same as the simultaneous self-restraint program in the Oji Paper case of twenty-three years ago? It clearly demonstrates that Japan's establishment has not changed a whit between twenty-three years ago and today.

In order to learn the identity of the parties plotting such malicious activities in the background, on December 30, 1999, I sent letters of inquiry to Kokusai Securities Hong Kong and Okasan Securities Hong Kong. A portion of these letters is given below:

> Moreover, you say that your measures on this occasion have been in accordance with instructions from the General Affairs Department of the head office, but it is strange why the General Affairs Department should intervene in an ordinary transaction. Normally it should be under the Business Department or the International Department. Given the fact that the General Affairs Department involved itself, one can only imagine that some sort of political agency is at work. In the past our company suffered losses in the Oji Paper case and the Katakura Industries case when the Ministry of Finance, the TSE, the "Big Four," and the issuing company colluded to exert improper pressure. On taking account of those matters, it can be surmised that some sort of pressure has certainly been involved in your company's measures on this occasion. This matter, which is exactly the same as around twenty years ago, when politicians, bureaucrats, and businessmen conspired to exclude us Hong Kong investors, means that things are being done the same way now, without any improvement.

Kokusai Securities had said that the General Affairs Department at the head office gave the instructions. One of the tasks of the General Affairs Department is to take countermeasures against *sokaiya* (the extortionists who threaten to disrupt or prolong general shareholders' meetings—*sokai*). Does Kokusai Securities believe me to be a scoundrel of that ilk? This is all the doing of the establishment, which falsely accused me, an innocent person, in the Oji Paper matter. Be that as it may, I have as yet to receive any answer from these companies. The fact that they are unable to respond seems to indicate to me that there is a hidden reason that they do not want to put into writing.

As of the publication of this book, the securities companies are still refusing to act as the custody agent for the Saibo shares. To try to correct this, I have made numerous attempts to receive assistance from the Securities and Futures Commission in Hong Kong, which I will deal with more fully in a later chapter.

In the meantime, Japan continues to hold our Saibo shares as hostages. This hostage situation has pretty much frozen up the trading activities in Saibo shares. However, there are still very minor trading activities of around 1,500 shares traded every 7–10 days just to satisfy the Tokyo Stock Exchange's minimum trading volume to avoid de-listing.

I can safely say that due to the pressure of Japan's Ministry of Finance, Japanese securities companies are afraid to touch or trade the Saibo shares. By preventing the Hong Kong investors from buying more at the price of ¥1,300, it also prevents the rest of Saibo's public shareholders from being able to profit by selling their shares at ¥1,300. Instead, the rest of the Saibo's public shareholders have to suffer the price decline due to the pressure to freeze the Hong Kong investor group's holdings.

The only way to resolve this frozen activity of Saibo shares is to catch and punish all the culprits who are responsible for the present situation. Once that happens, Saibo shares can be traded normally and the sale price will reflect the true value of the company. This would also serve as an example to other Japanese companies and as an example to the rest of the world that Japan can indeed take the proper steps to rectify its situation and begin to build faith in their system.

Continuing Efforts

Because the three different levels of the court system in Japan had denied my shareholders' lawsuit, I have tried in recent months to persuade the other major shareholders to join me in seeking justice. I have written letters to Toyoda Loom Works, the board of directors of the Asahi Bank, and various others.

I wrote personally two times to the Asahi Bank, which is the fifth major shareholder of Saibo, holding some 4.7% of Saibo's shares. I drew their attention to the unlawful activities committed by Saibo in seeking to dilute the shareholdings not only of my own company, but of theirs as well. I pointed out to them that they had fiduciary responsibilities to their own shareholders, who, because of the Asahi Bank's investment in Saibo, also had a stake in pursuing Saibo's wrongdoings. After no reply whatsoever from the Asahi Bank, on February 27th, 2001, my lawyer also wrote to them.

> It is rather obvious in the proper discharge of the duties imposed on the Board of Directors of your bank and in order to protect the rights and interest of your shareholders, you are obliged to take appropriate actions against Saibo in respect of the matters complained of above in the afore-mentioned letter to Saibo. Besides, the absence of any action against Saibo by companies such as your bank, may suggest that despite the apparent attempt by the Japanese government to bring about new changes and reforms to the Japanese financial and banking system, it somehow still operates very much as a closed shop with Japanese companies, banks, and financial institutions protecting and covering up for one another.

The letter to Toyoda Loom Works and the other major share-holders was essentially the same as the one to the Asahi Bank. Unfortunately, none of them have taken any action against Saibo for any of Saibo's illegal actions. It is sad to see that these Japanese corporations are not brave enough to stand up to one of their own. What they don't seem to realize is that companies such as Saibo—to say nothing of their own inaction—damages their own reputation in the eyes of the world.

In all of my correspondence with the other shareholders of Saibo, I included a copy of my lawyer's letter to Saibo that he sent on January 3, 2001. In this letter, I reiterated my problems with Saibo, their illegal self-dealings, and made mention of how similar all of this was to the Oji Paper and Katakura affairs. I restated my position on their self-dealings, the dubious sale of 100,000 shares by their president, Hirobumi Iizuka, and also pointed out to them the illegal activities regarding Chao Hui Trading in Taiwan and what I knew of their involvement—something that I had not yet pursued in court.

My lawyer closed with the following:

> However, what happened to Mr. Wang and his Hong Kong investor friends in your company did not necessarily apply to other Japanese companies. In the example of San Sui Electric, instead of blocking and seeking to interfere and hinder the investment of Hong Kong investors, it continuously issued substantial shares to Hong Kong investors. The quantities of shares issued to Hong Kong investors in December 1993 was 27,610,000 shares (equivalent to 12.89% of the entire issued capital of the company), which was at ¥163; in October 1994 another 12,660,000 shares (equivalent to 5.58%) at ¥300, and in June 1996 a further 13,770,000 shares (equivalent to 5.72%) at ¥218.

> According to Mr. Wang's experience in the Oji Paper, Katakura, and Saibo affairs, Japanese stock exchanges would not welcome the issue of substantial amounts of shares to Hong Kong investors. The only reason that Mr. Wang could think of was that the performance of San Sui was extremely unsatisfactory. In fact, the price of San Sui shares is currently about ¥8. The moral of this story tells us that the Japanese financial machine does not allow or tolerate foreign investors to share their benefit of success but would only readily allow foreign investors to take part in losing ventures.

It is truly regretful that this is the reality in dealing with the Japanese. I can only hope that one day, and one day soon, the citizens of Japan will wake up to what is happening in their country and take up the fight.

To this day, my problems with Saibo continue and the shares continue to be in cold storage.

Chapter Eleven

Efforts in Hong Kong

I am certainly not alone in my efforts to persuade the Japanese to reform, neither in the U.S. nor in Hong Kong. Though I have spearheaded the criticism of the Japanese way of doing business, some of my Hong Kong friends have been also involved, whether they were part of the lawsuits or simply supporting me in other ways.

Of my friends, Li Ka-shing is probably the most well known in Western circles. He holds several companies, Cheung Kong (Holdings) Ltd., Hutchison Whampoa Ltd., Cheung Kong Infrastructure Holding Ltd., The Hong Kong Electric Group, and tom.com. The market value of groups and companies under his control total HK$610.11 billion or US$78.219 billion. In the middle of the Katakura affair, I received the following letter of support from him.

1 October 1983

Dear Tseng Hsiang,

Thank you for forwarding the magazines and newspaper clippings and their contents have been noted.

It was unfortunate that you have been treated unfairly repeatedly in the course of your investing in Japanese companies. I have since been watching closely the development of the case and I feel that the action you take is on the right track. I hope your efforts will generate public opinions in response and in support to bring forth an early resolution to the case.

With my autumn greetings,

Li Ka-shing

When you're working against the system, there is a lot of room for self-doubt. His note of encouragement and support during the difficult times of the Katakura affair meant a great deal to me, especially that he believed in what I was doing.

Hong Kong

In addition to trying to bring pressure on Japan from the U.S., I have been trying to raise further awareness in Hong Kong of the problems with the Japanese financial system. I live part of the year in Hong Kong, and I have many friends and business associates there. Hong Kong is, of course, much closer to Japan geographically than is the U.S., and, as a result, Hong Kong knows more about Japan's economics than does the U.S. Also, since the Japanese securities companies had branches in Hong Kong and because the Oji Paper boycott, which made international headlines, included securities companies based in Hong Kong, my experiences are much better known there.

Hong Kong might be geographically closer and also much more financially tied to Japan than the United States, but that doesn't mean that it has any greater sway over the politics of Japan. It also doesn't mean that it's any easier to get any kind of action out of the authorities—which seems to be a universal problem.

In August of 2000, I decided that in addition to trying to raise awareness in the United States, I needed to focus attention on Hong Kong. On August 22, 2000, I wrote a letter to Mr. Andrew Sheng, who is the chairman of the Securities and Futures Commission, which is loosely comparable to the United States' Securities and Exchange Commission.

In my letter I raised complaints to the Securities and Futures Commission about the treatments that I received from the Japanese securities companies and their Hong Kong subsidiaries that acted in concert to obstruct my legitimate investments in Japan. I also wrote about the illegal activities of the Japanese securities companies and of the concerted actions involving the Ministry of Finance, the TSE, and the Japanese companies that had issued the stock. As part of my letter, I supplied him with information concerning my investments.

However, I received a reply dated October 23, 2000, that was not at all encouraging and which indicated to me that the commission didn't seem to understand the problems that were occurring. I then supplied Mr. Sheng with further information about my investments and the trouble I was experiencing.

My Hong Kong friends also sent similar letters to the Securities and Futures Commission that supported my position. My friends, who are all very famous and wealthy in Hong Kong, encouraged me in my actions and complaints against the Japanese Securities houses and against the Japanese authorities for their unfair treatment of foreigners. After all, some of them were part of these investments, and those that weren't directly involved certainly knew what was happening and understood the consequences of the actions of the Japanese.

Lee Shau Kee is another of my influential friends. He holds Henderson Land Development Co. Ltd., Henderson Investment Limited, Henderson China Holdings Limited, Hong Kong Ferry (Holdings) Company Limited, The Hong Kong and China Gas Company Limited, Miramar Hotel and Investment Company Limited, and Henderson Cyber Limited. His holdings have a market value of HK$137.88 billion, or US$17.68 billion.

On November 13th, 2000, he also personally wrote to Mr. Sheng to voice his support of my position.

Dear Mr. Sheng,

It has come to my knowledge that Mr. Cheng Yu-tung wrote to you on matters concerning Saibo, a Japanese stock, and would be grateful for your assistance.

I am also a good friend of Mr. Wang and have been party to the purchase of Japanese stocks, Katakura Industries and Saibo. I am currently holding 626,000 shares of Saibo and ranked seventh of the Company's largest shareholders. I now certify my authorization of Mr. Wang as my representative in handling all legal matters concerning my Saibo stocks. Mr. Wang will approach you shortly. Thank you for your attention.

With high respect and regards,

Lee Shau Kee

Dr. Cheng Yu-tung, whom Lee Shau Kee mentions in his letter, is the founder of New World Development Ltd.. More than twenty years ago, when it floated at the Hong Kong Stock Exchange, it was the largest among Chinese-owned realtors with a market value of US$2.2 billion.

I remember a conversation between Dr. Cheng and myself on one of our trips to the United States. On the plane, I advised him that as the market value of New World Development stocks was at a high of about US$2.2 billion, and the American bank stocks were low, he should trade them off for Citibank shares. I also told him at that time there were many outstanding managers at Citibank and his money would be safe and working for him after the trade-off. But Cheng said that New World Development was his baby and he couldn't bring himself to sell it simply for the sake of money. It would be unfair to the stockholders as well, he said. So he decided not to do the transaction.

If he had done that at the time, he would have been one of the major stockholders of Citibank today. Even now, Cheng is still busy working for his company every day. If he had carried out the trade-off, he would have been free to do whatever he likes to do, playing golf as he likes. The New World Development stocks were of a high value then and he still holds them today.

To his credit, he is a famous person in Hong Kong through commitment and hard work. He owns the Grand Hyatt Hotel, the New World Hotels chain, the commercial complex of New World Centre, etc., among many other real estate properties. He is the largest Hong Kong-based investor in China, with investments of over tens of billions of Hong Kong dollars. He has a secondary school in his hometown built with funds he donated. I have visited the place myself. It is very large, almost on the scale of a university.

On November 13th, 2000, he wrote:

Dear Mr. Sheng,

I am writing in support of my good friend, Mr. Wang Tseng Hsiang, who has recently submitted a complaint to your Commission.

In 1977, on the recommendation of Mr. Wang Tseng Hsiang, Mr. Chan Tsang Hei, Mr. Fung King Hei, Mr. Chung Ming Fai, and I made joint purchases of Japanese stock, Oji Paper, with Mr. Wang determining the purchase offer each time. Our wish to increase our Oji holdings was subsequently pre-empted by the eight Japanese securities companies based in Hong Kong who refused to accept our instructions to purchase, arousing much dissatisfaction on our part. However, they later guaranteed that such an incident would not recur thereafter and recommended Japanese stocks Katakura Industries and Saibo to Mr. Wang, and hence, Mr. Wang, Li Shau Kee, and I made joint purchases of such stocks. Saibo Company has recently caused problems and for which Mr. Wang wrote a letter of complaint to the Commission.

Chief Executive Mr. Tung Chee Hwa has strongly advocated the importance of free economy and fair competition in Hong Kong. It is my sincere wish that Mr. Wang's complaint could be handled fairly in your capacity as the Chairman of the Commission. Your serious attention to the matter will be highly appreciated.

With high respect and regards,

Cheng Yu-tung

Robin Y. H. Chan, GBS, LLD, JP, EOE, is another friend of mine who offered his support. He is the chairman & managing director of Asia Financial Holdings Ltd., the chairman & CEO of Asia Commercial Bank Ltd., the deputy to the Chinese National People's Congress, the chairman of the Chinese General Chamber of Commerce, Hong Kong, a council member of Hong Kong Trade Development Council, an advisor to the board of directors of Bangkok Bank Public Co., Ltd., and an advisor to the board of directors of the Tokai Bank Ltd., Japan. Needless to say, he is an extremely important and busy individual. But he still took the time to support me by writing his own letter to Mr. Sheng.

14 November 2000

Dear Mr. Sheng,

I am writing in support of Mr. Wang Tseng Hsiang who has recently submitted a complaint to your Commission and would be grateful for your assistance.

About thirteen years ago, through the connection of my good friend Mr. Wang Tseng Hsiang, Mr. Li Shau Kee, Cheng Yu-tung, and I jointly purchased shares of the Saibo Company. Saibo Company has recently caused problems and for which Mr. Wang wrote a letter of complaint to the Commission.

I now certify that Mr. Wang Tseng Hsiang is my representative in handling all legal matters regarding my Saibo
stocks. It is my sincere wish that the case could be fairly handled and resolved in your capacity as the Chairman of the
Commission.

Thank you for your attention.

With regards,

Robin Y. H. Chan

As you can see, I am clearly not alone in this and these other influential persons believe in and understand the importance of what I
am doing.

Despite all of this, Mr. Sheng's reply of December 6, 2000, was
again disappointing. So on January 8, 2001, I had my attorney write
to the Securities and Futures Commission. Here are some excerpts
from that letter.

> Your decision not to investigate Mr. Wang's complaint
> was, in our view, made without any in-depth understanding
> of the nature of Mr. Wang's complaint. Our client's com-
> plaint was made on the basis that Japanese securities compa-
> nies, their Hong Kong subsidiaries, and the Japanese author-
> ities embarked on a course of conduct with a view to, and did
> in fact, amongst other things, manipulate the price of
> Japanese securities, blocked and boycotted the disposal of
> the shares of Mr. Wang and his friends, and finally forced
> them to sell at prices which were suppressed by false infor-
> mation and publication.

> It appears that the basis of your decision not to take
> action was that the matter complained of "mainly revolved
> around the refusal of the brokers to provide services" and
> there was nothing under Hong Kong law giving sufficient
> ground for the Commission to initiate an investigation. We

respectfully beg to disagree in this regard. May we set out your statutory duties in this regard with reference to the Section 4 of the enabling Securities and Futures Commission Ordinance as follows:

1. One of your duties is to supervise and monitor the activities of exchange companies and clearing houses. This obligation clearly covers activities of the Hong Kong subsidiaries of Japanese securities companies in Hong Kong who chose to set up shop here conducting business in Japanese securities (Section 4(1)(d));
2. It is also your duty to take all reasonable steps to safeguard the interests of persons dealing in securities (Section 4(1)(e)). No doubt our client Mr. Wang and his friends who invested in Japanese securities through Japanese securities companies in Hong Kong were those intended to be safeguarded; and
3. You are also under the duty to suppress illegal, dishonorable, and improper practices in dealing in securities and the provision of investment advice or other services relating to securities (Section 4(1)(g)).

The true nature of our client's complaint is not the failure or refusal of Japanese securities companies to provide services. Instead, their failure and refusal to provide services to our client was only part of a scheme or plot with a view to stifle or obstruct our client's bona fide dealing in securities with a view to ultimately lock in his investments and to eventually force him to dispose of them at below the true market price. This was certainly not "commercial decisions made by the brokers in the course of their business" and they were certainly guilty of gross misconduct.

My lawyer then went over a list of more than a dozen enclosures I prepared for Mr. Sheng, including recent letters my attorney had sent to those who had acted against my friends and me in the Oji Paper, Katakura, and Saibo affairs. These enclosures included letters to the Ministry of Finance, the chairman of the Tokyo Stock Exchange, the securities companies, in addition to Oji Paper, Katakura, and Saibo. I also included two briefing papers and the transcript of Mr. Yoshida's testimony. Mr. Yoshida, you will remember, was the former Chief of the Distribution Market Section of the Securities Bureau of the Ministry of Finance of Japan.

The transcript contained evidence of Mr. Yoshida's testimony, making it quite clear that he was guilty of abuse of his statutory powers, which led to the imposition of the "Self Restraint Program" by the Japanese securities companies.

I further enclosed testimony of Mr. Hirobumi Iizuka (the president of Saibo), showing the Iizuka family's unlawful conduct and how they acted to retain control by diluting the other shareholders' percentages at a grossly undervalued sale to their own companies.

My lawyer then wrote about the Saibo case, which is still continuing and which the Hong Kong subsidiaries were and continue to be guilty of refusing to act as custody agents for my shares of Saibo:

> To further explain why we say the refusal of Hong Kong subsidiaries of Japanese securities companies to act as custody agent for Mr. Wang for his Saibo shares was not simply "a refusal to provide services" in the nature of a "commercial decision," please be advised that Mr. Wang in his previous letter of October 5th, 2000, set out the circumstances of the refusal, and he further pointed out that the concerted boycott by them not to act as custody agent for Mr. Wang literally turned his Saibo shares into worthless papers, because Mr. Wang will not be able to properly dispose of his shares in the Tokyo Stock Exchange if he has no custody agent. Certainly by seeking to sell them outside the Tokyo Stock Exchange was improper and Mr. Wang certainly will not do so.

It is quite clear that the refusal by the Japanese securities houses in Hong Kong was a concerted move and no doubt orchestrated by their head office in Japan, and probably with the participation of relevant authorities as in the previous Oji Paper and Katakura affairs. This sort of conduct can hardly be simplified as a legitimate "commercial decision" made by any securities broker whose very business it is to provide their services in order to earn commissions. How can this be regarded as a legitimate "commercial decision" if their refusal to accept business from our client will lead to the inevitable result that our client will not be able to lawful dispose of his shares and that his investment will be locked up unless this position is going to change?

...Viewing the situation as a whole, their actions or inactions in Hong Kong was part and partial of the bigger unlawful and tortuous scheme engineered by those in Japan.

It is the Commission's duty to supervise and monitor the activities of these Japanese securities companies, to take reasonable steps to safeguard the interest of our client and his friends who are part of the Hong Kong investing public, and further to suppress illegal and unlawful conduct. Since you are a regulating authority there is certainly no imposition on you to be satisfied to the same standard as the prosecuting authorities to have at least a prima facie case before taking any action.

Please kindly reconsider your position and give us a response at your earliest convenience. With the further materials we supplied above, we hope that you will be in the position to consider taking steps to investigate into the affairs and operations of the Japanese securities companies involved.

In all, my attorney sent him a five-page letter with more than a dozen enclosures, which amounted to roughly two hundred pages of material. We hoped that this would get the attention of the Securities and Futures Commission and that they would take appropriate actions against the securities companies once they understood the problem at hand. After all, if the Securities and Futures Commission truly understood the nature of my complaints, then they could hardly claim—as they originally had—that the Hong Kong subsidiaries of the Japanese securities companies had acted as they had merely out of commercial decisions. It was plain that they simply had not understood my previous letters because there was no way to understand the securities companies' action in the Saibo case as a mere "business decision." After all, whoever heard of a company refusing an honest commission only to claim they did so out of business concerns?

In response to our voluminous letter, Mr. Sheng replied on February 12, 2001, with the following:

Dear Sirs,

Thank you for your letter of 8 January 2001 and enclosures.

As indicated in my last letter dated 6 December 2000 to Mr. Wang, the Commission considered carefully all the material that he previously sent to us in support of his complaint against the Japanese brokers in question. Our decision not to pursue any further investigation was made having given due consideration to the totality of the evidence as revealed in the material supplied by Mr. Wang...

The Commission has no jurisdiction over matters that occur on Japanese markets. With respect to Saibo share matter, as I explained in my last letter, the Commission does not interfere with commercial decisions made by brokers in the course of their business, unless the brokers have been guilty of misconduct and their fitness and properness to remain as registered persons has been seriously impugned. It is clearly open to a broker not to act as a custodian of the shares in Hong Kong since it needed to deal directly with Japanese securities houses in Tokyo. The Commission has no power to act in these circumstances.

It seems as though the Japanese have invaded and made a colony out of Hong Kong. Or at least they have invaded the Hong Kong bureaucracy.

So here we see the two main reasons for Mr. Sheng's refusal to get involved in the matter. One, that "the Commission had no jurisdiction over matters that occur on Japanese markets" and that "the Commission does not interfere with commercial decisions made by brokers in the course of their business, unless the brokers have been guilty of misconduct and their fitness and properness to remain as registered persons has been seriously impugned."

As for the first reason, we were not asking for him to take jurisdiction over matters that happened on the Japanese markets. We were asking him to look at the conduct of the subsidiaries that are in Hong Kong. It is not as if the Hong Kong subsidiaries are embassies and have diplomatic immunity. They are registered businesses in Hong Kong and therefore liable to the laws of Hong Kong. The idea that the Securities and Futures Commission did not see that they had any jurisdiction because their actions were based on orders received from abroad would be like saying that if a murder happens in the U.S., though it was ordered from abroad, the local police have no authority to act on it. A crime is a crime, regardless of its origins.

As for the second reason, can the actions of the Japanese securities companies and their Hong Kong subsidiaries be considered anything less than being "guilty of misconduct"? Even the most recent example with Saibo shows their misconduct as their actions have turned my investment into worthless pieces of paper.

However, as we would point out, the course of actions involved in implementing the conspiracy were invariably completed or at least executed in Hong Kong by the subsidiaries of the Japanese securities companies. For this reason the courts in Hong Kong do have jurisdiction to deal with the matters under complaint.

Not one to give up, I tried again on March 12, 2001. My attorney drafted a 25-page letter to Mr. Sheng to once again try to persuade the Securities and Futures Commission to take some action. What follows are excerpts from that letter.

> In our respectful view, both reasons given by you seeking to justify your decision not to further investigate the matters under complaint are invalid. This erroneous decision reflects the fact that you either misinterpreted the evidence presented to you or you are simply shutting your eyes to the obvious colluded actions by the parent Japanese securities companies in Japan and their subsidiaries in Hong Kong...
>
> If you had given the matters complained of some thought, you should be able to discern the connection or link and come to the conclusion that whatever happened in Japan were part of the whole conspiracy which would even merit criminal sanction. But criminal sanction is not what Mr. Wang asks from the Commission, he is merely asking the Commission to discharge its statutory duties and obligations under the Securities and Futures Commission Ordinance to check against the unlawful conducts of these Hong Kong subsidiaries of Japanese securities companies to protect and safeguard the interest of Hong Kong investors, and to further regulate the business practices of Japanese securities companies in Hong Kong...
>
> As far as your comment that "the commission does not interfere with commercial decisions" in respect of the "Saibo Share matter" is concerned, you had probably not given due consideration to what we said in our last letter dated 8 January 2001 sent to you on behalf of Mr. Wang on the same subject. May we take this opportunity to point out again that the Tokyo Sock Exchange ("TSE") requires clearing of all shares sold within four days. But if Japanese securities companies did not keep the shares that were sold then

their authenticity would have to be verified by the issuing companies and this verification process would take seven days. Accordingly, if the shares to be delivered were not kept by a Japanese securities company as custody agent, the verification process would make it impossible for any foreign investors—although they could deliver the shares to Tokyo within the four days time limit—to complete any transaction.

It is therefore imperative that any foreign investor, who wishes to dispose of their shares in the market, would have to place or leave their shares in the custody of Japanese securities companies, so that this four-day time limit can be met. In fact, no investor in Japanese shares—whether Japanese or foreigners—would ever keep the shares bought by themselves and would invariably leave them in the custody of the securities companies through whom they had bought them. Besides, the investors would be able to obtain a credit margin of 50% on the shares in the custody of the securities companies, and the securities companies would welcome this as this meant secured business in the future when the investors wanted to sell their shares. As far as Mr. Wang is concerned, he always placed his shares in the custody of Japanese securities companies after he bought them over the last few decades and he had never once took physical possession of the shares...

Indeed, it can hardly lie in the mouths of these Japanese securities companies and their Hong Kong subsidiaries to say that they were entitled not to act as custody agent for Mr. Wang as this would amount to turning away business opportunities to earn substantial commissions involving such huge quantities of Saibo shares.

In contrast to your apparently indifferent attitude in relation to the matters complained of by Mr. Wang, the response from the U.S. SEC was much more positive than that demonstrated by your Commission. They immediately placed the matters complained of on file, expressed their interest, and further requested Mr. Wang to provide them with any additional information in the future...

Mr. Wang is of the view that it is about time that civil servants should come out from the antiquated colonial closet and shed their antiquated civil servant attitude. In particular, Hong Kong had returned to the motherland after the change of sovereignty in 1997. Your Commission is entrusted by the Securities and Future Ordinance to supervise and monitor the activities of securities companies, to safeguard the interests of investors, and, above all, to suppress illegal, dishonorable, and improper practices in the dealing of securities...

Your indifference in these complaints may be taken as a sign of weakness by those to whom the complaints were directed, and your failure to take any steps to look into the complaints may be considered by some as tarnishing the reputation of Hong Kong as a righteous and just society.

We hope the above may help you to change your views in respect of the comments you made in your last letter to us on behalf of Mr. Wang and that you may consider taking Mr. Wang's complaint further.

After more than two months of waiting, we received a response dated May 31st, 2001. In part, it read:

We have the following observations in relation to your client's complaint:

1. We note that your client has taken separate legal action against certain listed companies and brokerages in Japan, as well as some of the subsidiaries in Hong Kong (back in 1984). All these actions however appear to have either been unsuccessful or have been discontinued by your client on legal advice or otherwise.

2. Your client's allegation of conspiracy or collusion involves the Ministry of Finance, Tokyo Stock Exchange, a number of Japanese brokerages and their Hong Kong subsidiaries together with the Japanese listed companies whose securities were involved. Most of these alleged parties are, of course, in Japan. Any investigation carried out would, therefore, inevitably involve an exercise of obtaining evidence from witnesses and other alleged parties in Japan.

3. Two of the matters complained of occurred more than 20 years ago. In this connection, we have not been able to trace any record of complaints received from your client prior to September 2000, when these matters were first brought to the attention of the Commission. The age of these matters would, in any event, now pose difficulties to any investigation. Given the time lapse, it would be practically difficult for any regulator to seek to gather evidence from witnesses or retrieve the relevant documentation in relation to your client's allegations. In any event, it would be difficult even to establish a prima facie case without the co-operation of the Japanese authorities.

After considering the totality of the evidence, I regret that we remain of the view that Commission is not able to investigate your client's complaint in Hong Kong.

While I fully appreciate your client's grievances, I believe that it is appropriate for this matter to be dealt with by the relevant authorities in Japan. As previously indicated, I would be happy to forward your client's complaint, together with all the supporting documents, to the Financial Services Agency in Japan if he so wishes.

After all this time and effort, the Commission *still* did not seem to see how the securities companies' decision to refuse to act as the custody agent for the Saibo shares had turned our investment into worthless pieces of paper.

If I could only persuade the Commission to investigate even just one of the securities companies then it is likely that they would be persuaded to change their position on the boycott. For now, they continue to abuse their power simply because they are arrogant and believe that they can get away with it. After all, they know that they are unlikely to get caught and even if they do, then it is unlikely they will actually be punished. Such is the way with the justice system in Japan. Those responsible simply are not prosecuted unless it is a *truly* heinous crime, rather than face discipline for lesser acts. In this case, it is a crime that lies hidden. But the way to stop abusers is to expose them. And that is what I hope to do.

As part of my continuing efforts, after the completion of this book, I will be sending letters to the media in Hong Kong to try to draw attention to the abuse of power that the securities companies regularly engage in. Here's what I plan to send:

> It is encouraging to hear that Japan's Prime Minister wants restructure and reform but, to be frank, I'm skeptical that anything can be improved and changed if the culprits who contributed to the current mess in Japan are not caught and punished. In the case of the Savings and Loan bailout in the U.S. years ago—done so with taxpayers' money—more than 1,000 culprits were caught and jailed. However, in Japan, there is still no news of anyone in a position of power being caught and jailed. Meanwhile, Japanese taxpayers have to pay many times more than the U.S. taxpayers to save their own banking crisis.
>
> Since the Japanese authorities refuse to catch and prosecute those parties responsible for the current crisis, this alone raises doubts that Japan can have true reform. From my new book, you will find that even now there is still no change in the way Japan's financial sector and the brokerage houses do

business and continue to proceed in the old way. My investment in Saibo is an example to this still unfair and unjust
treatment.

I know and love the Japanese people, having spent my
youth in Japan and having invested in Japanese companies for
more than 30 years. As you will see, I have been trying to help
Japan change its system for the last 20 years and have met
with a great deal of resistance. I have saved over 1,500 newspaper and magazine articles discussing Japan's past scandals,
which I will make available for your review. The Japanese
public, in my opinion, is afraid to speak out for themselves
against the establishment. I have seen and experienced their
plight and am speaking out on their behalf. And speak out I
did. I have also recently sent faxes to the members of the
National Diet in Japan, voicing the need for a harsher action
against the culprits who have caused and continue to add to
Japan's current financial crisis.

Please join me in encouraging a strong reform in Japan by
using our public voice, our very own media.

In addition to writing to the Securities and Futures Commission,
and media, I have written to others in Hong Kong, including to the
Financial Secretary of Hong Kong. I explained to him my efforts,
including writing my books and speaking out on behalf of the
Japanese. By writing to him I hoped that "all the evils and anomalies
in the Japanese system will be fully exposed to the international world
who will come to realize that if Japan does not mend its ways, the
entire system in time will collapse giving rise to catastrophic effects
not only to Japan itself, but to the rest of the world's other leading
economies, including the U.S. and Hong Kong…When the inevitable
happens, no doubt Hong Kong will be adversely affected."

Finally, I will be approaching the *South China Morning Post* by letter
along with numerous enclosures regarding my efforts over the years
on behalf of the Japanese people. I am going to tell their readers how

the reforms being sought by Prime Minister Koizumi are supported by more than 90% of the people. And yet, until those who are responsible for the problems to begin with are caught and punish, no true reform will have ever taken place. I will cite the example of my still on-going problem with Saibo and offer them the use of my extensive newspaper collection of articles that discuss Japan's past scandals. I will tell them, too, how the Japanese people are afraid to speak out on their own and hoped that they would add their voice to mine in calling for reform.

No one can know the future. Will any of these efforts have any effect in Hong Kong and, as a result, in Japan? It's hard to say. Judging from the lackadaisical and mindless civil-servant responses from the Securities and Futures Commission, I have my doubts that the Commission will move forward and actually do something. But I do know this much: that if I don't try then I am assured of failing.

Chapter Twelve

The Future

It has been a very long road from the first days I spent on Japanese soil where I'd gone for school. I had not gone to Japan with the intention of starting a food importer business, or of buying my own ship to sail dangerous waters during World War II. Indeed, as I said in the beginning of this book, my life took an unexpected turn when I missed my school examination. But how fortunate indeed that I did; otherwise, I might have been lost in obscurity as a company clerk. It seems Fate had other ideas for me.

"The future is an undiscovered country," Shakespeare said. What will the future hold for the country of Japan? No one can say. I have done what I can and continue to try to reform a system that I have struggled with for many years. I hope that others soon will pick up the fight, both here in the United States and in other countries, otherwise the problems that Japan finds itself mired in may soon find their way to other shores. The fate of the Japanese people so far remains to be seen.

Despite all the years of struggle that I have had, there has been very little change to the entrenched ways of Japan's financial system. However, at least I can have the satisfaction of knowing that by my efforts, the Japanese public has been alerted to the problems and that there is a growing public interest in the problems that shareholders of Japanese companies have. I began this book with the intention of sharing my problems with readers in the United States and to expose the inner workings of the Japanese financial system—the "Economic Gang." I believe that the average American citizen (to say nothing of the average American congressman) thinks of Japan as a free market, much the same as we have here in the United States or in Great Britain or the other Western countries. I hope that in bringing out this book, I have at least opened the reading public's eyes to the injustices that are possible in the Japanese financial system and I hope that perhaps you, too, will begin to speak out on behalf of the Japanese people.

For the Sake of Japan

In March of 1999, an incident occurred at Bridgestone, the world-famous Japanese tire manufacturer. A 58-year-old former Bridgestone employee, who was laid off due to restructuring, committed hara-kiri in the company president's office as a way of protesting staff cutbacks. The suicide note that he left said:

> Thirty some years have passed since I entered this company as one part of a group sharing a common destiny with Bridgestone. We denied ourselves all the comforts of life and family in order to work for and support the company, building up Bridgestone to what it has become today. The way the company applies the rule that 'if you can't accept the way the company treats you, then quit' is an unpardonable act to the people who have supported Bridgestone for so many years. You administrators accept this policy without any resistance, just like lambs. Employees must unite against such managers who treat them like disposable garbage.

At large corporations in Japan, a storm of restructuring has been set loose. Bridgestone alone has reduced its work force by 3,000 in the past six years. Yet Bridgestone is the top tire manufacturer in the world. Its financial condition is excellent and its stock price is more than ¥2,200 per share. As a publicly listed company in Japan, it has enormous latent assets. It is simply an excellent company with increasing earnings per share that distributes extra dividends to shareholders. One can understand staff cutbacks or management restructuring at Japanese banks and general construction companies, which hold huge amounts of bad assets, but if a strong company like Bridgestone fires a large number of employees how good can this be for the regeneration of Japan? If other excellent companies follow Bridgestone and carry out reductions in their work forces, it will spur on social unrest.

In the current situation, many other large corporations are continuing to carry out staff cutbacks by the thousands. The total unemployment rate has reached 4.6%, which is the highest in Japan's history, and the number of unemployed exceeds 3,000,000. I am growing increasingly worried about the implications of surging unemployment for Japanese social cohesion.

Japan is in the middle of a great upheaval. Its bubble economy burst in the late 1980s but the Japanese government continued to prop up the economy in the 1990s and tried to maintain the lifestyle of its citizens with massive deficit spending. No one addressed the problems that led to the current situation. Banks have gone under or have been forced to merge with other banks. The government, in addition to having to spend to keep the current standard of living for the Japanese people, is now forced to deal with decades of abuse in the banking and financial sector and is spending trillions of yen just to bail out the system. This leaves nothing for new growth.

Recession, bankruptcy, restructuring, and unemployment have pounced upon middle-class salary men at big corporations, who up until now have been leading comfortable lives. The myth that you were guaranteed a cushy set-up for life if you latched onto a job at a large corporation is now a thing of the past. The newer white-collar workers who complain about losing their accustomed annual salary increases and bonuses are the lucky ones. For middle-aged and elderly white-collar workers, restructuring isn't just something that happens to other people. Instead they are faced with the very real possibility that they will lose their jobs and join the ranks of the unemployed. Many salary men are now in a situation where they are giving their all for the company even while the sword of restructuring is hanging over their heads.

Managers and employees of small and medium-sized companies are in an even worse situation than white-collar workers at large corporations. Because of the recession, they have no work. With the banks' unwillingness to make loans, there has been a sudden increase in the number of bankruptcies owing to a lack of working capital. To put this financial phenomenon in human terms, three presidents of small and medium-sized Japanese companies recently committed suicide by hanging themselves at the same time in the same hotel.

Grieving Over Japanese Society

Financial unrest gives rise to social unrest. Various incidents have shaken Japan after the collapse of the bubble economy, such as the elementary schoolboy murder case committed by a youth in Kobe and the bus hijacking and murder case perpetrated by a seventeen-year-old youth.

A social situation in which the future is unclear and people are forced to live in a stifling straitjacket has a negative psychological effect, particularly on young people. It is frightening how many recent juvenile crimes have been carried out by persons in a so-called *"kireta"* (blacked-out) psychological state in which they lash out and cause harm. Every time that I see the reports of cases that fall short of murder, such as school bullying or violence, or classroom breakdown, even I as a foreigner worry about the future of Japan. I still love Japan and the Japanese people and, for that reason, I can't help worrying about Japan's present condition and its future.

Why has Japan come to this state? In the past, the Japanese people were exceedingly polite, kind, warm-hearted and very virtuous.

They respected their elders and looked after their youth. Nowadays, it seems there are fewer and fewer such people in Japan and the moral fiber of the Japanese people has been destroyed. Where is their honor? Throughout the period of the bubble economy and its breakdown, I feel that the Japanese people have rapidly changed. The system of cozy relationships among politicians, bureaucrats, and corporate managers who have committed illegal acts for their own interests, and the justice system that tolerated their illegal acts, is rotting Japan from the core.

The regeneration of Japan does not only mean financial regeneration, but also social regeneration. To this end, without question bad practices must be eliminated, especially the cozy relationships among political, bureaucratic, business and financial elites. The Japanese government preaches Japanese regeneration, but I can only feel they want to preserve the system of cozy relationships unchanged. If Japan leaves this system of cozy relationships as is, Japan will become isolated from the world. Why don't the Japanese people protest the policies that save banks and a number of corporations at the expense of the citizens? It is what the Bridgestone employee meant when he said, "just like lambs." I believe this to be very true of the Japanese people who remain as silent at lambs in the face of the authorities.

I received a sympathetic letter from someone who had read my book *The Eve of the Financial and Securities Collapse*, which was published in Japan in 1998. He wrote, "while reading your book, my blood boiled over with righteous indignation many times...I can clearly understand such curt relationships among the people in positions of power."

This person was denied an appointment to a managerial position for a long time because he opposed one of his superiors in his company. In Japan, when a person disobeys managers or executives, they will often be treated coldly within the company. Therefore, Japanese white-collar workers submissively obey orders, even if the policies of the company are wrong. Not fighting against those in power is simply necessary to protect one's position.

Japan is now looking over the abyss of its survival as a major economic power. What is more, it has a chance to restore the fine societal customs appropriate for a great power. If Japan foregoes this opportunity, however, I fear there is no hope for its regeneration. Now is the time that the Japanese people must rise up and send a message to those in power.

Even so, I have not given up hope for the Japanese people. A Japanese publisher brought out my fifth book, *A Victim of the Establishment*, in April of 2001 and I will be publishing editions of it in Chinese. This book, in fact, is largely based on it. It is my hope that with the reading of these editions by people throughout the world, the issues that I have been raising with Japan for many years will become part of an international dialogue.

I would like to present a letter that was sent to me by a reader of the Japanese edition:

> I have read your works with a great deal of interest. I share your sentiments so much that I feel like shouting: "That's just what it's like!" The details of the various cases described in your latest work, *A Victim of the Establishment*, have provided a thorough briefing on what goes on at trials. The authorities in Japan cannot deal with it by dismissing it as being ridiculous and cheap. The people in Japan's establishment are extremely angry.
>
> I understand that absurd things have been done to Mr. Tseng Hsiang Wang as a result of the fading of the moral vision and the loss of the spiritual nobility of the Japanese establishment, which should be leading the Japanese state and society. Moreover, I also used to believe in the fairness of authorities such as the judiciary, but on learning of the details of the decisions against Mr. Tseng Hsiang Wang, I was astonished to find that the rot has advanced as far as it has.
>
> Patriotic sentiments are gaining strength in Japan's current situation, which is impervious to justice and righteousness.

Nonetheless, it is really shameful that even though the warning has been sounded by Mr. Tseng Hsiang Wang, a foreigner who loves Japan so much, we Japanese are at a loss about what to do.

In another of your works, you have written: "Doesn't a true spirit of love for one's company mean having the backbone to come down against illegal activities and trying to prevent them." I absolutely believe that to be the case. However, for the average Japanese office worker, such a course would require the kind of courage needed to leap off the top of a cliff. In such circumstances, they will waver at taking the first step. As a result, tremendous evils remain, the system of irresponsibility is blamed, and the brunt is borne by the weak. Since this is established on mistaken concepts, an adverse impact is produced on the society, on families and on the education of children.

The cause of everything such as the ruin of education produced by bullying in primary school, the deaths from overwork of loyal salary men, the misery of the restructuring of middle-aged and elderly white-collar workers and the problems of the aged is the tragedy brought on by the fact that individual Japanese have not strongly pressed the issue of what real justice is.

It's the same with the bailout of the banks. Given that the tax moneys of citizens are being used, there can be no confidence in it unless the information is first made public, clarification is given as to where the responsibility lies, and an accurate accounting is made of the past. Viewed from a different angle, the bailout of the banks amounts to a bailout of the problem society, but in regard to this matter you have proposed that "it would be advisable for a corporation seeking waivers of claims from a bank to issue shares whose value at market prices corresponds to the amount of the claims, and have them accepted by the bank." Truly, the scales fell from my eyes. I really believe that this is the right method for dealing with the problem. If this approach were pursued with the agreement of the citizenry, Japan's economic recovery could be achieved more rapidly. However, the actual state of affairs is that the issue is being handled with a lack of transparency, huge debts remain as a burden on the next generation, and family breadwinners have lost their jobs. It is a lamentable aspect of this country that many ordinary honest Japanese persons have sunk into the depths of despair.

Reading this book gave me heart. Let us return this country to its right and proper state. The strength of lone individuals is not much, but if a number of individuals link together, they can transform the world. It is your work that has given me such strength.

Perhaps it is presumptuous of me, but among us Japanese there are also those of us who take your warnings seriously; as a Japanese individual I would like to offer an apology for the many insults to which you have been subjected, and I hope that you will not lose your love for this country. I hope that you will not mind this request from one of your readers.

On reading this reader's letter, I felt greatly reassured to know that even in Japan there are people who understand my true intentions and who can listen to suggestions without covering their ears.

As long as there are readers like this, I am hopeful that Japan might be able to follow the path toward regeneration. If only they would choose to do so.

Hints of Reform

Both government actions and economic developments have given hints of a "controlled" liberalization of Japanese markets. The government's reaction to the summer of 1991's securities scandals included some reforms of security markets toward more liberal, free-market structures. Japanese securities and tax authorities sought to enforce civil and criminal sanctions against certain stock speculators, ranging from those embroiled by the Recruit scandal to Mitsuhiro Kotani and Sumitomo Bank officials.

But the government's actions in 1991 were not against those in authority nor were they targeted against government policies that allowed such scandals to occur in the first place. The steps they took hinted at reform but were not the wholesale change necessary to reform a corrupt system that continues to favor Japanese insiders.

Signs of change in Japan can frequently be misleading, and the forces arrayed against reforming the structure and operation of Japan's financial system are deeply entrenched. This is further complicated by what exactly "reform" means in Japan. Some observers have said that American and European hopes for reform are frequently dashed because of their fundamental misunderstanding of the true meaning—in the Japanese context—of perceived "signals" of reform.

What is also important to realize is that there is a vast difference between actions and words. The stated norms of behavior set forth in laws and regulations are what usually define acceptable behavior in accordance with what Americans would view as liberal or market-style approaches. In general, adequate laws are already on the books in Japan; problems lie in how they are interpreted and enforced in the Japanese context.

The problems in Japan are that many of those who have the power to create reform are those who are actually benefiting the most from keeping the current system. It is like the old saying of the fox guarding the chicken coop. Therefore, there is no desire on the part of the insiders for reforming the system to help the individual shareholder and ordinary citizen.

For example, the Ministry of Finance's relationship with the securities houses illustrates the common depth of the relationship between a Japanese ministry and the industry it regulates. The Ministry of Finance has at times displayed a breathtaking control over the securities industry, such as during the October 1987 market crash. According to various accounts, the Ministry of Finance and the Big Four, acting together, helped to avert an even worse global disaster by supporting the Tokyo market almost immediately following New York's twenty-three percent Black Monday freefall. This understanding reportedly was reached during a regular Tuesday meeting among Ministry of Finance and representatives of the Big Four, after which the Big Four—led by Nomura—began a major buying push.

One of the main problems lies in the fact that there is an element of mutual dependence in the relationship between the securities market and the Ministry of Finance, in which the Ministry of Finance's ability to regulate securities markets is constrained by professional and personal self-interest.

Ministry of Finance bureaucrats have personal incentives to protect and foster the financial sector. Senior bureaucrats are rewarded for their lifelong government service by *amakudari* (literally, "descent from Heaven"), which are privileged and frequently well-paid sinecures in the Diet or positions in the industry they previously regulated. Therefore, for personal as well as professional reasons, the Ministry of Finance and the securities industry have a mutual interest in maintaining a cooperative relationship.

The Big Four securities houses also would be in position to promote reform, but also stand to lose the most. The current market structure and operations permitted the Big Four to soar to global preeminence in the financial sector. They obviously have few, if any, incentives to tamper with such a regime.

As for the average citizen, there is very little that they can do. They are not organized toward cooperative actions against the government and as a society, they are not able to speak out.

Even those friends of mine in the government who would like to act for reform have their hands tied due to societal restrictions. This is undoubtedly a difficult concept for Americans to understand, since one of the foundations for the United States is the freedom of speech. But that was a hard fought right and the desire for it emanated from within. It has only been a little less than six decades since Japan stepped out from under imperial rule but, unlike the U.S., they did not fight for democracy. They lost a war and had democracy and all its ideals thrust upon them.

If the Japanese system will not change on its own, and if the Japanese people are unable to move for reform, then perhaps the U.S. and other countries must change their own policies in order to insist on fair and equal treatment and a true free-market system. This will then force the Japanese to change their system and put actions behind their words rather than to simply use a slight of hand that offers reform but that is in reality only an illusion.

I am trying to do what I can. While working on this book, I have continued to approach the Japanese government. I have been faxing the members of the National Diet on a daily basis, having sent as many as fifty-five different faxes under the title, "Culprit: The Ministry of Finance." Altogether, I will have more than a hundred messages for them from this series, so it looks as if I will be sending out faxes for the next couple of years. The fax charges alone are costing me ¥800,000 a month and I have two employees devoted entirely to keeping two fax machines busy every day. This undertaking only costs me money and won't earn me a single penny, but I do it because I know a Japanese person could not say the things that I say in these communications, because they will be ostracized or excluded if they do so.

The Call for True Reform

In order to attain financial stabilization over the last decade, the Japanese government has adopted all sorts of measures such as dumping huge amounts of public funds into the banks.

However, one condition should be required: banks that have applied sound management should be saved, while those that have committed any illegal act should not. Simply put, banks that have made poor financial decisions such as incurring a huge volume of non-performing loans through illegal financial maneuvers during the bubble economy should not be bailed out. Compared to other countries, Japan has too many banks anyway, so I think it would represent no problem for those that committed illegal acts to go out of business.

Further, everyone should be treated equally under the law. If managers of small banks are convicted of crimes committed during the bubble economy while managers of large banks are exempted from criminal liability for the same illegal actions, it cannot be said that everyone is equal under the law. Nor can equal treatment under the law be claimed when the government lends a helping hand not only to large banks, but also to manufacturers, trading companies, and retailers whose financial statements are worse because of recession, but ignores the small and medium-sized companies that comprise the backbone of the Japanese economy. And yet this is what goes on.

Every time a scandal in Japan's financial circles comes to light, the blame is always foisted upon lower level officials and a public announcement is then made that the top management was unaware that there was anything improper going on. In this way, they constantly dodge not only the blame but also the opportunity to fix the problem.

When Fuji Bank liquidated one of its subsidiaries, Fuji International Cayman Limited, several years ago, the losses amounted to ¥41.7 billion. It is thought that Fuji Bank took this action to shift losses suffered in securities trading in New York over to a subsidiary that had been set up as a tax haven in order to cancel them. However, despite the fact that such large sums had disappeared from the banks' assets, no one in the administration took responsibility. In fact, although my son Robert sent a letter in his capacity as a shareholder seeking an explanation of where and how the losses were produced, he was unable to obtain any substantive reply at all. If the statement that "the bank has adopted the best plan" is allowed to stand unchallenged, there will then be no way to check on whatever improprieties or failures may have occurred with the bank.

When Daiichi Kangyo Bank suffered huge losses through blunders in foreign exchange dealings in Singapore, a veil was drawn over the affair by attributing it to the individual actions of a lower-level operative from the local subsidiary. In the Daiwa Bank affair, the upshot of massive losses of well over a hundred billion yen that shook the bank to its foundations was the branding of a single clerk employed by the local subsidiary as the culprit. If, as the leaders of the banks have publicly announced every time there has been a scandal, the misappropriations of such enormous sums have been perpetrated by mere office workers who succeeded in covering them up within the banks, then that means there is no place on earth as unsafe as a Japanese bank. No intelligent person would ever deposit funds in such dangerous places where the lowest bank employee can walk off with untold billions of yen. For that matter, how could corporations ever entrust their transactions to such insecure banks?

For Japan's economy to achieve healthy development, it will be necessary to do away with the outmoded conventions nesting in political, bureaucratic, and business circles. If that is not possible, Japan will be ruined. The Japanese are extremely diligent and devoted to their professions, and I have always respected that. And their individual abilities are outstanding, which has been the cornerstone of Japan's prosperity up to now. However, if the Japanese economy declines, this will cause enormous harm to millions of innocent people.

In April of 2001, Japan elected a new prime minister, Mr. Junichiro Koizumi. He was elected based on his hard line approach toward the economic crisis and his vow to reform the system. In a July 2001 article in the *South China Morning Post*, he vowed to push ahead with his tough reforms in order to revive the world's second-biggest economy. In this article, he said that pain was inevitable—with or without change.

Koizumi Warns of Pain

"Japan will be in dire straits if we do not press ahead with structural reforms," Mr. Koizumi said. "I do not think we can boost the economy by taking fiscal steps or issuing more government bonds. Instead, people will suffer even more because interest rates will rise and structural reforms will slow."

Since sweeping to power in April on a grassroots desire for change in his conservative and long-ruling Liberal Democratic Party (LDP), Mr. Koizumi has said he will tackle the mountain of bad loans held by banks that has been hanging over the economy for a decade.

Economists said he would probably prop up the economy with a sprinkling of extra deficit spending this year to prevent a public backlash that could dent his support and unravel his reform drive, with an announcement possible in September.

Mr. Koizumi...has sought fiscal discipline and structural reform rather than public spending to pump Japan's convalescing economy.

One of Prime Minister Koizumi's primary objectives is to set up a new economic structure reform mainly to resolve the huge bad debts created by the banking crisis in two to three years. But, in my opinion, this is a very difficult task in light of the fact that none of the parties responsible for creating these huge bad debts have been pursued and punished. If this is the case, how can any true reform take place? The culprits responsible will see that no one has been prosecuted, so they will either continue the path they have chosen, or they will circumvent the new "laws" because they can safely assume that no one will come after them. Such punishments are also needed, as Professor Kamimura pointed out in the Oji Paper cases, in order to restore faith in Japan's market system. Otherwise, how are investors to believe that anything has changed?

With no threat at all to those responsible, is it any wonder then that because of the continuing slumping economy many in Japan are already calling for "a return to the kind of government spending that has landed Japan with the industrialized world's worst debt burden— the exact policy Mr. Koizumi had hoped to stamp out when he took office" (*South China Morning Post* June 11, 2001).

In the Japanese magazine, the *Weekly Genday*, Mr. Masa Haru Goto said that the banking crisis in Japan caused by the huge bad debts write-off should be the responsibility of the Ministry of Finance and the banking officers.

In another Japanese newspaper, former LDP party secretary Mr. Hiro Mu Nonaka said that there should be no bailout of banks with taxpayer money until the parties responsible for creating such a huge bank bad debt be pursued and punished.

These two people above were very influential political figures in Japan. Yet, as of today, no one of any significance were pursued and punished.

Prime Minister Koizumi, who is deeply concerned that Japan will be ruined if things continue in the same fashion as they have, came up with structural reform and gained the support of the Japanese people to win a massive victory in the election for the House of Councilors. But a look at the newspapers reveals that if he tries to put his publicly pledged structural reform into effect, there will be fierce opposition from profiteers and retired bureaucrats turned businessmen who have plundered the state budget in the past. Moreover, these profiteers who are opposed to Prime Minister Koizumi's structural reform are the same people who supported it at the time of the election. In such circumstances, structural reform will never succeed. This is why I fervently hope that the selfish profiteers and retired bureaucrats will consider the interests of Japan as a whole and I hope they will revise their way of thinking and halt their opposition to this plan, which is in the national interest. But if the past is any indication, then there is not a great deal of hope for the future.

I have already discussed in previous chapters the incredible debt facing the Japanese government due to the banking problems and how they are faced with difficult choices, which will have significant impact on ordinary citizens. But in addition to bailing out the bad debts of banks, Japan is facing a double-edged sword of having to cut back spending. In the past, Japan would have relied on heavy spending in the various backbone industries such as construction companies and public works in order to boost the economy. Because of the tightening noose of looming bankruptcies, high unemployment, and an economy that continues to slide, this type of spending is no longer possible.

The following is another *South China Morning Post* article.

Japan Trims Budget Fat
Proposed $188b Spending Cut First in Four Years

The Japanese government has tightened the noose on the era of pork barrel public spending by cutting ¥3 trillion (about HK$188 billion) from next year's budget as part of Prime Minister Junichiro Koizumi's stringent reforms.

They are the first cuts in four years and a pillar of Mr. Koizumi's attempts to mend Japan's tattered public finances and use limited funds more efficiently to pull the flagging economy out of its decade-long stagnation...

Economists said the move was a clear shift from traditional expenditure on public works projects.

Mr. Koizumi has pledged to limit new government bond issuance to ¥30 trillion a year, as a first step towards a balanced budget, and promised to radically alter how cash was allocated to maximize the economic impact of taxpayers' money.

To keep that debt issuance cap, spending must be cut by about ¥3 trillion in the next financial year, according to February Ministry of Finance estimates.

However, those estimates were based on an assumption that the economy would grow by two percent—something of a fantasy now that almost all economic data suggest the economy has been contracting.

Japan's gross domestic product shrank by 0.2% in the first quarter and economists forecast a steeper decline in the second.

If there was ever a time that Japan could use an influx of foreign investment it is now. And yet who can safely invest in Japanese companies? Has Japan warmly welcomed foreign investors in the past? Unfortunately, they have treated foreign investors as unwelcome guests.

Unfortunately, in the article above there is once again no mention of the government seeking prosecution against those who got Japan in its current mess; until then, no true reform will take place and things will continue as they always have with a few insiders bilking the rest of Japan out of huge fortunes. Also, how will Japan attract foreign investment if the wrongs of the past are never corrected? Who can trust such a system?

There is little doubt that Japan is in a crisis. In a February 14, 2002 article in the *South China Morning Post*, it was announced that Prime Minister Koizumi ordered his ministers to draw up a comprehensive plan by the end of the month to battle deflation and revitalize Japan's "recession-mired economy." The reason for the move was that only hours before, "United States ratings agency Moody's Investors Service said it was considering downgrading Japan's sovereign credit rating by up to two notches—a move that would put the world's second-biggest economy on a par with economic minnows such as Latvia and Cyprus."

As part of its reforms, those who are responsible for getting Japan into the mess that it currently is in must be held accountable. If not, then the reform that is being touted as reform is not true reform at all. If no one is held accountable, then how long before those in power simply find a new way of taking money from the system? With a system that does not punish wrongdoers, it is only inviting trouble like the Japanese corporations who, when they do not like the intrusions of foreigners, simply print more money by issuing new shares to themselves. Or like Katakura who, when they found themselves pinched by the new law designed to open industries to foreign investment, simply changed "the rules" by having themselves designated a protected company. Simply put, what good are laws if they are never enforced?

Hope

Because I have had the blessing of wealth, I have been somewhat insulated from the true effects of the Japanese powers that be. I still have my wealth and I have not been so foolish as to invest all of my eggs in the Japanese basket. But my experiences have shown that no one is immune to the cruelty of the insiders who run this system. I have been ruthlessly attacked by the powerful insiders who wanted my wealth but did not want the responsibilities that came with the concept of being responsible to the shareholders who are the true owners of the company. I have suffered a great deal emotionally, psychologically, and I have spent millions of dollars on lawsuits, to say nothing of how much I have lost financially had the securities companies not interfered with my investments.

Due to a matter of procedure, I might be able appeal the decisions in the Oji Paper and Saibo cases. However, things do not look especially promising if I were to do so. They would be tried under a system that is ripe with collusion and where political reform is very slow indeed, particularly in the judicial system. Still, the plans are in the works and I am considering once again waging the fight, though I am growing very weary of it and deeply wish that others would take up the fight.

On April 4, 2002, I had sent a letter of inquiry to Saibo's auditor, Tohmatsu & Co. On April 16, 2002, I received a note through their lawyers, refusing to answer questions that I had posed to them. They merely said:

> Under Article 27 of the Certified Public Accountant Law of Japan, any accounting firm is prohibited from disclosing any information that it acquired in the course of its professional service to its client without justifiable reason, such as a case where the client agrees to such disclosure. Please note that [a] request for information by any shareholder of the accounting firm's client does not constitute such justifiable reason.

Not happy with their response, I have gone ahead and written a letter to the Tokyo prosecutor's office regarding Tohmatsu's actions. This is similar to reporting a crime to the local sheriff here in the U.S. In my letter, I said that the investing public was being misled by the false securities reports by Saibo in which Tohmatsu must have been an active participant. I reminded the prosecutor that they had made recent arrests of accountants due to these types of falsified documents and encouraged them to fully prosecute Tohmatsu in hopes that it would be a warning to others.

Will the Tokyo prosecutor take any action? It is hard to say. While I hope that they do, experience leads me to believe they may not. It will certainly be interesting to watch.

But the true victims of Japan's establishment continue to be the average citizens and investors like the worker from Bridgestone who worked his life away, believing that the system will take care of them. Instead, the government is forced to place each citizen in debts to the tune of thousands of dollars while no one is made to pay for the crime of bringing Japan to the edge of financial ruin. I feel sorry for the Japanese citizens who find that their hard-earned savings and investments are subject not to the ups and downs of a free market but the whim of insiders. If these insiders want to squander the company's assets—and thereby bring ruthless harm to average shareholders—then they will do so without a second thought because they know there is no culpability for insiders.

The question is, how many other victims must there be before something is done to protect them? How many other criminals will go unpunished while the damage they inflicted continues to harm innocent bystanders who, like myself, want nothing more than to make simple investments in companies that they believe will pay them a good return on their investment?

I truly hope that Japan will make the changes it needs to, not only for the sake of its own people but also for the rest of the world so that the damage it has done to itself will not ruin other countries as well. But whether or not Japan will make the changes it needs to before it is too late is a matter for the future to reveal. If this book helps in some small way to avert such a situation and contributes to the rebirth of a Japan that is once again respected in the world, then I will be greatly rewarded indeed.

Appendices

Appendix A

Testimony in the Oji Paper Trials: Tokyo District Court

Standing as a witness in the courtroom of Tokyo District Court in the Oji Paper matter was Mr. Tadao Kobayashi, the former director and head of the International Business Department of Nikko Securities. He testified on two occasions, September 28 and December 1, 1992, having first declared: "I swear to tell the truth according to my conscience, without concealing anything and without telling any falsehood." The following is an excerpt from that testimony.

Unless otherwise noted, the person asking the questions is my attorney.

The Leaking of False Reports at the TSE

What details and reasons did you hear about from either the head of the Trading Control Office or someone acting on his behalf with regard to the decision to adopt the measure of suspending acceptance of buy orders?

Kobayashi: As I started to explain awhile ago, I heard that the quantity of purchases of shares in Oji Paper by the Hong Kong investors had become large and all sorts of rumors were going around regarding that fact, such as that it was being done for a special purpose, that there had just been interrogations or forewarnings at that time from the Tokyo Stock Exchange and the Ministry of Finance and that the Trading Control Office had conducted a thorough investigation of dealings in Oji Paper Company, and that as a result of that thorough investigation, there were concerns that laws and regulations might have been violated, so it was decided that it would be best to refuse to accept orders for a while.

Among the things that you have just said now, you stated that the Tokyo Stock Exchange and the Ministry of Finance had conducted interrogations and issued forewarnings, but who was it that was interrogated by the Tokyo Stock Exchange or Ministry of Finance, that is to say, who went to the Tokyo Stock Exchange or the Ministry of Finance?

Kobayashi: I think this was handled by the Trading Control Office, but I don't know who went.

Did the facts that the volume had become large and that the transactions were being carried out frequently and continuously come from things said by the Tokyo Stock Exchange or the Ministry of Finance?

Kobayashi: Well, I heard an explanation to that effect from the Trading Control Office. I didn't hear that such things had been said by the Tokyo Stock Exchange or the Ministry of Finance.

Then who said them?

Kobayashi: I heard them from the Trading Control Office.

But what were the grounds on which the Tokyo Stock Exchange or the Ministry of Finance conducted interrogations?

Kobayashi: I think that the interrogations would have been conducted precisely because of the circumstances just mentioned.

So there would have been an explanation to that effect from the Tokyo Stock Exchange or the Ministry of Finance, wouldn't there? If not, people would not have been summoned for no reason.

Kobayashi: I think that it was probably more a case of an explanation being sought rather than of an explanation being given.

When you say that there is now talk in some circles about there being a special purpose, what circles are you talking about?

Kobayashi: I think that they would be investors in general, or the mass media or publishing companies, people like that.

Were there publishing companies that were also saying things like that?

Kobayashi: Whether or not publishing companies were saying it, what I meant by "the public" just now...rather than that, it would be those ordinary investors in the public or—

When you say "investors in general," I don't know what you mean. Can you specify whom you are referring to?

Kobayashi: No, I can't.

You spoke about a special purpose, didn't you? What was it?

Kobayashi: I believe that this indicates that there may have been purposes such as those falling under Clause 3 of Rule 59 of the Statutes of the Tokyo Stock Exchange or Article 125 of the Securities and Exchange Act, in short, buying at high prices through cornering the market, or else the manipulation of share prices.

From what events did suspicions arise that there might have been a special purpose? What are the grounds and the specific facts from which such suspicions arose?

Kobayashi: Since I didn't make a judgment based on a thorough investigation of the circumstances of the trading, I have no knowledge in that area.

And you didn't hear anything about that aspect from anyone in the Trading Control Office?

Chief Judge: He's not saying that he didn't hear anything at all.

What did the Hong Kong investors do that gave rise to suspicions about violations of the Statutes or violations of the Securities and Exchange Act? What kind of actions were these?

Kobayashi: As I said a little while ago, I believe that it would have been things like the fact that the volume of the buy orders of the

Hong Kong investors for Oji Paper Company was considerably greater than the scale for ordinary investors in Japan, or the fact that the purchases were made frequently or the fact that they were made continuously.

And specifically on the matter of greenmail demands, there was nothing like that, was there?

Kobayashi: I don't believe that there was anything like that.

There was nothing at all, was there?

Kobayashi: As far as I know, there was nothing.

It wasn't just as far as Nikko Securities heard, was it?

Kobayashi: I believe that is correct.

. . .

This is an article from the *Nihon Keizai Shimbun* dated October 14, 1977. Did you see the article at the time?

Kobayashi: At the time, I believe that I did read this article.

According to this article, Tokyo Stock Exchange Managing Director Yamashita was reported as saying, "Oji Paper came to us to explain the circumstances regarding the accumulation of their shares by a Hong Kong circle." Briefly put, at the time that you saw that newspaper, did you know that Oji Paper Company had gone to the Tokyo Stock Exchange to explain the circumstances regarding the investment in Oji Paper shares by the Hong Kong investors?

Kobayashi: I knew of it from the newspaper.

You learned from the article that Oji Paper had gone to report to the Tokyo Stock Exchange, but Oji Paper would have obtained information about the Hong Kong investors' investment in Oji Paper shares from [Nikko,] the [main] managing underwriter, wouldn't it?

Kobayashi: I believe that it obtained the information from various places.

Included in that was some information that had been collected from the managing underwriter, wasn't there?

Kobayashi: There may have been.

Had you heard what the contents of the report that Oji Paper Company made to the Tokyo Stock Exchange were?

Kobayashi: No, I hadn't.

This was known by the Corporate Affairs Department, wasn't it?

Kobayashi: I believe so.

Comments on this Testimony

Because we had acquired a large block of shares in Oji Paper Company, Oji's management had submitted a false report to the TSE in order to protect themselves. The Tokyo Stock Exchange—without conducting *any* investigation, had leaked the story to the mass media at the same time that it was reporting it to the Ministry of Finance.

The Ministry of Finance fully realizes the power it has, not only over the approval of new products and business but also the securities houses' personnel, the contents of their accounts, the amounts of dividends, and the amount and timing of increases in capital. Because the Ministry of Finance holds the licenses of the securities companies, they have absolutely no choice but to follow the Ministry's bidding. Otherwise, the Ministry of Finance will simply pull the license from the securities company that isn't behaving.

Collusion of the Big Four in the Forced Sale

In the second paragraph from the bottom on the second page, it states: "In considering the above position of Nikko Securities, they added that they could not collectively buy back Oji Paper shares that such overseas investors currently held or would come to hold." However, isn't this entry contradicted by the fact that you went to Los Angeles and advised the plaintiff's representative that you would like the Hong Kong investors to sell the Oji Paper shares that they held through Nikko Securities?

Kobayashi: No, it isn't.

Then how are we to understand this?

Kobayashi: When this letter was first issued, they had to suppose that subsequent developments would lead to requests for a buyback at a premium, and if something like that did transpire, there was no way that Nikko Securities, for its part, could handle the arrangements for a buyback. This is why they issued such a document. But after that, as time passed it was judged that the issue of a buyback at a premium had disappeared, so we pressed them to sell, soliciting the sale of the shares they held as an ordinary transaction.

In Party A's Exhibit No. 44, no particular mention has been made of the price, has there?

Kobayashi: No, there hasn't.

So, how many shares was it in all that you asked the plaintiff's representative to sell when you went to Los Angeles?

Kobayashi: I don't remember clearly, but I believe that the figure was in the neighborhood of 30 million shares…What I want to say is that I had been to Hong Kong before I went to Los Angeles, as I mentioned a while ago. In Hong Kong I was looking for people like Mr. Wang, Mr. Chan, or Mr. Fung of Sun Hung Kai Securities, but I learned that Mr. Wang had gone to Los Angeles.

In requesting the sale, did you mention a price, either how much they should be bought for or at what price they could be sold?

Kobayashi: I did. I asked if the sale price could be based on the original market price.

On that occasion did you tell Mr. Wang that you knew how much the purchase price of the Hong Kong investors was?

Kobayashi: I didn't say that I knew, but in all likelihood the Hong Kong investors, or including Mr. Wang, I believe that I heard how much the cost was from Mr. Wang.

Did you ask Mr. Wang?

Kobayashi: Yes.

And did Mr. Wang tell you?

Kobayashi: Yes, he did.

How much did he say it was?

Kobayashi: I don't remember now.

Comments on this Testimony

In this testimony, Mr. Kobayashi said that I had broached the selling price, but that is simply not the case. I know this because I remember clearly that when I heard his words, it suddenly dawned on me: "Ah, Nomura, Nikko, Yamaichi and Daiwa, the 'Big Four', are conspiring together!" He was the one who brought up the selling price. I knew this because Kobayashi should not have been informed about how many shares we had bought from which securities house at what price, since securities firms have the obligation of maintaining the confidentiality of information about their clients. Still less would they do something like leak the details of their clients' transactions to rival companies. However, he was quite familiar with the details of our transactions.

Testimony Continues

And from your side, you spoke just now about the market price. Was it your intention or plan to determine the price at which they would sell?

Kobayashi: Yes, since the original market price at that time was the base, and at the time in question there wasn't much movement in the share price on a daily basis, I asked how it would be if the price were around that level.

So as far as your intention was concerned at the time that you made this request to the plaintiff's representative, did you think that you could buy the shares back at a price below the average purchase price paid by the Hong Kong investors?

Kobayashi: With regard to the point of cost, for my part I took the view that there was no relationship with the purchase price. It was up to the people who held the shares whether or not to respond, and the price that I suggested was based on the current price on the TSE. That's what I said.

Now when you talk about the current price on the TSE, the major houses, the Big Four, were all underwriting managers for Oji Paper, weren't they?

Kobayashi: Yes.

Therefore, even if we consider the share of these four companies alone, it accounts for an extremely large portion of the transactions on the TSE, and if we include the affiliates of the "Big Four," it comes to more than half. Viewed in that light, there was considerable scope for manipulation of the market prices on the TSE by these four companies, isn't that so?

Kobayashi: That is absolutely mistaken.

At the time in question it was still all right to buy and sell as much as one liked; no percentage had been set.

Kobayashi: However, when you purchase a large quantity of shares, there are strict penal regulations in cases where there has been interference in the price.

The point I am trying to get at is whether or not the proposal of selling at the market price contains the implication that the purchase would really be made at a fair price for the Hong Kong investors.

Kobayashi: The current price on the TSE was the fairest price at that time. I have always thought that. I still do, even now.

Whenever the Hong Kong investors wanted to buy or sell shares through Nikko Securities, they did it through Nikko Asia, didn't they?

Kobayashi: That is correct.

Yet despite that, why did you yourself go all the way to Los Angeles to ask the plaintiff's representative to sell?

Kobayashi: As I said the last time, since I was the head of the International Business Department and the orders received by Nikko Asia would be handled through Nikko Securities, it was a good idea to meet the client myself and have a concrete discussion about the shares, and I did so.

Even so, wasn't the fact that you made a point of going all the way to Los Angeles and asking the plaintiff's representative to sell the shares in Oji Paper ultimately because you had been asked to do so by some parties who wanted to buy the Oji Paper shares from the Hong Kong investors?

Kobayashi: Not in the least.

If not, would you still have made it a point to go all the way to Los Angeles?

Kobayashi: Since it was a large volume deal, it was worthwhile to go.

And such a request to the plaintiff's representative for the sale of the Oji Paper shares would have been made only by Nikko Securities?

Kobayashi: No. I believe various companies did so.

You've just now referred to various companies. Which ones were they?

Kobayashi: Since I am definitely a competitor, I don't know for sure, but I heard from Mr. Wang when I went to Los Angeles that Mr. Tabuchi of Nomura Securities had spoken with him immediately prior to that, or at least not very long before.

Did you hear that Vice President Tabuchi of Nomura Securities went directly from the United States to Hong Kong around April 17, 1978 to visit the plaintiff's representative, and requested that he sell the Oji Paper shares?

Kobayashi: I didn't hear that.

According to what Vice President Tabuchi said to the plaintiff's representative, that sale request was made at the behest of Chairman Goro Koyama of Mitsui Bank and President Tanaka of Oji Paper Company, and Nomura Securities has admitted in this court that Mr. Tabuchi told the plaintiff's representative about this. Judging from such facts, it can be imagined that there was the same sort of request from Chairman Koyama and President Tanaka to Nikko Securities. How about it?

Kobayashi: I received no request.

However, according to your testimony the previous time, Nikko Securities was the managing underwriter for Oji Paper Company.

Kobayashi: That's right.

Therefore, there wouldn't be a case in which a request was made to Nomura Securities but not to Nikko Securities, would there?

Kobayashi: That would be conjecture. I didn't hear about it.

. . .

Has there been an example in the past where a deal concluded with one company has been shared with others?

Kobayashi: I've had no such experience.

The percentage of the shares differed among Nikko, Nomura, Daiwa and Yamaichi, didn't it?

Kobayashi: Yes.

Why was that?

Kobayashi: The total number of shares was divided up according to the managers' shares.

What does "managers' shares" mean?

Kobayashi: There were managers, weren't there? This means there were several securities houses that became underwriters for the shares, and there were cases in which their respective shares differed.

Was a decision regarding Oji Paper Company made at this time?

Kobayashi: No, it had been decided previously. This is something that varies, but when there has been an increase of capital just prior to or at the time of financing, if the shares don't change, then they remain at the same level for a long time. Those are what we call the managers' shares.

So, since the managers' shares can vary, it is possible for the issuing company to threaten the managing underwriter by saying it will do something with its share.

Kobayashi: If it wanted to do that, it would be possible, yes.

Therefore, it would be fair then, to take the view that in the end the percentages of the allocations in such cases are decided by the wishes of the issuing company, wouldn't it?

Kobayashi: No, I don't believe that that's correct. I was told by Vice President Haraigawa to make the allocations according to the managers' shares, and since I am a salaryman, I did as I was ordered.

Comments on this Testimony

In the above testimony, Mr. Kobayashi has committed grave perjury. He testified that the shares of the managing underwriters for Oji Paper Company "had been decided previously. This is something that varies, but when there has been an increase of capital just prior to or at the time of financing, if the share does not change, then it remains at the same level for a long time" and also "I was told by Vice President Haraigawa to make the allocation according to the manager's share, and since I am a salaryman, I did as I was ordered."

As he admitted in his testimony, the shares for the respective securities houses that he requested of me by telephone were 35% each for Nikko and Nomura, and 15% each for Daiwa and Yamaichi. In the same testimony, he has said that the managers' shares were decided by the most recent increase of capital. However, the managers' shares for the most recent increase of capital turned out to be 40% for Nikko, 25% each for Yamaichi and Nomura, and 10% for Daiwa.

Appendix B

Testimony in the Oji Paper Trials: Tokyo High Court

Mr. Tadaaki Yoshida was serving in the post of the Chief of the Distribution Market Section of the Securities Bureau of the Ministry of Finance at the time of the Oji Paper matter. The examination of this witness was held on February 16, 1996 at the Tokyo High Court. Unless otherwise noted, the person asking the questions is my attorney.

Around September 1977, there were interrogations of the local Hong Kong subsidiaries of eight companies owing to trading in the shares of Oji Paper Company by the Hong Kong investors, weren't there?

Yoshida: Actually, I don't remember clearly whether the month was September, but the Distribution Market Section did conduct interrogations.

Were these eight companies called in at the same time and interrogated at the same time? Or were they summoned one after another and interrogated individually?

Yoshida: The person who handled the interrogations, Assistant Section Chief Yokota, who was in charge of that matter, summoned the persons from the securities companies directly, and I don't remember clearly, but since under normal circumstances there were hardly any cases in which they would come in together, and I don't recall whether it was people from those eight companies or from four of them, but I do remember that they came and spoke to Assistant Section Chief Yokota individually.

So then, you yourself didn't conduct the interrogations directly?

Yoshida: No, I didn't.

Were such interrogations regarding transactions in the shares of a particular stock held frequently?

Yoshida: According to my two years of experience, I don't believe that there were too many.

On the course of events leading up to those interrogations, what would have been the circumstances that resulted in their being conducted?

Yoshida: I will describe them based on what I remember. In normal circumstances, the Securities Bureau of the Ministry of Finance did not interact directly with the traders concerned. Since the Distribution Market Section of the Ministry of Finance primarily carried out administrative work based on data or reports that came from the Trading Investigation Office of the Tokyo Stock Exchange on matters involving investigations of trading in particular, and given that at the very beginning the basic rules of the TSE were involved, and moreover that it was an exceptionally voluminous draft report, that there was that report from the TSE to the Distribution Market Section, that purchase volumes of such magnitude were involved, and indeed, that it was being reported in the newspapers every day with reporters constantly coming to the Section Chief's office to gather news, the perception of a problem probably originated as a result of such events. This is the way I remember it.

So you're saying that the interrogations were conducted after you came to have the perception of a certain kind of problem from information that was submitted from a TSE report and also from newspaper reports and the like, aren't you?

Yoshida: Yes, that is the case.

What kind of problem did you come to have a perception of?

Yoshida: This is just an example from my personal experience, but for a period of four years before I took up the post of Distribution Market Section chief, I was seconded to the Ministry of Foreign Affairs and served for four years as Consul for Economic Relations at the Japanese Consulate General in Hong Kong. During that period I became well acquainted with Hong Kong's economy and with many persons in Hong Kong's economic circles. And speaking from this point of view, one instance of a perception of a problem, one thing in the background that I became strongly aware of, is that if you look at the nature of investment in Hong Kong, it is of a kind that looks to quite short-term returns. And then, another problem I perceived is that the four securities companies or eight companies might be canvassing for sales a bit too competitively under the influence of the Hong Kong side. So overall, broadly speaking, I had a perception of these two problems, and considering that in my capacity as administrator in that area, I had to have a full understanding of the circumstances as to whether a situation involving the Charter of the TSE had already developed or whether there was a concern that this would happen, and I resolved on the interrogations for such reasons.

In referring to the TSE Charter just now, did you mean Clause 3, Article 59 of the TSE Charter?

Yoshida: Yes, I believe that it was Clause 3.

And you had a doubt or a concern, as it were, that it had been violated?

Yoshida: I thought that there was a danger of that possibility; this was the problem that I perceived.

Among the factors figuring in your decision that you had come to perceive such a problem, did you take it as a fact that the Hong Kong investors were requesting concerned parties at Oji Paper to buy back the shares?

Yoshida: I may have read about such things in newspaper reports and other such places and taken them as the starting point for my administrative work, but as far as I remember now, I don't believe that I took such information as the basis for deciding on the interrogations.

Is it the case that no facts had been adduced either in the report mentioned awhile ago from the TSE Trading Investigation Office to indicate that there had been any greenmail requests from the Hong Kong investors?

Yoshida: With regard to that point, I have no recollection that there had.

It is said that when Assistant Section Chief Yokota was conducting the interrogations, he terrorized everyone with his ferocious scowl. Was that really the case?

Yoshida: I have no memory of having heard reports like that at the time.

What facts, what circumstances came to light as a result of the interrogations conducted by Assistant Section Chief Yokota?

Yoshida: My memory isn't clear on this, but as for what I expected from him in the first interrogations, I conveyed my perception of a problem, telling him I wanted him to thoroughly familiarize himself with the facts, the actual state of affairs and the detailed circumstances, and in the second and subsequent interrogations, he was to obtain a description of the data or an explanation of the circumstances from the various securities companies, and to consider our response as administrators. This was my own idea of the schedule, and in the first interrogations by Yokota, I said that their purpose was to get a grasp on the perception of a problem here and on the facts; this is the way I was thinking.

As a result of repeated interrogations, did the doubts, or the concerns, or the possibility of a violation of Article 59 of the TSE Charter about which you said you perceived a problem a while ago become stronger? Or did all of that disappear?

Yoshida: Actually, according to my memory, if I am not mistaken, I believe that I had no contact with the interrogations except on just one occasion. On such a point, I have no recollection that the interrogations were repeated.

Comments on this Testimony

Mr. Yoshida shows his bias against foreigners in this testimony by saying that Hong Kong investors had rather dubious (in the Japanese mindset) investment purposes in that we looked "to quite short-term returns."

What does it matter if we looked for short-term results and how would that have justified the Ministry of Finance's actions? The Ministry is supposed to step in when there are *illegal acts* taking place, not because they don't like a certain type of investing. Aside from that, this statement was ridiculous because the same type of short-term investment also exists in Japan. So it can only be that the Ministry took the actions that they did because we were short-term *foreign* investors.

It is truly unfortunate—and should be a matter of embarrassment to all of Japan—that the entire Oji Paper Company matter came about due to a mistaken perception rooted in racial discrimination.

What is most amazing to me is that he said we had never made any overtures of greenmail. If that is so, then why would he have judged that there was a "danger" of us becoming greenmailers and implement the self-restraint program? The only logical explanation is that either he or someone else had predetermined to force us to sell our shares and that they'd used greenmail as an excuse to do so.

Lack of Responsibility

This is documentary evidence from [your television interview with] NHK-TV entitled, "Financial Scandal." The contents of an interview with you appear in here, don't they?

Yoshida: Yes.

You've read this, have you not?

Yoshida: Yes, I have.

In your answer to a question regarding the, so to speak, fore-warnings, or administrative guidance in this matter, on the tenth line on page 220, it is written: "Mr. Yoshida: 'Therefore, it could be viewed as having been anticipated in the scenario that we prepared'." Isn't that so?

Yoshida: Yes.

Now these are the contents of what you answered in the interview, and judging from the answers in this interview, weren't you saying that the Ministry of Finance or the Distribution Market Section was in some sense anticipating that the various companies would adopt the self-restraint program and was leading them in that direction?

Yoshida: I believe that this NHK interview article has in fact been recorded according to what I said. However, as far as this interview is concerned, there was no indication in advance that the theme would be about the issue of Hong Kong, and I wasn't fully prepared when I was suddenly being interviewed on matters regarding general administrative guidance. Now, on looking at this wording, I have been reflecting that I did indeed use an expression that has undoubtedly given rise to misunderstandings. What I was trying to say, I believe that I used this expression in the sense, call it the judgment or anticipation on the securities side, that the securities companies conjectured or imagined that the Ministry of Finance had drawn up such a scenario.

On the third line from the end on page 220, you also answered: "I believe that it is unavoidable that the historical position will be taken that in the end we took strong administrative action," didn't you?

Yoshida: (Nods)

What does this mean?

Yoshida: I believe that I wanted to give vent to a sense of frustration, that up to that point I had not had such an opportunity to present an explanation in this court, and that it was not very likely that there would be one in the future either, and since I had not expected that there would be such an opportunity, however much I said I wouldn't be able to convey my true intentions as the section chief at that time, and that I would in no way be able to explain myself for the historical record regarding the state of affairs that the only thing that remained was the fact that the securities companies launched into the self-restraint program immediately after the Ministry of Finance held its interrogations.

Comments on this Testimony

The shiftiness here of Mr. Yoshida is a typical example of testimony by Japan's bureaucrats. While speaking about the self-restraint program during a TV interview, Mr. Yoshida had said, "Therefore, this may have been what they anticipated in the scenario that we imagined." Confronted with his assertions in court, he tried to excuse his remarks by saying, "When I was suddenly being interviewed…I indeed used an expression that no doubt has given rise to misunderstandings."

But his assertion that such an expression came out because he was suddenly being interviewed and couldn't prepare is nothing more than sophistry.

No matter how he tries to explain away the statements in his TV interview, it can only mean that the Ministry of Finance had prepared some sort of scenario to prevent the Hong Kong investors from acquiring Oji Paper Company shares and the eight securities houses had anticipated that scenario in the form of the self-restraint program. And no matter how he tries to explain it away or shift the blame to the securities companies, it is clear from his testimony that he was very aware at the time that he had taken an exceptionally strong administrative action.

Unfortunately, in Japan there is no way to call him to account for his actions. With this in mind, is it any wonder that Japanese officials feel little remorse for their actions and take no responsibility for them?

Starting a Fire and Looking the Other Way

When did you come to know that the eight companies had implemented the so-called self-restraint program?

Yoshida: I don't remember this clearly either, but the assistant section chief conducted the interrogations, and, subsequently, I don't remember at all whether it was the next day or several days after that when I received a report through him that the eight securities firms were about to adopt self-restraint. But I have no recollection at all of when the timing of that was.

Given the purport of the remark that they were about to adopt self-restraint, you knew about the self-restraint program before it actually began, didn't you?

Yoshida: As far as the expression I used is concerned, it may be a lyrical expression with the meaning that the eight securities houses had already started or a polite expression saying that it seemed they were doing it, but in fact I did not know about it before they started, and I think—to the best of my memory—that I received the report after they had started.

Are you saying that the eight companies sent reports to the Ministry of Finance?

Yoshida: As far as that is concerned, since it was through Yokota, I don't remember at all now what kind of reports I received.

Didn't it occur to you that the adoption of the self-restraint program by the eight companies was an activity that was not permitted under the Securities and Exchange Act?

Yoshida: At that time, I was surprised at its unexpectedness, but I didn't think that it was a legal issue. Since it was a question of a business transaction between private parties, as an administrator I felt that if it came to this stage, it was not a matter in which I should intervene. I remember that subsequent contacts with regard to this matter ceased as a result.

Didn't either the Distribution Market Section or the Securities Bureau conduct an investigation on the problem of [whether this violated] the Securities and Exchange Act?

Yoshida: As far as I remember, I have no recollection that an investigation was conducted after we received this report on the self-restraint program. I don't believe that there was one.

Judging from the fact that the eight securities companies adopted the self-restraint program simultaneously, it could be supposed that they spoke together or cooperated; did you also think that?

Yoshida: There may have been cases when answers from the eight respective companies came in together, but as a matter of common sense, I believe that I made a common sense judgment that that this was probably the result of a certain degree of internal contact among the eight companies.

Didn't you consider that that would constitute a problem under the Antitrust Act?

Yoshida: I don't believe that such a notion or perception of a problem occurred to me at the time.

If we look at the article from *Nihon Keizai Shimbun* in Item 1 of Party A's Exhibit No. 2, it reads as if you approved the self-restraint program in this case, or allowed it, saying that it was an unavoidable measure. Is that the case?

Yoshida: Yes. I received the report on the self-restraint program, and since no response was adopted in regard to it, I believe that I kept my hands off as it was not an administrative matter.

Comments on this Testimony

In his testimony, Yoshida was acknowledging that the self-restraint program was a collaborative effort among the eight companies and yet didn't believe it to be a legal issue. Once again, we see him shift blame for something he started. Since their actions—denying right of access—was illegal under the laws of Japan, this was most definitely a legal issue. As the chief of the Distribution Market Section of the Securities Bureau of the Ministry of Finance, Yoshida was in a position that *obliged* him to put a stop to the illegal self-restraint program.

And yet he said, "As an administrator I felt that if it came to this stage, it was not a matter in which I should intervene." This was a complete abdication of his duties.

William L. Reynolds, Professor of Law at the University of Maryland, who is an authority on antitrust laws, has come to the following unequivocal conclusion:

> Such a conspiracy [by jointly adopting the self-restraint program] would violate the U. S. antitrust laws for three separate reasons: It would constitute a conspiracy to fix prices to engage in a group boycott to allocate Mr. Wang's purchase of Oji Paper stock and it would be illegal whether tested under the *per se* rule or under the rule of reason, with no plausible defense seeming to exist.

What kind of defense would Mr. Yoshida make on reading this opinion of Professor Reynolds? Now that Japan's practices are turning into an international debate, perhaps Mr. Yoshida should reflect on the fact that he is the very one who brought about this public disgrace. Other Japanese bureaucrats would also do well to begin accepting responsibility for their actions. This is the same as someone starting a fire and then, when a huge forest fire breaks out, claiming they didn't know anything about it.

Furthermore, when my lawyer asked, "Given the contents of the remark that they were about to adopt self-restraint, you knew about the self-restraint before it actually began, didn't you?" Yoshida could only give a far-fetched excuse that the expression "were about to" might be either a lyrical or a polite expression.

However, in Japanese the expression "were about to" is an expression in the future tense meaning "plan to." In other words, he had received a report that they planned to implement the self-restraint program. Fully advised of the situation, he did nothing to stop it.

Every time I read the testimony of this Ministry of Finance bureaucrat, it makes my blood boil all over again.

Further Bureaucratic Testimony

Party A's Item 52 is an article from *Nihon Keizai Shimbun* dated May 25, 1978. It is an article about a large drop in the recurring profit of Oji Paper Company for the current quarter, isn't it?

Yoshida: (Nods)

Party A's Item 53 is an article from *Nihon Keizai Shimbun* dated September 29, 1978, about four months after that. The article involves a turnaround to profit at Oji Paper Company, doesn't it?

Yoshida: (Nods)

Do you remember Oji Paper Company making such public announcements at that time?

Yoshida: I have no memory of that at all. The fact is that I first learned that this had occurred only on reading the record of the first trial.

In the case of Party A's Exhibit No. 52, this is an article dating from before the Hong Kong investors parted with the shares in Oji Paper Company, while the article in Party A's Exhibit No. 53 dates from after they had done so; from the viewpoint of the Hong Kong investors, they feel that this was quite deliberate. Even if it is just an impression, what do you think on looking at them now?

Yoshida: As far as my current individual standpoint is concerned on looking at these two articles, I believe that when one takes these two announcements side by side, if I were a shareholder I would want to learn more about where and how the explanations or announcements of the circumstances changed over this period.

Only the four major companies, Nomura, Nikko, Daiwa, and Yamaichi, were the managing underwriters for Oji Paper Company, weren't they?

Yoshida: I don't remember whether all four companies acted as managing underwriters.

If these four companies spoke to one another and decided upon the self-restraint program, and then asked the other four to follow suit, judging from the power relations within the industry, I think that the reality within the industry would mean that the other four companies would have no choice but to get on board. What would be your opinion on that?

Yoshida: This is related to the organization of the securities industry at the time, and generally speaking I would not deny that; however, I really cannot comment on whether or not that was the case.

I referred to the four companies, but Nikko Securities was the lead manager, wasn't it?

Yoshida: According to my memory, I believe, as you have just said, that Nikko Securities was the managing underwriter at the time that I had that perception.

Therefore, one would presume that Nikko Securities would have played the leading role with regard to the self-restraint program and the cancellation thereof as well, but what is your opinion?

Yoshida: I can well imagine so, but with regard to that, I don't believe that I am in a position to comment on whether or not that was actually the case.

Comments on this Testimony

These are the contradictory *Nihon Keizai Shimbun* articles that first reported a downturn in Oji Paper Company because of the appreciation of the Yen, and then an upturn in their profits for the same reasons. Regarding this matter, Harvard University Professor of Law Howell E. Jackson severely condemned Oji Paper Company, saying,

"Intentional distortion of Oji Paper stock price in May, 1978 would constitute fraud and manipulation under U. S. securities laws."

Professor Jackson further stated that:

> The aspect of this fact pattern that would most clearly constitute a violation of U. S. securities laws is the manner in which Oji Paper (acting with the knowledge or assistance of some of the securities firms involved in these transactions) allegedly misrepresented the future prospects of Oji Paper. In the United States, any person who intentionally disseminates materially misleading information about the value of a security listed on a major stock exchange would violate numerous provisions of the federal securities laws and would be subject to prosecution by the Securities and Exchange Commission as well as civil liability from certain injured parties.

Professor Jackson pointed out that if these acts had been committed in the United States, it is certain that lawsuits for compensation for damages would have been lodged by nearly all of the shareholders who had suffered injury.

More Testimony from the Appeal to the High Court

The following testimony has to do with an incident that was reported to me by Mr. Inoguchi of Wako Securities.

Mr. Inoguchi had told me how Wako had been disciplined by Oji for preparing the survey report and giving it to us in the first place. Wako took this seriously enough that the president, President Saito, took a friend of his from the Mitsui Group to meet with Oji and to apologize profusely.

The witness here is Mr. Tomio Miyanaga, the former person in charge of Wako Securities Hong Kong. The following testimony was given on April 18, 1996, at the trial of the Oji Paper Company case in the Tokyo High Court. We pick up the testimony after my lawyer had just handed him one of our exhibits.

This is a confidential report by Wako International Limited regarding the shares of Oji Paper Company, isn't it?

Miyanaga: (Nods)

I'm showing the translation. It would be correct, wouldn't it, that this was prepared at the time by Wako International Hong Kong and delivered to Mr. Wang of Newpis Hong Kong?

Miyanaga: Well, I was not directly involved in this.

Although you weren't directly involved, what do you think on looking at this document?

Miyanaga: I have the impression that I've just seen it for the first time.

Chief Judge: Is this something that you're seeing for the first time today?

Miyanaga: Yes, so, in fact I went to Hong Kong in the spring of 1974, and then a few months later another staff member came from Japan. That staff member succeeded me in taking care of Mr. Wang's account and he may have passed it on.

Chief Judge: What you are saying is that you didn't know about it until today because you were not personally involved, aren't you?

Miyanaga: Yes, I am. At that time I was already looking after institutional investors such as Hong Kong institutional investors or the so-called British affiliated institutional investors, and another staff member had taken over Mr. Wang's account.

That staff member was a person named Inoguchi, wasn't he?

Miyanaga: Yes.

From what it says here, if we assume that this was prepared by Wako International Hong Kong, on looking at page twenty-five, it says that the total asset value of one share in Oji Paper Company is ¥2,561, doesn't it?

Miyanaga: Yes.

Indeed, this is a statistical expression, as it were, of the latent asset value that you referred to a while ago, isn't it?

Miyanaga: Yes, it is.

Therefore, if we assume that Wako passed it over to Mr. Wang, when all is said and done, it would be fair to interpret this as recommending investment in these shares, wouldn't it?

Miyanaga: Rather than calling it a recommendation, I would just say that it was a stock whose latent asset value was being looked at in comparison with the actual share price.

You spoke of stock value a little while ago, didn't you? That this was just the asset value?

Miyanaga: It is the value considered in terms of the assets.

Mr. Wang has said that he heard that Oji Paper Company had reduced Wako Securities' percentage of underwriting the former's corporate bonds as a penalty for preparing the present confidential report and recommending investment in Oji Paper Company to Mr. Wang. Do you know about that?

Miyanaga: No, I don't.

Let me ask about President Saito of Wako Securities. Mr. Wang heard that President Saito had asked a friend at Mitsui Bank to go with him to offer an apology to Oji Paper Company regarding this matter. Do you know about that?

Miyanaga: No, I don't.

Comments on this Testimony

Even though I have verified from several sources that the apology and subsequent disciplining of Wako did indeed take place, Mr. Miyanaga denied it. Perhaps he was worried that if he had, Wako would have met with further reprimands. However, by not revealing it, he has only allowed the abuse to continue. Certainly, their situation is no better than it was; Wako is still held in Oji's iron grip. The only way to break that is to expose the abuse that happened and continues to happen.

Appendix C

Legal Opinions on the Oji Paper Trials

During the Oji Paper trials, I sought legal opinions on the cases from various authoritative sources. These opinions offer greater insight into not only the cases themselves, but also into the entire situation. Unfortunately, due to length, I am unable to give all of the opinions that I sought. What follows are samplings of these legal opinions.

Opinion of Atsuo Mihara on the Self-Restraint Program

On November 17, 1996, Atsuo Mihara, an Economic Analyst, issued a paper entitled, "A Few Comments on the 'Self-Restraint Program' Involving Oji Paper Stock." Following are excerpts from this paper.

> First of all, it may be worthwhile mentioning here, I believe, that under the Japanese securities laws, any entity which desires to engage in the "securities business" is required to obtain not a registration with but a license from the Minister of Finance. It is therefore needless to say that

Ministry of Finance, its Securities Bureau in particular, did and does hold the power of life and death over each and every securities firm in this country.

[At the time in question,] the position of banks or that of business corporations which were considering raising funds from the securities market was [still] stronger than that of securities firms...Under those circumstances, it was quite understandable and therefore should not be disregarded that the Japanese securities firms were not in the position to oppose the intention of the Ministry of Finance or their main banks which was behind them...It is not too difficult to imagine that in the world that was governed by such powerful business relationships any reckless acts that would otherwise be considered inconceivable in the light of the guiding principles of a free market such as the self-restraint program in the present case could happen.

In other words, because the securities companies were subservient to Ministry of Finance, to the banks, and to the company for which they were underwriters, they were to do what they were told. It did not matter if what they were told to do was illegal or not. Nor did it matter if what they were told to do was essentially a contradiction of their very existence (i.e., providing access to a free market) or if it was a bad business decision. In such a situation, the Japanese securities companies did what they were instructed to do with no questions asked. Indeed, they would never have dared to speak up against such a practice, even if they wanted to. They had been told to do it and they did it.

It is not an overstatement to say that until Japan's "Bubble Economy" disrupted in the early 1990s, few businessmen paid serious attention to the corporate asset management concept...In my recollection, what the Japanese businessmen was most concerned about a decade or two ago was how to improve their corporations' equity ratio as quickly as possible by internally retaining as much earned surplus as possible rather than to improve their respective return on investment or return on assets. The inter-company equity ownership system, which effectively connected all major Japanese corporations with each other, and the main bank system were the two main factors that significantly helped the Japanese business executives achieve this goal.

Therefore it seems obvious that Mr. Wang's company's purchase of as much as 13.5% of the issued and outstanding shares of Oji Paper Company—which was one of the nation's most prestigious companies—invited strong repulsion not only from the management team of Oji Paper itself but also from the nation's paper manufacturing industry and financial circles. Under those circumstances, his company's investment, was, I believe, regarded [by Oji Paper Company's management] as so fearful a threat to their policy of building and maintaining a stable shareholder base that they…decided to design and implement the series of the problematical actions against Mr. Wang's company. Under those circumstances, it was probably a matter of course, I believe, that Oji Paper Company applied direct and indirect pressure upon the securities firms…

The real purpose underlying the self-restraint program was, I believe, to prevent any foreign investors or any Japanese companies which were not [in Oji's *keiretsu*] from acquiring the controlling interest in Oji Paper Company…This explains the reason why they did not hesitate to resort to various illegal actions (including [the leaking of false and negative information to the press] to cause huge financial losses to Mr. Wang's company when they knew that his company was still trying to maintain the huge block of shares in Oji Paper Company…

It seems therefore that no Japanese parties involved in the present case took any notice of the right of investors to expect and pursue appreciation of the value of their investment because they were just too busy in building and maintaining Oji Paper Company's shareholder base in a way they liked it for their own benefit or, to be more specific, in a way to guarantee that the then current management team of Oji Paper Company could remain in their position.

Therefore my conclusion based on my analysis of the present case is that the present case can be characterized by too excessive preference given to the idea of "having as many docile shareholders and as less critical or opposing shareholders as possible" over the investors' right to expect and pursue appreciation of the value of their investment. Thus the sale [by his company] of its shares in Oji Paper Company was, I believe, the only alternative left to it as a shareholder to be eliminated.

U.S. Legal Opinions:
Professor Steve H. Hanke

In addition to seeking Japanese legal opinions, I also sought opinions from U.S. legal experts. One of those whom I consulted was Professor Steve H. Hanke of Johns Hopkins University who gave me his opinions in an affidavit.

He based his opinions on: the judgment of the Tokyo District Court, briefs filed in the Tokyo High Court, and other affidavits and briefs from the case.

Regarding the false statements by the Big Four he said, "It appears that the Big Four may have consistently engaged in deception, material misstatement, and omissions to force the Hong Kong investors to divest their legally held minority position in Oji Paper."

As for their assertions that they did not know me prior to the forced sale of Oji Paper on June 12, 1978, he said:

> [The Big Four's] assertion appears implausible in light of several facts. First, individual members of the Big Four brokered substantial business transactions on behalf of the Plaintiff [(Newpis)] and the Plaintiff's representative [(myself)] over ten years prior to June 12, 1978… Second the members of the Big Four were clearly aware, prior to June 12, 1978, that the Plaintiff was controlled by Mr. Wang. In a memorandum dated October 9, 1977, over eight months prior to [the sale], T.H. Wang is listed as "president of Newpis Hong Kong, Ltd."[(This is a reference to the meeting I had with representatives of the Big Four on October 9, 1977 to try to resolve the issue.)] Third…if there was no relationship between the Big Four and the Plaintiff, Mr. Wang, or the other Hong Kong investors, would the Big Four send representatives to meet with the Hong Kong investors regarding their stake in Oji Paper? The apparent explanation, based on the preponderance of the facts, is that such a relationship did exist. Yet, inexplicably, the Big Four continue to assert that they did no business with the Plaintiff prior to June 12, 1978.

Regarding Daiwa's allegation that I had physically transferred the stocks to them, Professor Hanke, after reviewing the facts, came to the conclusion that it was highly unlikely that the sale had occurred the way that Daiwa had claimed. "Daiwa appears to have created a transparent fabrication in an effort to bolster the fiction that its relationship with the Plaintiff began on June 12, 1978. The fabrication, however, does not seem to comport with the reality of the marketplace with respect to foreign stock trades."

As for the allocation of commissions and Mr. Kobayashi's claims—at first that it was too large a transaction for Nikko to handle alone and his later sworn testimony that the commissions were divided according to the managers' shares—Professor Hanke said the following (one section has been summarized due to length):

> Neither Mr. Kobayashi's first nor his second explanation withstands close scrutiny. First, it is unusual that in the highly competitive brokerage industry, a brokerage firm would share a transaction with another firm because the transaction is too large to handle. Indeed, in response to the question, "Is there any precedent that trades once concluded with the firm [are] later shared by other firms," Mr. Kobayashi admits that he has "No such experience."
>
> [Second, the division of commissions was not allocated according to the managers' shares, which he declared under oath to be 35-35-15-15, because the truth was that the managers' shares at the time were actually 40-25-25-10. Instead, each securities company had been rewarded or punished according to the level of their faithfulness to Oji Paper.] Thus, Mr. Kobayashi's sworn statement that he "allot[ed the shares] according to the managing underwriters' share" is erroneous.
>
> Given that the Hong Kong investors were unsuccessful in their attempts to purchase the paper company stock in good faith and with offers that exceeded the market price, we can conclude that the Hong Kong group was being discriminated against and literally prohibited from making those purchases...The foregoing suggests a pattern of behavior that, if proven to be illegal, is consistent with stereotypes of entrenched Japanese managements. Such entrenchment occurs where management is not subject to the normal discipline imposed by a well functioning capital market such as the one in the United States or the one in the United Kingdom.

Professor Tatsuo Kamimura on the High Court's Ruling in Oji Paper

Professor Kamimura Faculty of Law, of Waseda University is one of the top legal minds in Japan. He specializes in commercial and securities and exchange laws. His opinion focused a good deal on how the High Court could confirm the illegality of the self-restraint program and yet dismiss my complaint because it did not see any causation between the two. In this, he felt the Court simply did not understand the implications of the self-restraint program and how such an action could have devastating affects on a free market system—to say nothing of how it was illegal. Due to length, parts of his opinion have been summarized. In this opinion, "Appellant" refers to our side.

> The High Court failed, obviously because of its lack of understanding of the seriousness of the implications that [the self-restraint program] could possibly have, to realize how serious the injury caused by the self-restraint program was in the sense that as a result thereof Appellant, who honestly believed that the stock market in this country was an open, free, and competitive market, was flatly denied and deprived of the right of free access thereto…
>
> In its decision, the High Court found that there was no proximate causal relationship between the sale by Appellant of the shares and the self-restraint program and refused to make any finding as to whether or not the Appellant suffered any loss or damage as a result of the self-restraint program. While it definitely held that the self-restraint program was illegal, it gave no careful consideration at all [as to] why Appellant felt that it was forced to sell the shares.
>
> [Such an approach] seems as if the High Court is saying that it has totally abandoned making any findings with

respect to any causality-related dispute cases or wrongful damage cases of the type peculiar to the stock market.

The High Court found that the self-restraint program as planned and implemented by the Big Four was illegal. Obviously, the High Court's lack of understanding of how the self-restraint program could potentially be harmful to the purposes for which the Securities and Exchanges Act was enacted had significant influence on the High Court's decision...

If one views securities firms licensed to act as such under the Act merely as one of the parties to a sale and purchase contract or brokerage service contract and its relations with its client investors from the perspective of law of contract alone, then one would tend to overlook the roles that the securities companies are expected to perform as a major part of the support and driving force of the securities market of this country. They are licensed to act as such under the Act *to the exclusion of all others* (emphasis added) so that they can make positive contribution to the sound and proper operation of the nation's economy. The boycott by the Big Four against Appellant in this case was one of the worst actions that they could possibly take against their clients in violation of the purposes of or the principles underlying the Act. By implementing it, they have almost renounced the idea of a free and competitive investment market and let the market commit "suicide."

The Act has been enacted for, among other purposes, the purpose of ensuring that the securities market will fully perform, among other duties, the function of assuring the formation of a fair market price for each and every issue traded on the market. Second, the securities firms have the responsibility to provide investment assistance and advice to their client investors to help them make proper *bona fide* investment decisions for each and every issue traded on the market to allow the market to form a fair market price for it. Third, the securities companies have the responsibility to relay all the *bona fide* investment decisions made by their client investors with respect to any particular issue traded thereon straight to the market so as to fully reflect the formation of a fair market price.

Thus, each and every securities firm that is licensed to act as such under the Act is—as main support and driving force of the free market mechanism—invariably under the obligation to relay all *bona fide* buying and selling orders placed with it by its principals to the market for execution. A market price for any particular issue traded on the market at a given time must be formed by the accumulation of *bona fide* competitive investment decisions made by numerous willing sellers and willing buyers of that particular issue at the time. Therefore, if securities firms were permitted to take any unauthorized arbitrary action on their part to prevent *bona fide* investment decisions made by their principals with respect to any particular issue from reaching the market in a timely manner, then the market mechanism would totally fail to function properly.

Because no securities firm has the right to reject arbitrarily any orders placed with them [it is important to understand] that no single securities firm can be free from these responsibilities even if it is acting by itself alone, let alone the four major securities firms who designed and implemented the self-restraint program against Appellant in the form of "concerted action." They are, I believe, also subject to the Anti-Monopoly Act.

Regarding the decision by the Big Four to enact the self-restraint program, the court believed it was "put into operation by the defendant securities companies based on nothing else than their own initiative. (It should be noted here, however, that this Court does not, by this view, necessarily mean that the forewarning [given by Ministry of Finance] would not and could not possibly be determined to be illegal, though no such determination is sought in the present case.)" This means, I believe, that the High Court wanted to strongly yet impliedly emphasize that the Ministry of Finance's warning in question was illegal.

What we can learn from this Case is that in the Japanese securities market there existed no such thing as freedom of access to the market, which was and is one of the most fundamental market rules common to the securities markets in the rest of the world. What is important here is not the right or wrong of the purposes underlying Appellant's investment in shares of Oji Paper Company, but the fact that Appellant alone was totally denied the benefits arising out of the foundation upon which the securities market in this country was considered to have been based.

In Professor Kamimura's opinion, the court also failed to see any causal relationship between the implementation of the self-restraint program and the sale of the shares; however, in order to make this claim, the Court would have had to make the rather broad assumption that the market had indeed fully recovered from the effects of the implementation of the self-restraint program. But in order to say that the market had *fully* recovered, someone should have been punished for their actions in order to reassure the investing public that all was well with the market and that such illegal activities would not occur in the future.

His opinion continues:

Absolutely no such penalty actions were ever taken to restore the order of the market in this Case. Surprisingly enough, on the contrary, the four major securities firms dared to declare at the time that their self-restraint program—which was later held to be illegal by both the Tokyo District and the High Court—was a proper action for them to take; that securities brokers had the right to accept or reject orders from their clients at their own discretion. Actions like the self-restraint program in this case were not exceptional emergency actions but were proper and normal actions for them to take in the course of exercise of the arbitrary rights and privileges they had. In other words, they virtually publicly declared that they had a license to do illegal things and that Tokyo Stock Exchange was a market where traditional illegal practices were still prevailing.

It was quite natural then for Appellant to think that they might even deny Appellant the right and chance to sell the shares on the market even just to recoup the money he had invested. On a market such as the Tokyo Stock Exchange where such intimidation or blackmailing-like statements were allowed to be made openly, anything could go. And the only wise alternative left to Appellant was to leave the market as soon as possible before they got fatally hurt, no matter whether they invested into Oji Paper Company for a long-term investment purpose of for a short-term capital gain purpose.

The High Court said their claims that they could refuse orders at their discretion was not a threat for future action but that they were merely explaining why they had taken the action in the first place. But how could they possibly have any plausible reasons for the self-restraint program, which the High Court itself finds illegal? The High Court, it seems, unduly and excessively made light of the seriousness of this particular question by allowing the four major securities firms to use such an essentially and fundamentally illegal view as an excuse for their illegal boycott.

The High Court says that while it may be true that [if the situation had been different] Appellant would not have sold its shares [at the time that it did], Appellant's sale in this case could still be considered to be in line with its investment objectives since it in fact realized some capital gains out of the sale, though it was in Appellant's view no greater than the then current commercial bank interest. Therefore, the High Court reasons, as long as Appellant sold the shares at profit, it should not be allowed to maintain that the sale was still out of its investment objectives and that therefore it was made against its own free will. It seems to me as if the High Court were saying that even if an investor is a victim of any illegal conduct committed by a licensed securities firm, he will not be entitled to any claim for damages against the securities firm as long as he successfully recoups the cost of his investment.

[The Big Four had also failed to disclose to the Hong Kong investors the fact that they were in a conflict of interest situation, which was a serious matter indeed.] From late September 1977 and on, the four major securities firms were working not for or on behalf of Appellant and its fellow investors but for and on behalf of Oji Paper Company alone. The Appellant and its fellow investors, who did not know this, naturally continued to do business with the four major securities firms during that period, blindly believing that they were still working for and on behalf of them with all due care to help them achieve their investment purposes. When [the securities companies] advised Appellant and its fellow investors to sell their shares in Oji Paper Company, they were not acting for the benefit of Appellant but for the benefit of Oji Paper Company. Additionally, even if they had fully disclosed to Appellant and its fellow investors in a timely manner that they were in fact in a conflict-of-interest situation, it would have been impossible for Appellant and its fellow investors to find any other [Japanese] securities firm or firms in Hong Kong that would be willing to work for them.

What bothers me very much in this case is that none of the four major securities firms had any effective Chinese Wall between their own underwriting and brokering departments. Because of the absence of an effective Chinese Wall between them, each of those securities firms made a serious mistake of mixing their positions as underwriters and broker houses. In other words, they totally forgot to clearly distinguish in their mind whether they were working for Oji Paper Company or Appellant and its fellow investors. Worse still, while they were implementing the self-restraint program against Appellant and its fellow investors, they continued not only to provide brokerage services to their other clients [in the sale or purchase of Oji Paper stock] but also to buy or sell [Oji Paper stock] on their own behalf in their dealing operations. Thus, they were in a conflict-of-interest situation in many respects. These problems are not peculiar to any particular securities firms but still common to the Japanese securities industry as a whole. That means that the rights and interests of individual brokerage clients tend to be easily neglected.

[In conclusion,] when the High Court considered those conducts by [the securities companies], it should not have placed the primary focus on the self-restraint program alone, but should have considered all of them as a series of unlawful conducts designed to unlawfully prevent Appellant's legitimate investment activities and that as such they, as a whole, constitute one big tortuous act. By avoiding the task of holding and declaring that those conducts committed by [the securities companies] in this case as a whole constituted a tortuous conduct, which, I agree, would be a very difficult task for it to accept and perform particularly under the pressure of the traditional ways of thinking which are still prevailing in this country, the High Court seems to have failed to grasp the inner true meaning of the matters at issue in this case.

Professor Kamimura's Review of the Appeal Judgment

I also requested Professor Kamimura to review the High Court's judgment on my appeal, and then went ahead with the appeal procedure to the Supreme Court, appending his written opinion to the reasons for the appeal. Professor Kamimura's opinion is quite a long piece, running to 15,000 characters, so what follows are merely extracts.

> The original judgment, even while ascertaining the illegality of the joint conduct by the securities firms and other defendants involved in the case (Mr. Fumio Tanaka, Oji Paper Company, the 'Big Four' securities houses) of refusing to broker purchase orders (hereinafter this shall be referred to as the 'self-restraint program'), denied a cause-and-effect relationship between this illegal conduct and the sale of the shares in the case by the appellant (T. H. Wang) and rejected the appellant's claim.
>
> First, because the original judgment conspicuously lacks any understanding with regard to the gravity of a situation in which the freedom to conduct securities transactions in a free, competitive market is taken away by the joint action of securities companies, which should be the upholders of the market structure, there is a failure to understand the self-restraint program's depriving investors of the freedom to deal in securities, which is premised on the existence of a free competitive market, as a major infringement of rights. It is

clear that this is a misinterpretation of Article 709 of the Civil Code and of Article 719, Clause 1 of the Civil Code, and that this violation affected the judgment.

Secondly, the original judgment denied the cause-and-effect relationship between the self-restraint program and the action of the sale and therefore took the position from the outset of not determining whether or not there was a loss. Although it acknowledged the illegal conduct of the self-restraint program in the case itself, its absolute failure to take any account of the circumstances in this case that compelled the appellant to make the sale or to make any attempt to determine the losses of the appellant constituted a total annulment of the characteristic cause-and-effect relationship between compensation for losses involving the market and of the acknowledgment of the amount of such losses. It is clear that this is a misinterpretation of Article 719, Clause 1 of the Civil Code, and that this violation is considered to have affected the judgment.

Thirdly, the chain of actions taken by the defendants around the time of the self-restraint program in this case can be viewed as a chain of comprehensive illegal joint actions aimed at preventing the acquisition of a certain scale of shares by the appellant and causing him to sell the shares that he possessed. While the original judgment recognized such a chain of acts as 'a type of conduct obstructing investment', it denied a sufficient cause-and-effect relationship between such chain of actions and the sale of the shares in this case by the appellant. It is clear that this is a misinterpretation of Article 709 of the Civil Code and of Article 719, Clause 1 of the Civil Code, and that this violation is considered to have affected the judgment...

The self-restraint program in this case constitutes exceedingly grave illegal conduct. Strictly speaking, the securities houses and executives committing such actions are subject to fines or imprisonment, and order in the market must be fully restored by the imposition of such measures as civil sanctions (in the case of the United States) or a fine [or other such measures to restore faith in the market]...

In an age when it is necessary to exclude administrative intervention before the fact and to arrange for the redress and remedy of private law after the fact, the expectations toward the Supreme Court are rising in the fields of legislation for large-scale publicly owned companies and for the securities and financial markets and of industrial legislation. In particular, Japan is a country in which not even one case of compensation for losses related to markets has been acknowledged. If compensation for losses is denied in such a case as this as well, the result can only be the lodging of civil claims for compensation for losses in other even more complicated cases. For the sake of forming a fair and healthy corporate culture in the fullness of time, courageous decisions are to be asked of the Supreme Court.

Appendix D

Testimony and Comments from the Saibo Trials

The following testimony, regarding the pricing of the newly issued shares, is from Mr. Hirobumi Iizuka, the president of Saibo, and took place on April 9, 1997 at the Urawa District Court.

The testimony here begins after my lawyer handed him an exhibit, which was Mr. Iizuka's own written statement regarding the issuance of the new shares.

As mentioned in pages five to six here, the pricing of the newly issued shares in this case was set at ¥801 on the basis of the transaction prices during the month immediately preceding the decision to issue new shares. Is that correct?

Iizuka: Yes.

The turnover for that month was 14,000 shares, wasn't it?

Iizuka: That is correct.

In other words, you used the month of transactions involving 14,000 shares as the basis for deciding the issue price for the two million new shares. That's less than one per cent of that number. Didn't you experience some doubts about that fact?

Iizuka: As far as the standard for determining the price was concerned, I was aware that the standard would ultimately be the market price, since the company was listed on the Second Market of the Tokyo Stock Exchange.

So you are saying that you personally felt no doubts about this?

Iizuka: Yes.

In regard to the average transaction price of ¥870 in the market recorded on page five of this exhibit, the plaintiff contends that it was not appropriate to take this as the basis for deciding the issuing price because the price was too low when compared to the asset value of the land and the securities owned by Saibo. Weren't either of those factors taken into account at the time?

Iizuka: No, they weren't.

Were any such doubts or opinions raised by anyone at meetings of the managing directors or the board of directors?

Iizuka: As I remember, there were none.

Comments on this Testimony

President Iizuka contends that "The standard for determining the price of the 2 million newly issued shares would ultimately be the market price," but there is considerable doubt about this. Saibo shares had an extremely small turnover rate, which is one reason why they were listed on the Second Market. As my attorney pointed out, the month before the issuance, the turnover was just a meager 14,000 shares. Was it really proper to price the 2 million newly issued shares on the basis of such a minuscule turnover?

Obviously not, since both the Urawa District Court and the Tokyo High Court both agreed with that the extremely low volume of Saibo shares being traded made it hard to determine whether such an evaluation would be fair, and the Tokyo High Court went further to say that it would have been nearly impossible to buy 2 million shares of Saibo at the price of ¥801 per share.

The trading volume for Saibo has been low for some time before the trial and has since continued to be low. From January 1999 to January 2000, for example, the trading volume for the entire year was a mere 285,000 shares—averaging only 21,923 shares per month. The most active month was in October when 74,000 shares were traded but there were two months that saw only 1,000 shares exchange hands. There was even one month, May 1999, in which there was no trading at all. Given this extremely low volume, it is highly questionable whether the Saibo stock even meets the listing standards of the Tokyo Stock Exchange.

Evidence of Illegal Conduct by the Board of Directors

My lawyer handed President Iizuka another exhibit, which was the Minutes of the Board of Directors Meeting of March 7, 1991, at which the resolution on the issuing of new shares was passed.

Saibo either owns or rents the land referred to here on page thirteen, doesn't it?
Iizuka: Yes.
The land that it owns itself amounts to a total of 245,664 square meters, doesn't it?
Iizuka: Yes.

. . .

My lawyer handed President Iizuka another of our exhibits.

This is an assessment of the value of the land owned by Saibo that was made by a property appraiser at the request of the plaintiff. According to what appears in the value assessment table on the third line, the evaluations given per square meter are ¥500,000 for the land at the head office and the main factory; ¥350,000 for the land at Kawaguchi Green City and the driving school/golf driving range in Kawaguchi City; and ¥110,000 for the land at the golf driving range in Hasuda City. As far as the overall assessed value is concerned, if we allow for the rather large drop of 40% in the prices for land in Kawaguchi City and take just 60% of the assessed values, can we take it that the breakdown would be more or less like this?

Iizuka: I don't know about the values.

The assessment of the unit price was made by taking both the market price and the posted price into consideration. Now, what do you think about these amounts of ¥500,000, ¥300,000, and ¥110,000?

Iizuka: I don't know.

. . .

My lawyer next handed President Iizuka a report on the prices of land owned by Saibo.

On comparing the area of the land of the head office in the securities report of March 1992 with the area of the land of the head office in the securities report of March 1993, it has increased by 1,057 square meters. The increased portion would be the land at Maekawa, which was acquired in December 1992 for ¥487 million, wouldn't it?

Iizuka: I believe that that was part of it.

Was anything else purchased?

Iizuka: I don't recall clearly.

If we divide ¥487 million by 1,057 square meters this means it was purchased at approximately ¥460,000 per square meter. Was that roughly the price at which it was acquired at that time?

Iizuka: I remember that the amount was something like that.

Then the assessment a while ago on the value assessment table from Party A's Exhibit No. 1 that valued the land of the main factory and the head office at ¥500,000 per square meter is not all that different from your own reading of the value of the land, is it?

Iizuka: Kasahara's land is located on the side of the main plant closest to the prefectural highway and if it were converted into a commercial zone, I think that this plot would have the strongest selling appeal.

. . .

My lawyer gave another exhibit to President Iizuka.

Referring to the map in the Appendix on the sixth sheet, where is the land bought from Kasahara on this map?

Iizuka: It's the area referred to as the "Exclusive Parking Lot" near the Warabi-Hatogaya Prefectural Highway.

And where is the land for Saibo's head office on this map?

Iizuka: It's where "1F Saibo Office" is written on the lower left.

Aside from that, is nearly all of the northern side the main factory?

Iizuka: Yes. The sections where the words "Iitome Memorial Hall" and "Mukahidai High School / Saibo School" appear belong to the section for the head office.

Insofar as it is based on the assessment table from Party A's Exhibit No. 1, the land in Kawaguchi and Hasuda alone comes to ¥48,356,390,000 and when that is divided by the 12 million shares that were issued at the time, we get ¥4,029 per share. Did you make such a calculation?

Iizuka: No, I didn't.

So what are your thoughts now on hearing that the amount comes to ¥4,029 per share according to this calculation?

Iizuka: I think that it's extremely high.

. . .

My lawyer handed him a securities report, another of our exhibits.

In the column with information on the current prices of securities on page thirty-six of this securities report of March 1991, it is recorded that the current prices of the securities owned at the time by Saibo totaled ¥7,605,542,000. When the value of these securities is divided by the 12 million shares that were currently issued at the time, it comes to nearly ¥634 per share. Would such an understanding be correct?

Iizuka: I didn't look into that.

So let's see. If we take the combined value of the property according to the assessment table and of the securities, we get a total of ¥4,663 per share. But there is quite a large disparity when here when this figure is compared with the average transaction price of ¥870 per share during the month immediately prior to the issuance of the new shares that your company has used as its valuation. Why do you think that was?

Iizuka: I presume that there were several factors, but I couldn't say specifically what they were.

Comments on this Testimony

In their securities report, in the column for information on the current prices of securities, Saibo itself recorded that the value of the securities alone that they held came to more than ¥7.6 billion, and yet no entry was made in the column for the current value of the land. I dare say that Saibo was concealing the current value of the land that it owned. The failure to enter facts in a securities report is illegal.

Moreover, Saibo acquired the land adjacent to the company at approximately ¥460,000 per square meter. Based on this acquisition price, the land in Kawaguchi City and Hasuda City alone would come to ¥48,356,390,000. Dividing this by the total of 12 million issued shares at the time yields the figure of ¥4,029 per share that my attorney cited. Certainly, all of the directors must have known this, not least the president. Therefore, this corroborates the idea that the price of ¥801 determined by Saibo's board of directors was a fabricated price and utterly without foundation.

Maryland University Professor of Law Mark A. Sargent cited the following quotation regarding this decision of the board of directors in his paper, *A Legal Analysis of Securities Matter Involving the Saibo Company*: "[There] is a presumption that in making a business decision, the directors of a corporation act on an informed basis, in good faith, and in an honest belief that the action is in the best interests of the company."

This is the "business judgment rule." This rule is applied when an inquiry is conducted into a matter under dispute with regard to the propriety of an action taken by the board of directors. Professor Sargent went on to say, "For example, a showing that the board had a financial interest in a transaction that the board approved will shift the burden of proof to the board to show the entire fairness of the transaction."

How would the improper issue of new shares be handled if the Saibo case were being tried in an American court? He said:

> Under Delaware law, the authority of the board of directors to approve the issuance of shares is subject to the board's overriding fiduciary duty to the corporation and its stockholders. It has long been established that a court may intervene on fiduciary grounds if the issuance was approved for or with "improper motive or personal gain or arbitrary action or conscious disregard of the interests of the corporation and the rights of its stockholders."

Examining the Saibo matter even more closely, Professor Sargent said:

> Such issuance could be considered grossly inadequate, in violation of corporate fiduciary duty prescriptions, under either of two theories. First, the individual defendants failed to disclose the actual value of the shares given the substantial real estate and securities holdings of the company. Second, the thinly traded nature of Saibo shares meant that no fair market value existed for such shares. Consequently, if

Saibo had been a Delaware corporation, the directors' approval of the dilutive issuance of additional stock on March 7, 1991 at a grossly inadequate price would have constituted a breach of the fiduciary duty of loyalty.

In addition, Professor Sargent said that if it is assumed that Saibo's daughter companies (Saiei Fudosan and Saitama Kogyo) were controlled by and hence were affiliates of the directors who approved the stock issuance, then the issuance of the new shares in Saibo was self-dealing.

Furthermore, Professor Sargent remarked on the breach of the duty of care by Saibo's board of directors:

> There could exist a serious question as to the directors' obligation of care, however, with respect to the stock issuance. If the stock issuance was authorized by the directors without any effort to consider the real value of the shares, the directors may have failed to satisfy the requirement under *Van Gorkom* of making a fully informed decision. It would appear that the directors of Saibo issued stock at market value without any effort to take into account the value of Saibo's real estate assets, even though the directors should have known that such values far exceeded book value. This duty not to rely on market price and to make a fully informed valuation was further heightened by the thin trading of Saibo's shares, which made the market price of the stock a highly unreliable measure of value. [When considering the sheer volume of new shares to be issued,] the thin market should have alerted any reasonable, objective director to be especially careful with regard to the pricing of any stock issuance. Accordingly, the development of further facts in this case may support a finding that the directors breached their duty of care by making a highly uninformed valuation decision.

In conclusion, he said:

> In short, because approval of the stock issuance was an "interested transaction"(or self-dealing), the individual defendant directors would not have the protection of the business judgment rule. Instead, such directors would have the burden of proving the "entire fairness" of the transaction under section 144(a)(3). If they could not establish the fairness of the price, the court could void the transaction.

Professor Sargent issued this memorandum on November 21, 1995, which was quite a long time before this examination of the witness (April 9, 1997). On reading the testimony in this witness examination, it can be seen that everything indicated by Professor Sargent was borne out.

Massive Deficit Over Nineteen Years

The following is more testimony from that of President Iizuka's appearance before the Urawa District Court.

On the matter of Saibo's profit and loss, as the plaintiff understands it, there was a profit overall, but when this was divided into textiles and property, it was seen that the main business, textiles, was in the red, and this portion was reducing the profits from property. Such an understanding is correct, isn't it?

Iizuka: Ultimately the figures came out that way, but it doesn't mean that losses in textiles were eating into profits in property. Rather, it should be understood that the fruits of the history of the textile division, which had been built up assiduously up to then, were tied to the current profits in property.

Nevertheless, there is no mistaking the fact that the structure of profits and losses persisted in that vein for eleven years in succession up to March 1991, is there?

Iizuka: No, there isn't.

The situation of the main business division being in the red has continued since then up to the present, hasn't it? A matter of some seventeen years?

Iizuka: Yes. According to the figures, the losses have fluctuated quite a bit, but the trend is downward.

Haven't the managers of Saibo, including yourself, been deliberately keeping its profits down by means of such a profit structure or, if not deliberately, haven't you at least been tolerating such a profit structure?

Iizuka: No. That is the farthest thing from our minds.

There is a view that such a profit structure is the reason that dealings in the shares are not active and as a consequence, the transaction price has been depressed. What do you think about this?

Iizuka: As far as the background of the share price and its formation is concerned, I am aware that there are matters that do not come within our scope.

Comments on this Testimony

Although Saibo possesses enormous assets, profits haven't risen. An examination quickly reveals that textiles, the main business, is in the doldrums and has been producing massive losses every year, and that a profit is narrowly realized by virtue of the revenue from leasing property. The cumulative losses in the textile sector over a seventeen-year period reached ¥7.0 billion, which is eleven times the capital fund prior to the increase of capital. Obviously, the assets of the company are not being put to practical use in an efficient manner.

The renowned listed textile company Tachikawa, founded in 1906, decided to dissolve itself in July 1997, because it had produced losses for five years in succession, noting, "The shareholders are being inconvenienced." It was a decision made precisely because of the value placed on shareholders. Additionally, the president of Toyo Rayon, the major chemical fiber manufacturer, has said that he withdraws from businesses that show losses for three years in a row. The distribution giant Daiei has announced a policy principle for the year 2000 of settling and selling off the accounts of subsidiaries whose business is in the red.

Saibo's type of corporate management will never make a profit no matter how much time goes by, and the continued investment in the textile division was pointless. As Saibo's fourth largest shareholder with around 5% of its shares, I suggested to the management that they should withdraw from the loss-making textile sector and carry out the development of commercial and residential sites in order to put the land assets to practical use in an efficient manner. However, Saibo's management rejected all such proposals that I raised time and again.

Despite all this, on being asked whether such a profit structure might not be the reason for the depression of the share price, President Iizuka answered, "As far as the background of the share price and its formation is concerned, I am aware that there are matters that do not come within our scope."

What kind of irresponsible manager claims that the formation of his own company's share price is completely beyond his power? If his is part of the management of a publicly listed company, then it is his *duty* to have his management skills reflected in the price of his company's shares. If his leadership results in losses, then he must reconsider his management approach and, above all, he should withdraw from any loss-making sectors in order to improve the business of his company.

The Real Purpose of the Newly Issued Shares

Concerning the need for funds leading to this increase of capital, rather than this being a situation in which the decision for the capital increase was predicated on a need for funds, wasn't the process, in fact, one wherein the capital increase was decided first and a corresponding "need" for funds was thought up later as a use for the increase in capital?

Iizuka: At the very beginning, starting from a long time back, there was a desire to redevelop the main factory in a positive manner and in that connection we considered how the relocation of the existing plant should be carried out. At the same time, I believe that this was the period when the need for funds coincided exactly with a time of burgeoning prosperity, because sales were expanding smoothly.

It has been said that the board of managing directors ordered each department to look into needs for the funds. Whose suggestion was that?

Iizuka: It's not a question of one person. It was the proposal of the whole board of managing directors.

Do you remember which person on the board of managing directors made the suggestion?

Iizuka: I'm not clear on that.

Did the board of managing directors first decide the capital increase?

Iizuka: Yes.

Who in that board of managing directors took the initiative in making the proposal to increase the capital?

Iizuka: At that time, three of us—myself and two other directors—were the core of the board of managing directors, and I believe that it was mutually agreed upon by the three of us.

I believe that this kind of issue is usually handled from the bottom up with circulars from the planning department, the finance department, and so forth. Was the investigation for the need for funds and the decision on the increase of capital handled from the top down?

Iizuka: In the case of our company, I understand that to have been the case regarding the present matter.

On the method of procurement of the funds, didn't you give any consideration to selling some of the securities held at the time, whose current value was approximately ¥7.6 billion?

Iizuka: No, there wasn't. We made the decision after considering other methods of procurement.

What you are saying then, is that you decided to allocate the increase of capital to third parties and requested business connections, financial institutions, and life and liability insurance companies to subscribe, but there was no favorable answer. Is that what you are saying?

Iizuka: Yes.

Considering that none of the companies gave a favorable answer, doesn't this mean that they all felt that there was something wrong with the purpose of the capital increase and avoided subscribing to it?

Iizuka: That is something that we don't know.

If we take it that all the major shareholders, including business connections, financial institutions and life and liability insurance companies were all negatively disposed, in the normal way of thinking, I believe that the usual course would have been to give up the capital increase at that stage and arrange for the procurement of funds by some other method. What is the reason that you proceeded with the capital increase to the extent of going against the inclinations of all of the major shareholders?

Iizuka: The foremost reason was that there was a need for funds.

. . .

My attorney now showed President Iizuka the securities report for Saibo as of June 1991, which was some three months after the allocation of the new shares that had taken place on March 7, 1991.

On the lower half of page five it says, "However, there was no favorable answer except from Saitama Kogyo Co., Ltd. and Saiei

Fudosan Co., Ltd., and unavoidably, the two companies..." What kind of feeling is implied by "unavoidably"?

Iizuka: It was because we would have wanted the shares to be subscribed by other companies as well if at all possible.

You didn't ask the plaintiff—Newpis Hong Kong—to purchase the additional shares, did you?

Iizuka: No, we didn't.

Why was that?

Iizuka: I don't believe that there was any deep or special reason.

On page fourteen of this securities report for the sixty-eighth year, no mention at all is made of approximately ¥300 million for the present three-story factory building in the column on New Establishment, Major Expansion or Renovation of Facilities, or Plans Thereof, is there?

Iizuka: No, there isn't.

So, originally, there wasn't any plan at that time to invest ¥300 million to move the factory, was there?

Iizuka: Initially, the redevelopment of the main factory had come first and we had the idea of adjusting the timing of the factory relocation to coincide with that. Therefore, when there was a change in the circumstances surrounding the redevelopment of the main factory, the delay there caused a delay in the move.

This is a securities report as of June 1991. Now, if there was a plan such as you have just stated, isn't it strange that nothing is recorded in here about it?

Iizuka: I believe that it was because there was a time lag.

So what you are saying is that although there was such a possibility, the plans had not been settled on yet, is that right?

Iizuka: The precondition was that the preparation of the main factory site would be carried out first.

So you are saying that, taking the preparation of the main factory as a precondition, it was at that stage that you wanted to arrange the procurement of funding for the investment in the building that would ensue by allocating the increase of capital to third parties, aren't you?

Iizuka: That is correct.

. . .

My lawyer now showed another piece of evidence.

The uses of the funds are recorded on page six. Approximately ¥1.6 billion was produced through this increase of capital, but within the following year only ¥211 million was used for investment and improvement as you have testified and everything beyond that involves subsequent expenditures, doesn't it?

Iizuka: Yes.

In that case, why did you have the capital increase? It seems unnatural to have had an increase of capital for uses like those recorded here. What do you think?

Iizuka: We wanted to go ahead with the redevelopment more quickly.

In item six it says, "April 1993, Kurohama Golf reconstruction, ¥253 million," doesn't it?

Iizuka: Yes.

. . .

My attorney presented President Iizuka with another exhibit.

In the column on New Establishment, Major Expansion or Renovation of Facilities or Plans Therefore, on page fourteen of this securities report up to March 31, 1992 for the sixty-ninth year, there is an entry of ¥400 million budgeted for a golf driving range, isn't there?

Iizuka: Yes.

Is this the Kurohama Golf that was just mentioned under item six?

Iizuka: Yes.

However, in the column for Methods of Fund Procurement on page fourteen, it appears as funds on hand rather than funds from an increase of capital, doesn't it?

Iizuka: Yes.

Doesn't this conflict with your explanation?

Iizuka: I take it to mean that funds that were acquired by an increase of capital were then expressed as funds on hand after the change of year.

Comments on this Testimony

Let's try to find out from this testimony what the true motive was behind Saibo's allocation of the increase of capital to third parties.

First of all, it was extremely strange to have risked a capital increase rather than using the normal methods of raising new capital, such as borrowing from financial institutions or selling assets that Saibo owned. Since Saibo was a company without debts at that time, banks would have happily loaned them the funds they needed. Moreover, by selling some of the ¥7.6 billion in securities that they owned, Saibo would have easily been able to cover their funding needs. It can only be supposed that they arranged for the capital increase because of the "improper motive or personal gain or arbitrary action or conscious disregard of the interests of the corporation and the rights of its stockholders" referred to by Professor Sargent.

Secondly, it was also strange that the method they used involved the allocation of the capital increase to third parties rather than to shareholders. If I had been allocated shares in the capital increase with a value of more than ¥5,000 per share at a price of ¥801 per share, I would have taken them gladly, because at the time, we could not obtain the shares even at ¥1,300 apiece. But, as President Iizuka has testified, I was not even asked—despite the fact that I owned roughly five percent of the shares and was one of the more major shareholders. Even though I was not asked, I am certain that other shareholders with smaller stakes than mine would also have jumped at the chance to purchase additional shares at what was almost forty percent off the market price.

Thirdly, it is also strange that none of the major shareholders or other business connections that were supposedly asked declined the offer and that only to two companies, Saitama Kogyo and Saiei Fudosan—the daughter companies of Saibo—were favorable to the idea.

However, in Japan it is simply unbelievable that major banks and other stable shareholders would refuse to subscribe to an increase of capital through new shares. I consider this testimony to be utterly false. When proof of the refusal by the major shareholders was asked for, Saibo could only supply personal letters from those who were employees of these companies. As for not asking me, he did not give any reason at all. This is not only unfair and prejudicial towards me but also to all the other shareholders who were not asked.

Fourthly, there is considerable doubt as to whether the need for funding extended to the implementation of an increase of capital. Out of the capital increase, only a mere ¥211 million was used the following year for investment in equipment.

In view of this, the true purpose of the allocation of the capital increase to third parties was not to procure additional funds, but rather to place 2 million shares into the hands of two affiliates in order to increase the proportion of shares held by the Iizuka family.

More Establishment Intervention even after Twenty Years

According to the calculations of the plaintiff's side, the total number of shares held by Saibo's directors and inspectors with the surname Iizuka prior to this increase of capital came to 1.97 million shares, or 16.4%. Was it around that figure?

Iizuka: Yes.

When the shareholdings of the defendant Saitama Kogyo and the defendant Saiei Fudosan are combined with the number of shares held by officers with the surname Iizuka, the total is 3.4 million shares, or 28.4%. This would be generally correct, would it not?

Iizuka: I have the feeling the percentage might be a little higher.

Was it not the true purpose of this increase of capital to boost the percentage of shares held by the managers with the surname Iizuka and by the two companies, the defendant Saitama Kogyo and the defendant Saiei Fudosan?

Iizuka: There was absolutely no intention of that nature.

There is no doubt that the defendant Saiei is a corporation controlled and operated by the Iizuka family, is there?

Iizuka: I don't know whether that would be the right way to put it, but I admit that there is quite a bit of influence.

The defendant Saitama Kogyo is an associated company of Saibo, and is practically a subsidiary, isn't it?

Iizuka: Yes.

However, essentially, would it be a company over which the Iizuka family exercises considerable influence?

Iizuka: I don't think I would necessarily say that.

. . .

My lawyer handed him a copy of an exhibit, which forced him to change his vague answer on this point.

When we look at the officers' column in this certified copy of the register of the defendant Saitama Kogyo current at the time, the operation is totally under the management of the managers of Saibo, isn't it?

Iizuka: Yes.

My attorney then handed him still another exhibit.

When we examine the major shareholders column in the column for the defendant Saitama Kogyo on the third sheet of this appendix, since, aside from Saibo with 48.5%, it continues with the names of Shigeru, Naoji, Tadanobu, and Hirobumi Iizuka, doesn't this make it a corporation that is essentially owned and operated by the Iizuka family?

Iizuka: In certain respects, I do not believe that it would be entirely wrong to put it that way.

Around when was the plaintiff (Newpis Hong Kong) listed as a major shareholder?

Iizuka: I don't recall clearly.

Thereafter and up to the present the Hong Kong investors, including the plaintiff, have continued to buy Saibo stock, haven't they?

Iizuka: Yes.

As of March 1991, it would have been totally impossible for the Hong Kong investors including the plaintiff to buy 2 million shares on the stock market in light of the trading volume, wouldn't it?

Iizuka: In regard to that, there is no way to tell.

Since the trading volume is extremely small even now, isn't it the actual case that the Hong Kong investors can hardly buy any stock of Saibo, even at ¥1,300?

Iizuka: There is not a large volume every day but since it is definitely possible to buy a few shares at a time, I don't believe it can be said that there is no trading.

However, the two companies, the defendant Saiei and the defendant Saitama, were able to acquire 2 million shares at ¥801 per share through the allocation of the increase of capital to third parties in March 1991. Don't you think that this was unfair to the other shareholders?

Iizuka: Judging from the circumstances in which the issue price was set at the time, I do not feel that there was any particular discrimination.

Premised on the assessment table from Party A's Exhibit No. 1, in spite of the fact that the value of the assets owned by Saibo came to

¥4,662 per share, your increase of capital by as many as 2 million shares at ¥801 per share and the placement of the shares into the hands of two particular companies were arrangements made for the benefit of those two companies at the expense of the other shareholders. Didn't you consider this to be a breach of faith against the other shareholders?

Iizuka: I didn't take it in that way at all.

Are you aware that there was a transaction of 100,000 shares at one time on August 8th, 1996?

Iizuka: I don't remember.

Weren't you involved in that transaction?

Iizuka: I don't know.

Since the beginning of this year, has there been any case in which you have been interrogated or requested to submit data regarding investments by the Hong Kong investors from the Ministry of Finance or a related institution, or have you submitted any reports to them?

Iizuka: No.

Comments on this Testimony

As noted in this testimony, Daiwa Securities sold 100,000 shares in Saibo on the market at the bid price of ¥1,300 on August 8, 1996. However, Yamaichi Securities, which was Saibo's sole managing underwriter, promptly bought up these 100,000 shares at the bid price of ¥1,300. It is inconceivable that anyone other than the Iizuka family would have had Yamaichi Securities buy them up. That is because the Iizuka family, more than anyone else, knew that the value of the Saibo stock, even at present, was worth more than ¥1,300.

When asked, if he was involved in the purchase President Iizuka responded, "I don't know." If he was not involved with it, wouldn't have he replied, "No, I wasn't"? But perhaps being wary of perjury he answered, "I don't know," instead. It's easy to infer, then, that he really was involved in it.

Index

Note: American names are presented herein by surname. It is customary to write Chinese names by surname first, followed by given name(s), as in "Li Ka-shing," although Japanese names typically follow American order. Therefore, to avoid confusion, Japanese and Chinese names are presented as they appear in the text. However, instances when no first name is given, as in "Mr. Yamataka" or "President Suehiro," the entries are by surname.